Citizen Politics

Public Opinion and Political Parties in Advanced Industrial Democracies

Second Edition

RUSSELL J. DALTON
University of California, Irvine

CHATHAM HOUSE PUBLISHERS, INC.
Chatham, New Jersey

CITIZEN POLITICS
Public Opinion and Political Parties in Advanced Industrial Democracies

Chatham House Publishers, Inc.
Post Office Box One
Chatham, New Jersey 07928

PUBLISHER: Edward Artinian
PRODUCTION SUPERVISOR: Katharine F. Miller
ILLUSTRATIONS: D'Arts
COVER DESIGN: The Antler and Baldwin Design Group, Inc.
COMPOSITION: Bang, Motley, Olufsen
PRINTING AND BINDING: R.R. Donnelley & Sons Company

LIBRARY OF CONGRESS CATALOGING-IN-PUBLICATION DATA
Dalton, Russell J.
    Citizen politics : public opinion and political parties in advanced industrial democracies / Russell J. Dalton. — 2nd ed.
        p. cm.
    Rev. ed. of: Citizen politics in western democracies. © 1988.
    Includes bibliographical references (p.) and index.
    ISBN 1-56643-026-7 (pbk.)
    1. Political participation. 2. Political parties. 3. Democracy.
4. Public opinion. 5. Comparative government. I. Dalton, Russell J.
Citizen politics in western democracies. II. Title.
JF 2011.D34   1996
323'.042—dc20   96-4480
                                                                    CIP

Manufactured in the United States of America
10 9 8 7 6 5 4 3 2 1

For
VIRGINIA DEVAUGHN
and BIFF

Contents

Figures

Tables

Preface

When I began the first edition of this book in the early 1980s, many political scientists expressed open reservations about the viability of modern democracy. President Carter had lamented the malaise of the American spirit, and prognostications about the future crisis of democracy were commonplace.

Against this background, the first edition of *Citizen Politics* argued that democracy was alive and well—if one looked at its citizens. The citizens of advanced industrial democracies believed in the democratic creed and wanted their governments to meet these expectations. The first edition presented evidence that contemporary publics were becoming more active in the political process, more likely to participate in elite-challenging activities, more likely to vote on issues and other policy criteria, and more demanding of their representatives. If democracy was in crisis, it was a crisis of institutions and not the spirit of democracy or its participants.

This contrarian argument in support of democracy has been overtaken by a new conventional wisdom. With the collapse of the Berlin Wall and the Soviet Empire, there arose an unbridled and uncritical enthusiasm for democratic politics. Even those who proclaimed the limits of democracy a short decade ago now see a democratization wave transforming the globe.

This reversal of the conventional wisdom gives one pause. One possible response is to gloat; but I am skeptical of fads, even those that reinforce my own views. My approach to academic trends follows Will Rogers's view of politics. He said that politics was a little like keeping your balance on board a ship. When the ship leans left, you should lean right; when the ship leans right, you should lean left. Thus, in revising *Citizen Politics* I have highlighted the strengths of the democratic processes but also the problems we must confront if democracy is to meet the challenges identified in the last edition and the new challenges of today. The changing nature of citizen politics creates new opportunities to expand the democratic process, as well as new risks. Democracies must respond to these challenges if democratization is to continue. Indeed, I would argue that it is the ability to adapt that gives democracy its strength.

This book introduces students to the knowledge we have gained about citizen political behavior, the questions that still remain, and the implications of these findings. The analyses focus on citizen politics in four nations: the United States, Great Britain, Germany, and France. In addition, this new edition expands the comparative coverage to examine these four nations in a larger cross-national context. Students of comparative politics can examine the rich variety of public opinion in different democracies. Even those interested in only a single nation can benefit from comparisons that highlight the similarities and dissimilarities across nations.

I hope this book will be of value to several audiences, but it was primarily written for classroom use in courses on comparative political parties, public opinion, and European politics. The first half of the book (chapters 1–6) introduces the principles of public opinion and the broad contours of citizen action and citizen beliefs. The second half of the book offers chapters on party alignments (7–11) that could, in the second half of the school term, be combined with other texts on political parties. The book concludes with a discussion of citizen attitudes toward the democratic process.

Another new feature is the addition of a data supplement from the 1990–91 World Values Survey. These data are used throughout the book, and a subset of items is available to instructors using this text. The list of variables is described in appendix B. I find that computer-based research projects on public opinion both enrich the subject matter of the course for students and provide them with a firsthand opportunity to understand the process of public opinion research.

At the graduate level the book provides a useful core text for courses on West European politics or comparative political behavior. My intent was to summarize the existing knowledge in the field, as well as to introduce the controversies that at present divide researchers. I hope the instructor will find the materials facilitate discussion of the readings from primary research materials. Even senior scholars might find familiar data interpreted in new and thought-provoking ways.

Acknowledgments

As in the first edition, the research for this book has benefited from the advice and criticism of my colleagues, as well as students who have used this text. More than my own efforts, this book reflects the insights I have gained from working with other scholars. I will be forever indebted to Kendall Baker and Kai Hildebrandt for their collaboration on *Germany Transformed*. Many of the themes we first explored in that book appear in more comparative terms in these pages. I was also fortunate to work with an exceptional group of scholars on the *Political Action* project. This project shaped my understanding of political participation. More important, many of these individuals have become career-long colleagues and friends: Samuel Barnes, Max Kaase, Hans-Dieter Klingemann, and M. Kent Jennings. I am also indebted to Paul Beck and Scott Flanagan for their collaboration on *Electoral Change in Advanced Industrial Democracies,* which provided an initial assessment of how electoral politics in advanced industrial societies were changing.

During the writing of this book many others helped with advice, survey data, or moral support. Paul Abramson, Paul Beck, Scott Flanagan, Dieter Fuchs, Manfred Kuechler, Michael Lewis-Beck, Mary MacIntosh, Ian McAllister, Robert Rohrschneider, and Martin Wattenberg commented on the manuscript in either the first or second edition. An equal debt is due to the students at the University of California, Irvine, who have used this book and shared their reactions. I am grateful to the Center for German and European Studies at the University of California, which provided research assistance on this new edition, and to Alexa Cole for her assistance. Edward Artinian has been an enthusiastically supportive publisher and almost a new relative of the Dalton family.

I also want to acknowledge a special debt to Ronald Inglehart. Ron was my mentor at the University of Michigan, and his provocative views about citizen politics have deeply influenced my own thinking. I have constantly admired his enthusiasm for social research and his creativity as a scholar. In addition, he graciously provided early access to the 1990–91

World Values Survey that provides the empirical base of this revision. In innumerable ways, I am in his debt.

This book has a bold objective: to provide an overview of the nature of citizen politics in advanced industrial democracies. The task is clearly beyond the means of any one individual; but with a little help from these friends the resulting product can begin to outline the political changes, and political choices, that today face the citizenry in advanced industrial democracies.

1. Introduction

This is a book about people—as citizens, voters, protesters, campaign workers, community activists, party members, and political spectators, they are the driving force of the democratic process. We all watched in awe as the force of "people power" opened the Berlin Wall, led the Velvet Revolution in Czechoslovakia, brought democracy back to the Philippines, and created a democratization wave on a global scale. In the established democracies, the spectacle of an American party convention, the intensity of a French farmers' protest, the community spirit of a New England town meeting, or the dedication of an English environmental group creates an equally impressive image of the democratic process. Granting power to the people, even if that process is incomplete, is a radical development. Even with the recent spread of democratization, only a minority of the world's nations have democratic institutions and procedures.

This book presents a populist view of the democratic process, emphasizing the attitudes and behaviors of the average citizen. The analyses are therefore incomplete; we do not study the role of elites, interest groups, and other political actors. I do not presume that the public is all-knowing or all-powerful. Indeed, there are many examples of the public's ignorance or error on policy issues (as there are examples of elite errors). There are also many instances where policymakers disregard the public's preferences. The democratic process, like all human activities, is imperfect; but its strength lies in the premise that people are the best judges of their own destiny. The success of democracy is largely measured by the public's participation in the process and the responsiveness of the system to popular demands. As Adlai Stevenson once said, in a democracy the people get the kind of government they deserve (for better or worse).

The recent democratic transitions in Eastern Europe, Asia, and South Africa remind us how precious, and how fragile, democracy can be. These events are also a reminder of the importance of the public in sustaining the democratic process once it is established. While it is intriguing to look at these new democracies and their publics (and we will at times), our inquiry focuses on the nature of citizen politics in the established democracies of the West. These established democracies provide a model of success that might be relevant as new democratic states try to develop. Also, the process of democratization is open-ended, and even for the established democracies we shall argue that democratization and the expansion of citizen influence is a continuing process.

Before we proceed, I want to acknowledge the complexity of the topic we are studying. It is difficult to generalize accurately about public opinion and political behavior because the public is not homogeneous. There is not a single public. The public in any nation consists of millions of individuals, each with his or her own view of the world and the citizen's role in politics. Some people are liberal, some moderate, some conservative; others are socialist, reactionary, communist, or none of the above. We often find that opinion is divided on issues of contemporary political debate—this is why the issues are controversial and require a political decision. Some people favor strict environmental laws; some see environmental standards as excessive. Some favor international trade; some are skeptical of its claimed benefits. The study of public opinion underscores the diversity of the public.

Individuals also differ in the attention they devote to politics and the experiences they bring to the political process. Although a few individuals are full-time political activists, most people have modest political interests and ambitions. On some issues a broad spectrum of society may become involved; other issues are greeted with widespread apathy. The public's views generally define the acceptable bounds of politics, within which political elites resolve the remaining controversies. When elites exceed these bounds, or when the issues immediately affect people's lives, the potential for political action is great. The difficulty is to understand and predict which course of action the public will take.

In short, as social scientists we deal with the most complex problem of nature: to understand and predict human behavior. Yet this is not a hopeless task. The development of scientific public opinion surveys in the 1950s provided a valuable tool for researchers. With a sample of a few thousand precisely selected individuals, one can make reliable statements about the distribution of attitudes and opinions (Babbie 1990). Not only can we observe behavior, but with the survey interview we can inquire into the motivations and expectations that guide behavior. Furthermore, a survey can be divided into subgroups to examine the diversity in individual opinions.

Readers will find that this is a very empirical study, relying heavily on public opinion surveys. I do not claim that all we know about the public is found in the statistics and percentages of public opinion surveys. Some of the most insightful writings about political behavior are qualitative studies of public opinion. And yet, even insightful political analysts can make contradictory claims about the public. The value of the empirical method is that it provides a specific reference standard against which we can measure contrasting descriptions of the electorate. Surveys enable citizens to describe politics and their political actions in their own words, and thus survey research offers a tremendously valuable research tool for social scientists.

Drawing on an extensive collection of opinion surveys, this book examines the nature of public opinion in several advanced industrial democracies.[1] I describe how individuals view politics, how they participate in the process, what opinions they hold, and how they choose their leaders through competitive elections. These findings should further our understanding of citizen politics and thereby the working of the political process in contemporary democracies.

The Comparative Study of Public Opinion

This is an explicitly comparative study, exploring public opinion and political behavior in several democracies. Our goal is to strike a balance between attention to national detail and the general characteristics of citizens that transcend national boundaries.

There are several advantages to the comparative study of political behavior in Western democracies. A common historical and cultural tradition unites Europe and North America. Although these nations differ in the specifics of their government and party systems, they also share broad similarities in the functioning of the democratic process and the role of the citizen in the process. A comparative approach thus provides a basis for studying those aspects of political behavior that should be valid across nations. General theories of why people participate in democratic politics should apply to citizens regardless of their nationality. Theories to explain party preferences should hold for Americans and Europeans if they represent basic features of human nature. And yet, most of the major studies of public opinion focus only on one nation.

A comparative study of several nations provides a broad assessment of general theories of citizen political behavior. In most instances we expect to find similar patterns of behavior in different democracies. If our theories do not function similarly across nations, then we have learned something new and important. Science often progresses by finding exceptions to general theory, which necessitate further theoretical work. The same applies to social science.

Comparative analysis also allows us to examine the effects of political structures on citizen political behavior. For example, in what nations is class voting stronger than the average, and why? Or, does the nature of a nation's electoral system affect the public's voting behavior? Each nation produces a "natural experiment" where general theories can be tested in a different political context.

Finally, even if we are interested only in a single nation, comparative research is a useful approach. An old Hebrew riddle expresses this idea: "*Question:* Who first discovered water? *Answer:* I don't know, but it wasn't a fish." Immersing oneself in a single environment renders the characteristics of the environment unobtrusive and unnoticed. It is difficult to understand what is unique and distinctive about American political behavior, for example, by studying only American politics. Indeed, many students of American politics may be surprised to learn that the United States is often the atypical case in cross-national comparisons. American public opinion is unique in many ways, but we understand this only by rising above the waters.

The Choice of Nations

To balance our needs for comparison and attention to national differences, this study focuses on citizen politics in four nations: the United States, Great Britain, the Federal Republic of Germany (FRG), and France.[2] I based the choice of these nations on several criteria. By most standards, these are the major powers among the Western democracies. Their population, size, economy, military strength, and political influence earn them leadership positions in international circles. The actions of any of these nations can have significant consequences for all the others.

These nations also were chosen because they highlight many of the significant variations in the structure of democratic politics. Table 1.1 summarizes some of the most important differences. For example, Great Britain is a pure parliamentary system of government. The popularly elected House of Commons selects the prime minister to head the executive branch. This produces a fusion of legislative and executive power, because the same party and the same group of elites direct both branches of government. American government has a contrasting presidential system, with extensive checks and balances to maintain a separation of legislative and executive power. French politics functions within a modified presidential system; the president is directly elected by the public and so, too, is the National Assembly that selects the premier to head the administration of government. Germany has a parliamentary system, with the popularly elected

Bundestag selecting the chancellor as head of the executive branch. The German system, however, also contains a strong federal structure and a separation of powers that is uncommon for a parliamentary government. Excellent analyses of these contrasting institutional forms and their implications for the nature of democratic politics can be found in the research of Arend Lijphart (1984) and G. Bingham Powell (1982).

Electoral systems are equally diverse. Britain and the United States select the members of the national legislature from single-member districts, and a plurality is sufficient for election. Germany uses a hybrid system for Bundestag elections; half the deputies are elected from single-member districts and half are selected from party lists. The goal is to produce a modified version of proportional representation (PR) in which each party has a proportion of legislative seats equal to its share of the popular vote. The French electoral system is based on deputies winning a majority in single-member districts, with a second ballot (*tour*) if no candidate receives a majority on the first ballot. Rein Taagepera and Matthew Shugart (1989) have presented an excellent study of how such institutional arrangements can affect electoral outcomes.

The party systems in these four nations are also varied. Party competition in the United States is usually limited to the Democratic and Republican parties. Both are broad "catchall" parties that combine diverse political groups into weakly structured electoral coalitions. In contrast, most European political parties are hierarchically organized and firmly controlled by the party leadership. Candidates are elected primarily because of their party labels and not because of their personal attributes; in the legislature most party members vote as a bloc. Party options are also more diverse in Europe. Britons can select from at least three major party groups; Germans have five major parties in the Bundestag. French party politics is synonymous with diversity and political polarization. Jacques Fauvet described French politics in the following terms:

> France contains two fundamental temperaments—that of the left and right; three principal tendencies, if one adds the center; six spiritual families; ten parties, large or small, traversed by multiple currents; fourteen parliamentary groups without much discipline; and forty million opinions. (Ehrmann and Schain 1992, 231)

Although Fauvet was describing French politics in the late 1950s, much of his description still applies today. France, a nation of "perpetual political effervescence," provides the spice of comparative politics.

The contrasts across nations take on an added dimension as a conse-

TABLE 1.1

A COMPARISON OF POLITICAL SYSTEMS

	United States	Great Britain	Germany	France
Population (in millions)	225	57	78	55
Gross domestic product/capita	$23,240	$17,790	$26,180	$22,260
Political regime established	1789	17th century	1949	1958
State form	Republic	Constitutional monarchy	Republic	Republic
Government structure	Presidential	Parliamentary	Modified parliamentary	Modified presidential
Chief executive	President	Prime minister	Chancellor	President
Method of selection	Direct election	Elected by Parliament	Elected by Parliament	Direct election
Legislature	Bicameral	Bicameral	Bicameral	Bicameral
Lower house	House of Representatives	House of Commons	Bundestag	National Assembly
Upper house	Senate	House of Lords	Bundesrat	Senate
Power of upper house	Equal	Subordinate	Equal on state issues	Subordinate
Electoral system				
Lower house	Single-member districts	Single-member districts	PR and single-member districts	Single-member districts
Upper house	Statewide elections	Inheritance and appointment	Appointed by states	Appointed by communes
Major parties	Democrats	Labour	Democratic Socialists (PDS)	Communists
	Republicans	Social Democrats	Greens	Socialists
		Liberals	Social Democrats	Ecologists
		Conservatives	Free Democrats	UDF
			Christian Democrats/Christian Social Union (CDU/CSU)	Gaullist (RPR)
				National Front

quence of German unification. Western Germans have developed the characteristics of a stable, advanced industrial democracy; the former East Germany, like most of the rest of Eastern Europe, is just beginning this process. Democracy is a new experience for eastern Germans, and understanding of the democratic process and commitment to democratic norms are uncertain. By including western-eastern comparisons in our analysis of Germany, we can better understand what is distinctive about public opinion in an established democracy, as well as the prospects for democratization in the East. Furthermore, when possible, we broaden the scope of our cross-national comparisons to place our four publics in the context of citizens in other advanced industrial democracies.

As this brief outline suggests, these four nations provide a rich mix of sociopolitical conditions in which to study political behavior. Subsequent chapters often include survey data from other nations to highlight a specific point or place these four nations in a broader comparative context. In general, however, the bulk of the study focuses on the political behavior of American, British, German, and French publics.

A New Style of Citizen Politics

The reader will quickly realize that this volume emphasizes the changing nature of citizen political behavior. I maintain that these changes derive from the socioeconomic transformation of the four nations under study over the past fifty years and the political consequences of this development. Western democracies are developing a set of characteristics that collectively represent a new form of *advanced industrial* or *postindustrial* society (Bell 1973; Inglehart 1977, 1990).

The most dramatic changes involve economic conditions. An unprecedented expansion of economic well-being has occurred since World War II. Economies in Western Europe and North America grew at phenomenal rates in the postwar decades. In France, for example, the economic expansion between 1950 and the mid-1960s exceeded the total growth during the sixty-five years of the Third Republic (1875 to 1940). Analysts describe the astonishing expansion of the West German economy as the *Wirtschaftswunder* (Economic Miracle). Income levels in our four nations are two to four times greater than at any time in prewar history. By almost any economic standard, the four nations of this study rank among the most affluent nations of the world.

With increasing affluence has come a restructuring of the labor force. The size of the agricultural workforce has decreased dramatically in most Western nations, and industrial employment has remained stable or declined. Advanced industrial societies are characterized by a marked shift in the labor force to the service sector. In addition, because of the expansion of national and local governments, public employment now constitutes a significant share of the labor force. All four of the core nations in this volume have passed Daniel Bell's (1973) threshold for postindustrialism: half of the labor force employed in the service or governmental sector.

Advanced industrialism is associated not only with changes in the relative size of the three principal employment sectors but also with changes in the context of the workplace and the residential neighborhood. The continuing decline of rural populations and the expanding size of metropolitan centers stimulate changes in life expectations and lifestyles. Urbanization means a growing separation of the home from the workplace, a greater diversity of occupations and interests, an expanded range of career opportunities, and more geographic and social mobility. With these trends come changes in the forms of social organization and interaction. Communal forms of organization are replaced by voluntary associations, which in turn become less institutionalized and more spontaneous in organization. Communities are becoming less bounded; individuals are involved in increasingly complex and competing social networks that divide their loyalties; and institutional loyalties are becoming more fluid.

Educational opportunities have also expanded rapidly over the past several decades. European governments historically restricted university education to a privileged few; the vast majority received minimal education (often only four years). In the late 1930s the proportion of university students among 20–24 year olds was only 1 percent in England, 1 percent in Germany, and 3 percent in France (Flora 1983, 553ff.). Education received a higher value following World War II. Minimal education standards were increased, and university enrollments skyrocketed. By 1975 the proportion of university students among college-age youth was 7 percent in Britain, 14 percent in West Germany, and 20 percent in France (Flora 1983). Even the United States, with initially higher university enrollments, experienced a tremendous growth in its university population, to nearly 50 percent of the 18–24 year olds. This expansion of educational opportunities has fundamentally changed the educational composition of contemporary mass publics.

These increases in education have been accompanied by parallel increases in information resources. The growth of the electronic media, especially television, has been exceptional. Access to other information sources, such as books and magazines, has increased. Even more revolutionary is the growth of electronic information processing: computers, information and retrieval systems, the Internet, and related technologies. Information is no longer a scarce commodity. The contemporary information problem is how to adapt to life in cyberspace, managing an ever-growing volume of sophisticated knowledge.

Western democracies have also changed in the extent of the government's involvement in society. Two world wars and the Great Depression expanded the government's role in economic and social activities. Western publics now hold the government responsible for protecting and managing society. Governments increased their control over their national economies, and government programs became the guarantor of social needs. Many European societies developed the characteristics of a welfare state, where an extensive network of generous social programs protect the individual against economic or medical hardship (Heidenheimer and Flora 1981). Unemployment, illness, and similar problems still cause hardships, but the consequences under the welfare state are less dire than during earlier periods. Publics in advanced industrial societies enjoy both a high level of affluence and relative security.

Despite these trends, the 1990s have seen a mounting public concern in Europe, North America, and Japan about whether this developmental trend can continue. Everywhere, it seems, there has been a retrenchment in government social programs. Increased international interdependence means that periods of recession now have a global reach. The euphoria about the end of the Cold War and the democratization of East Europe now have been tempered by worries about growing nationalism, ethnic conflict, and the financial burdens that modernization will require. These are real worries that have at least partially revived earlier economic problems and have revived reactionary political groups.

Admittedly the miraculous economic growth of the postwar era now seems like distant history. The trajectory of growth is not continuing, at least for now. And yet the transformation of Western democracies is more than simply the politics of affluence. Changes in the occupational and social structure are continuing, and with them an alteration in life conditions and lifestyles. Expanded educational opportunities represent an enduring trait of modern societies. The information revolution is continuing; in fact it is growing at an amazing rate. Even economic recession has not removed the gains of the past; it has only moderated the rates of future growth. Advanced industrial societies are still dramatically different from their prewar predecessors.

This book maintains that one result of these social changes is the development of a new style of citizen politics. As the socioeconomic characteristics of these nations have changed, so too have the characteristics of the public. More educational opportunities mean a growth in political skills and resources, producing the most sophisticated publics in the history of democracies. Changing economic conditions redefine the issues of concern to the public. The weakening of social networks and institutional loyalties is associated with the decline of traditional values and social norms.

The elements of this new style of citizen politics are not always, or necessarily, linked together. Some elements may be transitory; others may be coincidental. Nevertheless, several traits coexist for the present, defining a new pattern of citizen political behavior. The goal of this volume is to present a systematic study of public opinion that explores this pattern of political thought and action.

One area of change affects the public's involvement in politics (chapters 2–4). Greater public participation in economic and political decision making has become an important social goal. This development is closely tied to the spread of protest, citizen action groups, and unconventional political participation; but it involves more. Citizens are less likely to be passive subjects and are more likely to demand a say in the decisions affecting their lives. The new style of citizen politics includes a more active participation in the democratic process.

Another broad area of change involves the values and attitudes of the public (chapters 5–6). Industrial societies aimed at providing affluence and economic security. The success of advanced industrialism fulfills many basic economic needs for a sizable sector of society. Thus concerns are shifting to new political goals (Inglehart 1977, 1990). Several of these new issues are common to advanced industrial democracies: social equality, environmental protection, the dangers of nuclear energy, sexual equality, and human rights. In some instances historical conditions focus these general concerns on specific national problems, for example, racial equality in the United States, regional conflicts in Britain, or center-periphery differences in France. Many of these issues are now loosely integrated into an alternative political agenda that is another element of the new style of citizen politics.

Partisan politics is also changing (chapters 7–11). Until recently, comparative party research has emphasized the stability of democratic party systems. This situation has changed in the past decade. Stable party alignments are weakening, producing increased fragmentation and fractionalization in most Western party systems. Declining class differences in voting behavior reflect the general erosion in the social bases of voting. Studies in the United States, Britain, and other nations document a decline in the public's identification with political parties and growing disenchantment with parties in general. In another place (Dalton et al. 1984, chap. 15) we describe these patterns as the *dealignment* of contemporary party systems.

These trends are at least partially the result of the addition of new issues to the political agenda and the difficulties the established parties have had in responding to these issues. New parties have arisen across the face of Europe—ranging from green parties on the New Left to New Right parties at the opposite end of the political spectrum—and new political movements seek access to the Democratic and Republican parties in the United States. Increased party volatility is also caused by the changing characteristics of contemporary publics. Unsophisticated voters once relied on stable social-group and partisan cues to make their political decisions. Because of the dramatic spread of education and information sources, more citizens are now able to deal with the complexities of politics and make their own political decisions. Consequently, issues are becoming a more important basis of voting behavior as the influence of traditional group and party allegiances wanes. The new style of citizen politics includes a more issue-oriented and candidate-oriented public.

Finally, evaluations of political institutions and political leaders are constantly being reassessed (chapter 12). Evidence from several nations shows a decline in trust of political elites and institutions. The conflict over new issues and new participation patterns may be a partial explanation of these trends. In addition, emerging value priorities that stress individualism and political participation produce skepticism of elite-controlled hierarchical organizations (such as bureaucracies, political parties, and large interest groups). Some observers suggest that a more demanding and assertive public will be a continuing feature of the democratic process in advanced industrial societies.

The post–Cold War era has witnessed a global wave of democratization and an enthusiasm for democratic politics that has not been seen since the end of World War II. The emerging democracies of Eastern Europe and Asia are trying to develop the political norms and procedures that will enable their new systems to endure. In the established Western democracies there is also a new belief in the vitality of democracy that sharply differs from the worries of democratic malaise and distemper that were common a decade ago. Yet even in established democracies the democratic process is changing and evolving. Democracy is not an end state, but an evolutionary process.

The development of this new style of citizen politics strains the political systems of advanced industrial democracies. Protests, social movements, partisan volatility, and political skepticism are disrupting the traditional political order. Adjustment to new issue concerns and new patterns of citizen participation may be a difficult process. More people now take democratic ideals seriously, and they expect political systems to live up to these ideals. The new style of citizen politics is a sign of vitality and an opportunity for these societies to make further progress toward their democratic goals.

Notes

1. I acquired most of the data in this volume from the Inter-university Consortium for Political and Social Research at the University of Michigan, Ann Arbor. Additional data were made available by the Zentralarchiv für empirische Sozialforschung, University of Cologne, Germany; ESRC Archive, University of Essex, England; and the Banque de Données Socio-Politiques, University of Grenoble, France. See appendix A for additional information on the major data sources. Neither these archives nor the original collectors of the data bear responsibility for the analyses presented here.

2. For a brief review of these nations, see Almond and Powell (1996). More detailed national studies are found in Rose (1989) for Britain, Dalton (1993a) for Germany, and Ehrmann and Schain (1992) for France.

PART ONE

Politics and the Public

2. The Nature of Mass Beliefs

Any discussion of citizen politics is ultimately grounded on basic assumptions about the political abilities of the electorate—the public's level of knowledge, understanding, and interest in political matters. For voters to make meaningful decisions, they must understand the options on which they are deciding. Citizens also must understand the workings of the political system if they intend to influence and control the actions of their representatives. In short, for citizen politics to be purposeful, the electorate must have at least a basic level of political skills.

Examining the sophistication of voters also improves our understanding of the public opinion data presented in this book. With what depth of knowledge and conviction are opinions held? Do survey responses represent reasoned assessments of the issues or the snap judgments of individuals faced by an interviewer on their doorstep? It is common to see the public labeled as uninformed (especially when public opinion conflicts with the speaker's own views). Conversely, the electorate cannot be wiser than when it supports one's own position. Can we judge the merits of either position based on the empirical evidence from public opinion surveys?

Despite several decades of public opinion polling, analysts still disagree in their evaluations of the public's political sophistication: knowledge about politics, involvement in the political process, understanding of policy issues, and understanding of the democratic process. This controversy involves normative assumptions about what level of public sophistication is required for democracies to fulfill their political ideals, as well as differences in evaluating the empirical evidence.

The Supercitizen

Historically, many theorists have maintained that democracy was workable only when the public had a high degree of political information and sophistication. Mill, Locke, Tocqueville, and other writers saw these public traits as essential requirements for a successful democratic system. Moreover, most theorists claimed that the citizenry should support the political system and share a deep commitment to democratic ideals such as pluralism, free expression, and minority rights (see chapter 12). Otherwise, an uninformed and unsophisticated electorate might be manipulated by misguided or unscrupulous elites. In a sense, these theorists posited a supercitizen model: the public must be a paragon of civic virtue for democracy to survive.

This ideal of the democratic supercitizen was often illustrated by the American electorate.[1] A popular lore grew up about the sophistication of Americans. Alexis de Tocqueville (1966) praised the social and community involvement of Americans when he described the United States in the nineteenth century. Voters in early America supposedly yearned for the stimulating political debates of election campaigns and flocked to political rallies in great numbers. The New England town hall meetings became a legendary example of the American political spirit. Even on the frontier, it was claimed, conversations around the general store's cracker barrel displayed a deep interest and concern with political matters.

While these democratic norms were initially of European origin, history painted a less positive picture of the citizenry in many European nations. The right to vote came much later to most Europeans, often delayed until the beginning of the twentieth century. The aristocratic institutions and deferential traditions of British politics limited public participation beyond the act of voting and severely restricted the size of the eligible electorate. In France, the excesses of the French Revolution raised doubts about the principle of mass participation. In addition, the instability of the political system supposedly produced a sense of *incivism,* and people avoided political discussions and political involvement.

Germany presented the most graphic example of what might follow when democratic norms fail to develop among the public. Authoritarian governments ruled during the Wilhelmine Empire (1871–1918), and people were taught to be seen and not heard. The democratic Weimar Republic (1919–33) was but a brief and turbulent interlude in Germany's nondemocratic history. The frailties of popular democratic norms during the Weimar Republic contributed to the system's demise and the rise of the Nazis. For the next several decades, many social scientists tried to answer the question of why Germans allowed democracy to fail and be replaced by the horrors of Hitler's Third Reich. A strong democratic culture eventually developed in the postwar Federal Republic of Germany. Yet these historical experiences strengthened the belief that a sophisticated, involved, and democratic public was a requirement for democracy to succeed.

The Unsophisticated Citizen

The start of scientific public opinion surveying in the 1940s and 1950s provided the first opportunity to move beyond the insights of political theorists and social commentators. We could finally test the lofty images of the democratic citizen against reality. The public itself was directly consulted.

In contrast to the classic image of the democratic theory, early surveys painted an unflattering picture of the citizenry. The political sophistication of the public fell far short of the supercitizen model. For most people, political interest and involvement barely extended beyond casting an occasional vote in national or local elections. Furthermore, people apparently brought little understanding to their participation in politics. It was not clear that the electorate based its voting decisions on rational evaluations of candidates and their issue positions. Instead, voting was conditioned by group loyalties and personality considerations. The seminal work in the area succinctly summarized the findings:

> Our data reveal that certain requirements commonly assumed for the successful operation of democracy are not met by the behavior of the "average" citizen.... Many vote without real involvement in the election.... The citizen is not highly informed on the details of the campaign.... In any rigorous or narrow sense the voters are not highly rational. (Berelson et al. 1954, 307–10)

A landmark study, *The American Voter,* substantiated these early findings (Campbell et al. 1960). Campbell and his colleagues documented a lack of ideological understanding by the American electorate. In an influential essay on mass belief systems, Philip Converse (1964) spelled out the criteria for judging political sophistication. As modeled in figure 2.1, Converse maintained there should be a basic *structure* at the core of individual political beliefs. An ideological framework such as liberalism or conservatism presumably provided this structure, at least at the highest level of sophistication. In addition, Converse held there should be *constraint* between individual issue positions. Constraint was measured by the strength of the linkage between specific issues and core beliefs and by the interrelationship among issues. A person who was liberal on one issue was expected to be liberal on others. Furthermore, opinions on one issue should be ideologically (or at least logically) consistent with other beliefs. Finally, Converse said that issue opinions should be relatively *stable* over time so that voters held firm beliefs that consistently guided their behavior. The overall result should be a tightly structured system of beliefs like those depicted in the figure.

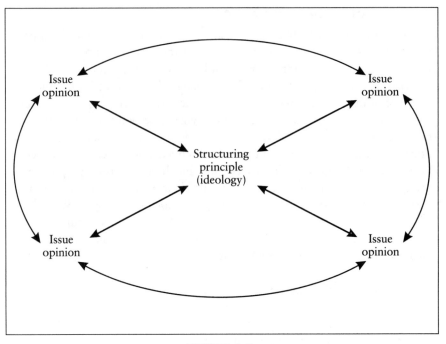

FIGURE 2.1

MODEL OF A STRUCTURED BELIEF SYSTEM

In testing this model, Converse found that Americans appeared deficient on most of these criteria. First, public opinion apparently lacked a general ideological structure. Most individuals did not judge political phenomena by a broad ideological framework, such as liberalism/conservatism or capitalism/socialism. Converse reckoned that barely a tenth of the American public used ideological concepts to structure their belief systems. Second, there seemed to be only a weak relationship between issues that presumably were connected. For example, voters who felt taxes were too high nevertheless favored increases in spending for many specific government programs. Third, issue beliefs were not very stable over time. An analysis of the same group of individuals interviewed in 1956, 1958, and 1960 found that the opinions of many people seemed to vary capriciously. The lack of structure, constraint, and stability led Converse to conclude that public opinion researchers were often studying "nonattitudes" (Converse 1970). On many issues of long-standing political concern, many voters apparently lacked informed opinions or any opinions. *The American Voter* also concluded that the electorate "is almost completely unable to judge the rationality of government actions; knowing little of the particular policies and what has led to them, the mass electorate is not able either to appraise its goals or the appropriateness of the means chosen to secure these goals" (Campbell et al. 1960, 543). This research was soon followed by a series of surveys showing that many people could not name their elected representatives, were unfamiliar with the institutions of government, and did not understand the mechanics of the political process (more recently, see Delli Carpini, and Keeter 1991, forthcoming). The image of the American voter had fallen to a new low.

Political scientists generalized this view of the unsophisticated citizen to Western Europeans. Once one moved beyond election turnout, political involvement in Europe was frequently lower than in the United States. Converse and Dupeux (1962) found that French political interest was lower than in the United States, despite the tumultuous and polarized nature of the French party system. French voters also lacked well-formed opinions on the pressing issues of the day (Converse and Pierce 1986, chap. 7). Similar evidence emerged from surveys of the British public (Butler and Stokes 1969). Sixty percent of Britons did not recognize the terms Left and Right as they applied to politics. There were again the telltale signs of nonattitudes—weak linkages between opinions on related issues and excessive opinion instability over time. Gabriel Almond and Sidney Verba (1963) conducted a widely read survey of public opinion in five nations —the United States, Britain, West Germany, Italy, and Mexico—during the late 1950s. They found that only a minority in each nation discussed politics frequently and that few people regularly followed news accounts of politics and government.

Other research raised doubts about the public's commitment to political tolerance and other values underlying the democratic process. The general public displayed support for democratic ideals in the abstract, but not when applied to real political groups and movements, such as communists, Nazis, atheists, and political nonconformists (Prothro and Grigg 1960; Stouffer 1955; McClosky 1964; McClosky and Brill 1983). Again, the empirical reality apparently fell short of the democratic ideal.

Having found that most citizens failed to meet the requirements of classic democratic theory, political scientists faced a paradox. Most individuals were not "good" democratic citizens, and yet democracies such as the United States and Great Britain had existed for generations. Gradually, an *elitist theory of democracy* developed as scholars tried to interpret these survey findings in a positive light (Berelson et al. 1954, 313–23; Almond and Verba 1963, chap. 15). The new theory contended that democratic politics might prove unworkable if every person was active on every issue at all times. Images of the centrifugal forces destroying the Weimar Republic were fresh in many minds; this generated concerns about the possible effects of excessive participation. These scholars suggested that the model citizen "is not the active citizen; he is the potentially active citizen" (Almond and Verba 1963, 347). These researchers argued that people must believe that they can influence the government and must be willing to make an effort if the issue is sufficiently important. Few will realize this potential, however. This balance between action and potential presumably assured that political elites had enough freedom to make necessary decisions, while keeping the public interest in mind.

Another element of this theory stressed the heterogeneity of the public. "Some people are and should be highly interested in politics, but not everyone is or needs to be" (Berelson et al. 1954, 315). From this perspective, the responsiveness of the political system was assured by a small core of active citizens and political elites, leaving the rest of the public blissfully uninformed and uninvolved. This mix between involved and indifferent voters reportedly assured the stability and flexibility of democratic systems.

The elitist theory of democracy was drawn from the realities of political life—or at least from the hard evidence of survey research. It is, however, a very undemocratic theory of democracy (cf. Barber 1984). The theory maintains that "the democratic citizen ... must be active, yet passive; involved, yet not too involved; influential, yet deferential" (Almond and Verba 1963, 478–79). The values and goals of democracy were at least partially obscured by a mountain of survey data.

Accepting this new creed, some analysts used this evidence to justify an extreme elitist model of the democratic process (Dye and Ziegler 1970; Crozier et al. 1975; Huntington 1981). These critics of the public implied that citizen activism is undemocratic and politically destabilizing. Thomas Dye and Harmon Ziegler (1970) bluntly claimed:

> The survival of democracy depends upon the commitment of elites to democratic ideals rather than upon broad support for democracy by the masses. Political apathy and nonparticipation among the masses contribute to the survival of democracy. Fortunately for democracy, the antidemocratic masses are generally more apathetic than elites. (328)

Thus if a supportive and quiescent public ensures a smoothly functioning political system, then it is virtually the duty of the individual to remain uninvolved. When the public began to challenge political elites during the turbulent 1960s and early 1970s, these political scientists cautioned that democracy required a public of followers who would not question political elites too extensively. They argued that too much democracy could threaten the democratic process.

Despite these claims, I believe that the elitist theory overlooks the complexities of the democratic process and takes an unsophisticated view of the evidence. For instance, this theory ignores the inconsistencies that exist among political elites. Members of the U.S. Congress routinely endorse formal budget limits and then act to circumvent these same limits in the next piece of legislation; in one vote they endorse strict measures to limit crime, in the next they refuse to ban assault weapons.[2] Such inconsistencies are illustrations of the complexity of politics when talking about elites; for the public these are signs of their lack of unsophistication. In addition, the elitist critique of the public's abilities has been challenged on both normative and empirical grounds in recent years.[3] The picture of the public's abilities is not nearly as bleak as that painted by early survey research. As our scientific knowledge has increased, so too has our respect for the electorate and its abilities. Thus a reassessment is necessary.

Political Sophistication Reconsidered

Our challenge to conventional descriptions of an unsophisticated electorate is based on several points. Advanced industrial societies have undergone profound social and political changes in the postwar period that have increased the public's political abilities. In addition, we now have a more refined knowledge of the methodological strengths and weaknesses of survey research. Finally, and most important, past research has enriched our understanding of how voters actually think about political matters. Each point deserves detailed attention.

A Process of Cognitive Mobilization

During the past thirty years there has been a dramatic transformation in the characteristics of the public in advanced industrial democracies. The political skills and resources of contemporary electorates—traits such as education, media exposure, and political awareness—have been vastly improved since the 1950s. These trends have contributed to a growth in the public's overall level of political sophistication, or what is described as a process of *cognitive mobilization* (Inglehart 1990, 1977, chaps. 10–12; Dalton 1984). Cognitive mobilization involves two separate developments. First, there has been a decrease in the cost of acquiring information about politics. Second, there has been an increase in the public's ability to process political information. Cognitive mobilization thus means that more citizens now have the political resources and skills necessary to deal with the complexities of politics and make their own political decisions.

The public's access to political information has increased in many ways. The expansion of the mass media, especially television, is the clearest example of this increased access to political information. The average citizen once might have suffered from a lack of information; today, there is a nearly unlimited supply and variety of political news. The growth of the mass media is a well-known fact, but it is easy to forget how much has changed in the past few decades.

Thirty years ago, an individual had to make a great effort to remain informed about politics. One could read newspapers or magazines, but this was a time-consuming task, especially for an electorate with limited education. Particularly in Europe, the printed press was of uneven quality, and many mass newspapers were little more than scandal sheets. Radio expanded access to information, but the major change came with the introduction of television.

Television is a ubiquitous part of contemporary life, although in the early 1950s it was still a novelty to most Americans and a luxury to most Europeans. Only half of American homes had a television set in the early 1950s, less than 10 percent in Britain and France, and less than 5 percent in the Federal Republic of Germany. The expansion of television ownership over the next two decades was closely paralleled by the public's increasing reliance on television as a source of political information (figure 2.2). In the 1952 American election, 51 percent of the electorate used television news as an information source. By 1960, this had risen to a plateau of about 90 percent. In 1961 only 50 percent of the West German public depended on television for political information; by 1974, the Germans also reached the 90 percent plateau. The available data from Britain and France present a similar pattern.

As television viewership has increased, so also has the amount of political information provided by the medium. The now-standard American nightly half-hour national news program began only in 1963. Since then, technology and viewer interest have increased the television programming devoted to news and political affairs. Today, news reporting is instantaneous and done on a worldwide scale. Most Americans now have access to news on a twenty-four-hour-a-day basis; CNN, C-SPAN, and other cable channels have created a new media environment.

European television contains an even larger proportion of political information because government supervised national networks devote more time to news, politics, and current events. Political information accounts for about a third of all public network programming in France and Germany and about a quarter in Britain. Moreover, new information technologies and the competition from new private channels are transforming the

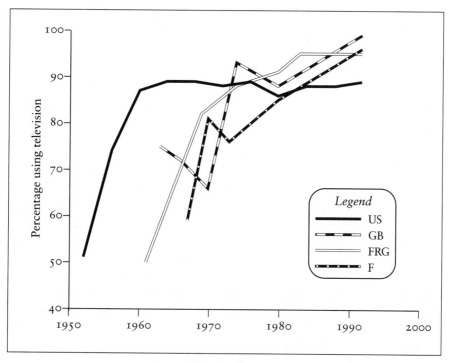

FIGURE 2.2

THE GROWTH OF TELEVISION AS A SOURCE
OF POLITICAL INFORMATION

SOURCES: *United States*, 1952–92, American National Election Studies. *Great Britain*, 1963–74, British Election Studies; 1980–92, Eurobarometer 15 and 37. *Germany*, 1961–69, German Election Studies; 1980–92, Eurobarometer 15 and 37. *France*, 1965–74, Gallup (1976b); 1980–92, Eurobarometer 15 and 37.

media environment in Europe. More than half of all Europeans can receive cable channels, ranging from the government networks to CNN or BBC World News to a host of private channels. Government restrictions on television have gradually weakened, and the media are playing a larger political role. For example, before the 1964 election, the British government prohibited the BBC from carrying election news during the campaign period. Now television coverage is a central part of British campaigns as well as German and French elections (Semetko et al. 1991; Semetko and Schoenbach 1994). A further expansion in television usage and greater diversity in television programming thus lie ahead.

As a result of these trends, television now plays a primary role in informing Western publics (table 2.1). People uniformly cite television as the most frequently used source of political information.[4] However, the high ranking for television does not mean that other media are used less often. Except for radio, public usage of most media apparently has remained stable or increased over the past twenty years (Graber 1993; Semetko et al. 1991). Opinion surveys routinely find that large majorities of the public regularly watch television, read newspapers and magazines, and hear news on the radio. Contemporary publics thus have access to an array of media sources that would have been unimaginable a generation ago. These increases in the quantity and quality of political information provided by the media should improve public awareness of political affairs.

Recent research has also pointed out that politically relevant information comes from our daily life experiences (Fiorina 1990; Popkin 1991). During the past thirty years governments have assumed an increasing role in society, and their performance of this role is often apparent to the citizenry. In simple economic terms, the government's share of the gross domestic product (GDP) increased significantly in all four of the nations under study (Heidenheimer et al. 1990, chap. 5). In 1990 public expenditures accounted for over a third of the GDP in the United States and almost half in Britain, Germany, and France. Thus economic performance is a straightforward, and meaningful, measure of how to judge the incumbents. Similarly, governments now take a more activist policymaking role in a wide variety of noneconomic areas—from setting health standards to family and

TABLE 2.1

MOST IMPORTANT SOURCE OF POLITICAL INFORMATION

(IN PERCENTAGES)

	United States 1992	Great Britain 1989	West Germany 1989	France 1989
Television	69	53	56	44
Newspapers	43	30	37	24
Personal discussion	6	19	26	15
Radio	16	12	20	13
Other	4	5	18	7
Total	100	119	157	103

SOURCES: *United States*, Stanley and Niemi (1994, 74). *Other nations*, Eurobarometer 31A (June 1989).

NOTE: Responses in British, German, and French surveys total to more than 100 percent because multiple answers were possible.

social programs to new energy and environmental policies. Public opinion data suggest that citizens recognize the increasing impact of politics on their daily lives. When a commuter notes that highways are deteriorating (or being improved) or parents note improvements (or deterioration) in their children's schools, these are significant political facts. Political information is virtually unavoidable.

The expansion of political information provides an opportunity to the citizenry, but this information may seem like an increasing cacophony of noise unless the public is able to process and evaluate the information (Graber 1988; Ferejohn and Kuklinski 1990). Thus it is important that the public's political skills also increase.

The most visible change in political skills involves the educational levels of the citizenry. Advanced industrial societies require a more educated and technically sophisticated electorate, and postwar affluence has provided the funding for an expanded educational system (see chapter 1). University enrollments grew during the 1950s and then exploded upward in the 1960s. Between 1950 and 1975, university enrollments increased by 347 percent in the United States, 472 percent in Britain, 503 percent in West Germany, and 586 percent in France—far outstripping population growth rates. These trends are producing a gradual change in the educational level of contemporary electorates. Older, less-educated generations slowly are leaving the electorate and are being replaced by better-educated young people. For instance, almost half of the 1948 American electorate had a primary education or less, and only a tenth had some college education. By 1992, the portion of the electorate with some college education grew to outnumber the voters with only primary education by an eight-to-one ratio, and the college-educated made up almost two-thirds of the electorate. Parallel changes are transforming European publics. In the postwar Federal Republic of Germany, for example, the number of citizens with only primary schooling exceeded those with a secondary school diploma (*Mittlere Reife*) by about five to one. Today, the number of better-educated Germans is nearly twice as large as the lesser educated.

There is not a direct one-to-one relationship between years of schooling and political sophistication. Nevertheless, the evidence from survey research broadly shows that education is linked to a citizen's level of political knowledge, interest, and sophistication (Converse 1972). Paul Sniderman, Richard Brody, and Philip Tetlock (1991) have presented persuasive evidence that educational levels are related to the modes of political decision making that citizens use. Samuel Popkin (1991, 36) suggests that rising educational levels increase the breadth of citizens' political interests, even if they do not raise overall levels of institutional knowledge or issue constraint by the same amount. Thus better-educated individuals come closer to the classic model of ideological citizens and are more knowledgeable in their behavior. A doubling of the public's educational level may not double the level of political sophistication, but some increase should occur. Contemporary electorates are clearly the most educated in the long history of democracies, and this should contribute toward making a more sophisticated electorate and a new style of citizen politics.

Philip Converse (1972, 1990) has argued that political attention is an even more important indicator of the public's political skills. Reflecting and reinforcing the general development of cognitive mobilization, interest in politics and government affairs has increased in many democracies. Figure 2.3 presents several measures of general political interest tracked over time.[5] Interest in specific elections may vary from campaign to campaign, but these data suggest a trend of increasing politicization. General political interest has grown most steadily in the Federal Republic of Germany, partially for the reasons cited above and partially because of the nation's resocialization to democracy (Baker et al. 1981, chap. 2; Conradt 1980). Yet there are similar trends of expanding interest in Britain and France. American interest in campaigns, the only question extending back to the 1950s, exhibits initially high levels that grow slightly over the next forty years. Evidence from other nations also conveys of pattern of generally increasing political interest (e.g., van Deth and Horstmann 1989; McAllister 1992, chap. 2; Richardson and Flanagan 1982, 232; Inglehart, forthcoming, chap. 8). The available data are often incomplete, and different survey questions are used in each nation, but the trend of increasing political interest in advanced industrial democracies is unmistakable.

This process of cognitive mobilization has affected several areas of citizen beliefs. The debate over the electorate's sophistication has focused on the public's ideological awareness, determined by whether citizens use ideological concepts in judging political parties (Converse 1964). Time-series data from the United States and Germany show an increase in this highest level of ideological sophistication (figure 2.4). In 1956, at the time of *The American Voter*, only 12 percent of the American public actively used ideological concepts in evaluating the Republican and Democratic parties. This group of ideologues increased to 27 percent during the tumultuous years of the mid-1960s, and in the 1980s stood at nearly double the 1950s level (Knight 1992). The German trend also moves upward throughout the 1970s and 1980s, only dipping in the nonideological context of the postunification election in 1990. Suggestive evidence from Great Britain shows growing ideological sophistication among its citizens. We see shortly that even this definition of ideologues may significantly underestimate the

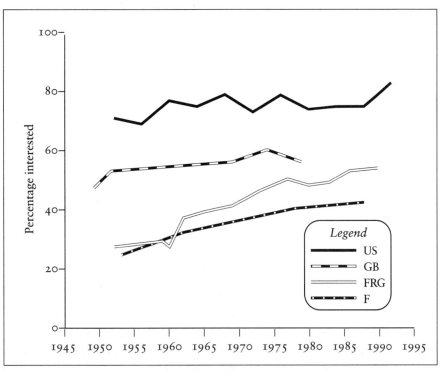

FIGURE 2.3

INTEREST IN POLITICS

SOURCES: *United States,* 1952–92, American National Election Studies. *Great Britain,* 1949, Gallup (1976a); 1963–79, British Election Studies. *Germany,* 1952–90, Noelle-Neumann and Koecher (1993, 617–18). *France,* 1953 and 1978, Charlot (1980); 1962, Gallup (1976b); 1988 (Michelet 1992).

sophistication of contemporary electorates.

Signs of a changing electorate are visible in other aspects of citizen politics. The present level of issue voting is generally higher than during earlier periods. Cognitive mobilization is also expanding political participation to include more demanding forms of political activity. Many of these specific trends are examined more closely in the following chapters, but the stereotype of an unsophisticated voter is clearly much less applicable today than during the 1950s.

Problems of Measurement

Researchers also have challenged the methodology of the studies that describe the public as unsophisticated. In the simplest case, the issue is

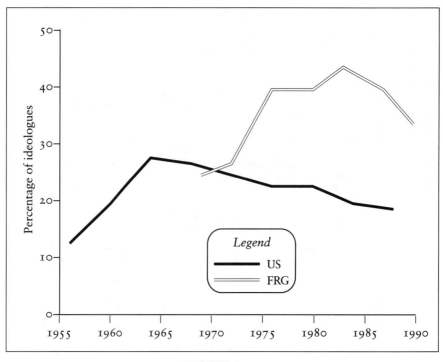

FIGURE 2.4

PERCENTAGE OF POLITICAL IDEOLOGUES

SOURCES: *United States,* 1956–80, Pierce et al. (1982); 1984–88, Knight (1992). *Germany,* 1969, Klingemann (1979); 1972–90, Hans-Dieter Klingemann, personal communication.

whether surveys are asking the proper questions. For instance, early surveys found that few voters could recall the name of their congressional representative—an apparent sign of a poorly informed public. When the task is name recognition rather than recall, however, most electors (more than 70 percent) can identify their representative (Mann 1978). Mann argues that the name recognition question more realistically measures the necessary level of political knowledge, thus dramatically altering our conclusions about the public's political sophistication. One could make this same argument for most measures of political (and nonpolitical) knowledge.[6]

Another measurement controversy involves the concept of issue constraint. During the 1970s, researchers found evidence of large increases in constraint between various issues in American opinion surveys (Nie with

Andersen 1974; Nie and Rabjohn 1979). Subsequent analyses showed that improvements in question wording and format contributed to these findings (Sullivan et al. 1978; Bishop et al. 1978). Critics of citizen sophistication therefore argued that political sophistication was not growing as rapidly as others claimed. More recent research finds that further improvements in survey question methodology can produce even higher levels of constraint and predictability in issue opinions (Krosnick 1991). In addition, John Zaller (1992) points out that even responses to a single issue item draw upon a mix of values, and thus it is not surprising to find some real fluidity in survey responses.

The debate on the format for survey questions sometimes misses a major lesson of this research. Even if the electorate has not become as consistent as some methodological studies suggested, citizens were not as inconsistent as researchers had initially thought (Niemi and Weisberg 1993, chap. 4).

Evidence on the public's supposedly limited commitment to democratic values is also open to question. Paul Sniderman and his colleagues (1991) analyzed data from a Canadian survey and the early McClosky study on the political tolerance of elites and the general public. They found that a general characterization of the citizenry as less tolerant than elites ignores the variations in opinions within both groups. Elites in several Canadian parties were actually less tolerant than some groups of party voters. Similarly, self-identified conservatives in America display less tolerance than the public as a whole and even conservatives among the public at large. They conclude "the differences in commitment to civil liberties between competing groups of elites eclipse in size and political significance differences between elites and the public as a whole" (Sniderman et al. 1991, 365). Thus the statistical evidence in support of this aspect of the elitist conception of democracy is very questionable.

Another important methodological debate concerns assessments of the public's ideological sophistication. The longitudinal analyses displayed in figure 2.4 show that the proportion of ideologically sophisticated Americans have increased since the time of *The American Voter* study. Eric R.A.N. Smith (1989) directly challenges this conclusion. By redefining the meaning of the concept, Smith argues that the sophistication of the American electorate has remained virtually unchanged in the three decades since *The American Voter*. Smith reinforces the theme of the limited sophistication of mass publics, but his evidence is flawed in two important ways. First, his analyses actually measure how much people say about politics. He uses the number of responses to the open-ended questions about what people like and dislike about the parties and candidates, rather than the content of these responses. By substituting quantity for the quality of response, Smith ignores what sophistication is supposed to measure (see Luskin 1987).

Second, there is convincing evidence that the active use of ideological concepts depends heavily on the political context. Cross-national evidence shows that political sophistication is not a fixed or a sharply restricted characteristic of public opinion (Klingemann 1979; Dalton 1988, 25).[7] For instance, the polarized nature of Italian politics (including a large Communist Party) yields high levels of ideological usage and recognition, although Italians are less educated and politically interested than many other Western publics. Conversely, the moderate American political climate leads to a low level of ideological expression when compared to most other nations. The low ranking for the United States is ironic, since the American electorate has been the primary basis of research on citizen political sophistication. This finding also underscores the importance of rising above the context of a single nation when making generalizations about the intrinsic political abilities of citizens.

Debates over question wording and format highlight a more basic concern of opinion researchers. By most standards, survey research is a blunt tool for measuring public opinion. Surveys simplify complex beliefs to categories such as "agree" or "disagree." The dividing line between response categories often is imprecise. What exactly is the difference between following politics "sometimes" versus "now and then? It is easy to imagine how a person may give different responses to the same question even if his or her interest in politics remains essentially constant. Faced with unclear or insufficient question options, the public's responses to survey questions may appear as inconsistent or unstable. The imprecision of the survey instrument (measurement error) thus contributes to perceptions of an unsophisticated electorate.

The size of the measurement problem can be substantial. Angus Campbell, Philip Converse, and Willard Rodgers (1979, 185), for example, found a .71 correlation between two identical questions measuring satisfaction with housing asked thirty minutes apart in a survey. Clearly, most people know whether they are satisfied with their own homes, and little should change in such a short time. These researchers attributed instability largely to the imprecision of the housing-satisfaction question. Yet this instability is not much different from the stability of some political opinions over a two-year period, which Converse (1964; Converse and Markus 1979) interprets as evidence of a lack of political attitudes.

Social psychologists and survey methodologists are well aware of the results of measurement error, and advanced statistical techniques can adjust for these measurement problems. When measurement error is taken into account, the stability of political opinions is much higher than previously recognized (Judd et al. 1981; Wyckoff 1987; cf. Converse 1980). In addition, the relationships between opinions in different policy areas is much stronger (Judd and Milburn 1980). We now realize that opinion instability and limited issue constraint are at least partially a product of imprecise measurement.

The methodological evidence thus points in the same direction. As our expertise in survey research methods has improved, so too has our evaluation of the public's political sophistication.

Sophistication versus Satisficing

It probably was inevitable that early empirical studies would reach negative conclusions about the public's political sophistication. Analysts judged citizens against the lofty ideals of classic democratic theory, and reality fell short of the theoretical ideals. When this occurred, analysts stressed the shortfall. We need a more balanced view of the topic; stripping away the idealized standards of classic democratic theory and the rationalizations of elitist democratic theory—looking instead at politics from the perspective of the voter. Recent research has devoted less attention to assessing the absolute level of the public's political abilities and has focused on how individuals actually deal with the political decisions they face.

To the surprise of some political science professors, politics is only one part of people's lives. Because of the pressing needs of family and career, people can devote only a limited amount of time to politics. The typical American, British, German, or French citizen cannot afford to keep informed on all political issues—few political elites or political scientists attempt this task. Similarly, people must balance participation in politics against their other time commitments. Citing these factors, the elitist theorists argue that many (or most) citizens are overwhelmed and become political dropouts, and democracy is better for it. In contrast, Morris Fiorina (1990, 335) has made the provocative argument that the more surprising fact is that citizens have as much information as they do, since the acquisition of political knowledge cannot be justified by narrow rationalist calculations of the value of that knowledge in influencing government policy.

While politics is complex, it still has important effects on one's life. Most citizens thus do not drop out of politics. Instead, they find a means of balancing the costs and benefits of political activity. Anthony Downs (1957) wrote of the "shortcuts" that a rational voter makes to manage the complexities of politics; current political scientists emphasize the same point by claiming that voters use "heuristics." For instance, Samuel Popkin writes (1991, 218) that "the use of information shortcuts is ... an inescapable fact of life, and will occur no matter how educated we are, how much information we have, and how much thinking we do." The political science literature has identified three potential methods that citizens might use as information shortcuts.

One approach suggests that citizens specialize their interests. Instead of following all issues, citizens concentrate their attention on a few topics of direct personal relevance or interest. The total electorate thus is divided into several partially overlapping *issue publics* (Converse 1964). Simply expressing an opinion is not enough to establish membership in an issue public, since many people will state an opinion to an interviewer even if they have given little prior thought to the topic. A member of an issue public has devoted prior attention to the issue and has firm beliefs. Many farmers, for example, closely monitor government agricultural policy while paying scant attention to urban renewal programs. Parents with school-age children may display considerable interest in educational policies, while the elderly may show a special concern for social security. The largest issue publics generally exist for topics of broad concern, such as economic policy, taxes, and basic social programs. At the other extreme, only a few voters regularly follow issues of foreign aid, agriculture, or international trade. Very few citizens are interested in every issue, but most citizens are members of at least one issue public. To paraphrase Will Rogers, "Everybody is sophisticated, only on different subjects."

The concept of issue publics has basic implications for the study of political sophistication. When citizens are allowed to define politics according to their own interests, a surprising level of political sophistication often appears. Robert Lane's conversations with a group of working-class men found coherent individual systems of political beliefs that sharply conflict with the findings of survey research (Lane 1962). David RePass (1971) documented a high level of rational issue voting when citizens identified their own issue interests. Opinion stability also is higher among members of the relevant issue public (Converse 1964, 244–45; Schuman and Presser 1981, chap. 9; Feldman 1989). Thus low issue constraint and stability in public opinion surveys do not mean the electorate is unsophisticated; the alternative explanation is that not all citizens are interested in all issues.

Philip Converse views issue publics as a negative aspect of mass opinion because a proliferation of distinct issue groups works against policymaking based on a broad, coherent ideological framework. Converse's criticism may be overstated, however. If citizens limit their issue interests, this does not mean that they fail to judge these issues using a broad political framework. Different clusters of issue interests still may emanate from a common underlying set of values. In addition, Lane (1973, 1962) pointed out the potential negative consequences of an overly structured belief system, for example, dogmatism and intolerance. In a slightly different context, analysts maintain that the existence of many competing political groups, with overlapping and cross-cutting memberships and shifting political alignments, is an essential characteristic of pluralist democracy (Dahl 1971). In some instances, therefore, issue publics may be a positive feature of citizen politics.

A second model of satisficing behavior generalizes the idea of issue publics into a broader framework of "schema theory" (Conover and Feldman 1984; Peffley and Hurwitz 1985). Instead of viewing belief systems as interconnecting a diverse range of political attitudes, as originally proposed by Converse, schema theorists maintain there is a *vertical structure* (or network) of beliefs within specific political domains as illustrated in figure 2.5. A broad organizing structure is linked to general political orientations; specific issue opinions are derived from one or more of these general orientations. For instance, attitudes toward government programs assisting minorities might reflect both orientations toward the role of gov-

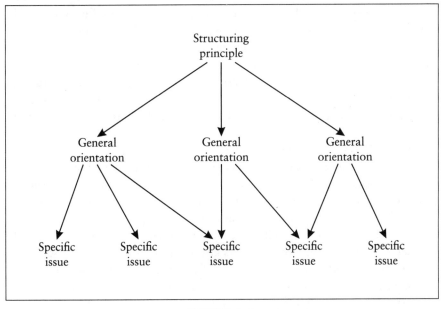

FIGURE 2.5

A HIERARCHICAL MODEL OF BELIEFS

ernment and attitudes toward minorities (Sniderman, Brody, and Tetlock 1991). At the same time, even if opinions on specific issues are strongly linked to broader political orientations, the model posits that relationships between specific issue opinions can be weak because they are not directly linked together. Thus this model lacks the direct linkage between opinions on different issues posited in *The American Voter* model (see figure 2.1, p. 18).

Furthermore, the specific political attitudes included within a schema, and the structures used to organize information, might vary across individuals. Some voters' beliefs will include only one part of the structure of figure 2.5, such as the issues on the left of the figure. Another person's schematic structure might include another subset of issues and general orientations. Thus the growing literature on schema theory has tried to identify specific cognitive structures (or schema) that are relevant for subsets of issues, such as a foreign policy schema, a racial schema, or a schema for judging political candidates.[8]

In short, a complex belief system might exist within an issue public, linking issue positions to a broad structuring principle such as Left/Right position—even if schema are not linked across issue publics. The existence of such structures provides voters with a method of managing information and making political judgments. Thus even if citizens are not sophisticated on all political topics, they may have logical and structured beliefs within specific domains that enable them to manage political decision making.

A third model of satisficing involves the use of reference standards to simplify political decisions. This research is compatible with schema theory, offering alternatives to the development of a sophisticated structuring principle. Instead, citizens rely on political cues, or heuristics, to orient themselves to politics (Sniderman, Brody, and Tetlock 1991; Ferejohn and Kuklinski 1990).

Social groups provide one common source of political cues. Many policy issues can be cast as conflicts between class, religious, ethnic, or other social groupings. Membership in a social group, either formal or through psychological ties, can be a valuable guidepost in dealing with policy questions. The French steelworker, for example, might prefer nationalizing industry because he feels it will benefit working-class interests; an avowed French Catholic presumably supports government aid for religious schools. These voters might not explain their policy preferences with sophisticated ideological arguments or reference to specific legislative proposals, but they still are making reasonable political choices.

Early voting studies emphasized social groups as a source of voting cues. Lazarsfeld and his colleagues (1948) constructed an *index of political predisposition* based on social class, religion, and rural/urban residence. This index was a potent predictor of American voting behavior. The highly stratified nature of Western European societies produced even stronger group differences in European voting patterns (Lipset and Rokkan 1967; Rose 1974). Furthermore, studies of ideological sophistication find that group references are frequently a basis of party evaluation (Converse 1964; Klingemann 1979). For many less educated citizens, group references may reflect broad political orientations that they have difficulty explaining in the terminology that would classify them as sophisticated ideologues. When social conflicts are salient, and the parties take clear positions on these conflicts, then social characteristics can provide effective cues for orienting oneself to politics.

An even more powerful source of political cues is partisanship. Many citizens develop a psychological bond to a specific political party that may persist through an entire lifetime (Campbell et al. 1960, chap. 6). This *party identification* sometimes is based on emotional and nonrational criteria, such as simple inheritance of parental partisanship, and may serve as a surrogate for social-reference-group cues. Party attachments also usually contain a rational evaluative component that incorporates past political experiences (Fiorina 1981; Downs 1957, 85).

The usefulness of social-group cues is limited to topics directly related to group interests, but party identification has broader applications. Parties are central participants in democratic politics, so most political phenomena can be judged within a partisan framework. Party attachments obviously can simplify voting choices, since most elections involve a choice between parties. In Western Europe, where parties act as cohesive units, party voting is an effective and efficient method of decision making. The heterogeneity of American parties lessens the policy value of party voting, but the complexity of American elections still makes party a valuable voting cue. Partisanship is also an important force in shaping evaluations of political leaders and new political issues. If voters are unsure about an issue, party cues can suggest where their interests lie. An issue supported by one's party is more likely to benefit the individual, while the policies of the opposition are suspect. In sum, because of its ability to make sense of distant, complicated, and often arcane political phenomena, party identification frequently is viewed as the central thread connecting the citizen and the political process.

Left/Right orientations may serve as another source of political cues. Most voters do not express sophisticated ideological views, but they still can locate themselves within a broad ideological family, or *tendance* (Klingemann 1979; Fuchs and Klingemann 1989; Westholm and Niemi

1992; Jacoby 1991). This Left/Right orientation provides a reference structure for evaluating political objects. In most nations partisanship and ideological orientations exist side by side and have reinforcing effects. But Left/Right orientations hold special importance in political systems where party cues are weak; for example, in France. The French party system is notoriously volatile, which undercuts the continuity and value of partisanship. Ideological tendance thus plays a larger role in guiding the political behavior of the French and can bring some order to an ever-changing political landscape (Fleury and Lewis-Beck 1993; Michelat 1993).

The diverse criteria that people use in making political judgments is suggested by the results in table 2.2. Citizens in several nations were asked to describe the good and bad points of two major political parties in their nation. In general, only a few people actively employ ideological concepts in judging the parties. This does not mean, however, that the remaining individuals are devoid of political judgments. About 40 percent of the American, British, and German electorates evaluated the parties according to social-group alignments. Even more voters judged the parties by their organization and political competency. Outright policy criteria were mentioned in nearly half of the survey responses. Even the broadest and most frequently used criteria—judging parties by the nature of the times—can provide a meaningful basis of evaluation (Fiorina 1981; MacKuen et al. 1992). In short, far from suggesting that citizens are uninformed and unsophisti-

TABLE 2.2
BASES OF PARTY EVALUATIONS
(IN PERCENTAGES)

Criteria based on	United States	Great Britain	West Germany
Ideological concepts	21	21	34
Social groups	40	41	45
Party organization and competence	49	35	66
Policy concepts	45	46	53
Nature of the times	64	59	86
Political figures	40	18	38
Intrinsic values	46	65	49
No content	14	18	6
Total	319	303	377

SOURCE: Political Action Study, 1974–75.

NOTE: Totals exceed 100 percent because multiple responses were possible.

cated, these data display a diversity and complexity of public opinion that often is overlooked.

Politics and the Public

This chapter has focused on trends that are affecting all advanced industrial democracies: the rise of political interest, cognitive skills, and information resources. There are, of course, important differences in these traits across nations. Political interest and involvement apparently are more extensive in the United States than in Britain, Germany, or France. Conversely, politics and public opinion generally are more ideological in Europe than in the United States. While subsequent chapters draw out these national differences in more detail, this chapter has described a broad pattern of increasing political sophistication that is common to publics in most advanced industrial democracies.

Although political sophistication has increased, democratic electorates will never match the political sophistication posited by classic democratic theory and displayed by political elites such as members of Congress or Parliament. It makes little sense to debate this point. Instead, the findings of survey research more meaningfully describe how citizens actually perceive and evaluate politics, and reach political decisions—how publics deal with the decision-making tasks they face. Despite the criticisms of the naysayers, citizens are regularly making political choices and finding diverse criteria on which to make these decisions. How are these choices made?

The evidence of this chapter describes a pattern of public opinion that Donald Kinder and David Sears (1985) term the "pluralistic roots of political beliefs." People rely on various methods to manage the complexities of politics. Many voters focus their attention on a few issues of particular interest, rather than devoting equal attention to all issues. Thus the electorate is composed of overlapping issue publics, each judging government action on different policies. The bases of evaluation also vary within the electorate. Some citizens judge politics by a broad ideological framework, but this is only a minority of the public. Many more citizens depend on political cues, such as social-reference groups or party attachments, to guide their behavior. By limiting their issue interests and relying on other decision-making shortcuts, the average voter can balance the costs and benefits of political involvement and still make reasonable political decisions.[9]

Some of the most persuasive work on this topic comes from Sniderman, Brody, and Tetlock (1991; also Moon 1990). They find, for example, that better-educated individuals are more likely to use ideological criteria as a basis for their political choices. At the same time, other citizens use group references or other political cues to make their decisions. In both cases the decisions broadly reflect their interests. Even more telling is Arthur Lupia's (1994) research on voting on insurance initiatives in California. He finds that a small attentive public was well informed on the initiatives and made choices appropriate for their defined interests. In addition, a larger group of voters used group cues, which proposals were supported by Ralph Nader and which by the insurance industry, and also made rational voting choices. This is pluralistic decision making in practice.

This pluralistic model has several implications for our study of public opinion in later chapters. We should not interpret unstable or inconsistent issue opinions as evidence that voters lack any attitudes. Survey questions are imprecise, the public's issue interests are specialized, and a complex mix of beliefs may be related to a single issue (Zaller 1992). In addition, we must be sensitive to the diversity and complexity of mass politics. Simple models of political behavior that assume a homogeneous electorate might be theoretically elegant and empirically parsimonious, but they are also unrealistic. Citizens function on the basis of diverse criteria and motivations. We should try to model this diversity, instead of adopting overly generalized theories of citizen politics. Finally, we must not underestimate the potential for change. As this chapter has documented, the electorates of advanced industrial democracies have undergone a major transformation during the postwar period. Public opinion reflects a dynamic process, and we should avoid static views of an unchanging (or unchangeable) public.

We should not, of course, be guilty of overestimating the sophistication of Western publics. There will always be instances when the electorate holds ill-advised or ill-informed opinions; some citizens will remain ignorant of all political matters. Such is the imperfect nature of human behavior. While few individuals deserve the rating of full ideologues, however, an equally small number are devoid of all bases for making meaningful political choices. The important lesson is not to ignore or belittle the varied criteria citizens rely on in dealing with politics.

The ultimate question, then, is not whether the public meets the maximum ideological standards of classic democratic theory, but whether the public has a sufficient basis for rational political action. Phrased in these terms, and based on the evidence presented in this chapter, we can be more optimistic about the nature of belief systems in contemporary publics.

Notes

1. There were, of course, dissenting voices. Bagehot (1978), Schumpeter (1943), Wallas (1908), and Lippmann (1922) were highly critical of a participa-

tory view of democracy. For a review of this literature, see Eckstein (1984).

2. For other examples of such inconsistencies, see Arnold (1990). Furthermore, the elitist theory ignores the problem of democratic accountability if its assumptions are true, and it ignores the evidence on the abuses of power among even democratically elected elites (e.g., Green et al. 1984).

3. For example, subsequent research has questioned the evidence that elites are more politically tolerant than the general public (Jackman 1972; Sniderman et al. 1991).

4. The European nations used the same question: "Which sources of information are most helpful at election time?" The question in the United States asked about the use of information sources for news about what's going on in the world today.

5. The British, German, and French questions measure general interest in politics, although the question wordings and response options are different in each nation. The American question asked about interest in campaigns. Because of the differences in question wordings, the absolute levels of political interest should not be compared across nations; for such comparisons, see Jennings and van Deth (1989) and Inglehart (1990).

6. Critics of the public's level of knowledge often ignore parallel findings among elite groups. For instance, Zimmerman (1990, 1991) found that newspaper editors and elected politicians displayed surprisingly low levels of knowledge about historical and scientific facts.

7. Similarly, figure 2.4 (p. 28) shows that the contextual influences on ideological sophistication also can change over time. The American public's ideological sophistication increases sharply during the polarized years of the mid-1960s and then declines in the 1970s as political conflict moderates.

8. This literature is quite diverse in its applications (see Hurwitz and Peffley 1987; Sniderman, Brody, and Kuklinski 1984; Graber 1988; Miller, Wattenberg, and Malanchuk 1986; Rohrschneider 1993a). For a critique of schema theory, see Kuklinski, Luskin, and Bolland (1991).

9. The public's reliance on various decision-making shortcuts is similar to the pattern of "satisficing" behavior common to decision makers in business and government (Cyert and March 1963). Nevertheless, the democratic elitists would denigrate this when the public adopts satisficing behavior on political matters.

3. Political Participation

Democracy should be a celebration of an involved public. Democracy requires an active citizenry because it is through discussion, popular interest, and involvement in politics that societal goals should be defined and carried out in a democracy. Without public involvement in the process, democracy lacks both its legitimacy and its guiding force. When Germans take the time to cast informed votes, British electors canvass their neighbors, or Americans write their president, the democratic process is at work. The recent global spread of democratization has brought these democratic freedoms to millions of people. The jubilation that accompanied the first democratic elections in Eastern Europe or the open elections in South Africa attests to the value that citizens place on this right.

Although the objectives of participation may be similar for American, British, German, and French citizens, the actual methods and contexts of citizen input often vary across nations. This chapter examines several methods of "conventional" citizen action. By this we mean voting, campaigns, group activities, and other methods normally associated with democratic politics. We are not implying that unconventional forms of participation (protests, demonstrations, etc.) are unimportant; they are, in fact, examined in the next chapter. Instead, the sources and motivations of conventional and unconventional participation are sufficiently distinct to deserve detailed and separate attention.

The Modes of Participation

Most discussions of citizen action equate the public's participation in politics with the act of voting. Voting is the most visible and widespread form of citizen action, but it is not the only means of citizen input. The public's participation in politics is not limited to elections, nor is voting the most effective means of influencing the political process. Moreover, in cross-national comparisons, voting is an imprecise measure of the public's overall involvement in the political process.

A rich set of cross-national studies has explored the different forms of conventional political action in which citizens may participate (Verba et al. 1971, 1978). These researchers find that people do not use various activities interchangeably, as many early analysts assumed. Instead, people tend to specialize in activities that match their motivations and goals. Specific kinds of activities frequently cluster together. A person who performs one act from a particular cluster is likely to perform other acts from the same cluster, but not necessarily activities from another cluster. They labeled these clusters of activities *modes of democratic participation.*

Researchers have identified several distinct modes of activity: voting, campaign activity, communal activity (working with a group in the community), and contacting officials on personal matters (table 3.1). Separate participation modes exist because political activities differ in the requirements they place on participants and the nature of the action. Sidney Verba and his colleagues (1978) classified the differences between participation modes by several criteria: (1) whether the act conveys information about the individual's political preferences and/or applies pressure for compliance; (2) whether the act is directed toward a broad social outcome or a particular interest; (3) the potential degree of conflict involved in the activity; (4) the amount of effort required; and (5) the amount of cooperation with others required by the act.

Voting, for example, is a high-pressure activity because it determines control of the government, but its policy content is limited because an election involves many issues. Voting also is a reasonably simple act that requires little initiative or cooperation with others. Involvement in political campaigns makes much greater demands on the time and motivation of individuals. Although campaign work occurs within an electoral setting, it can be more policy focused than the simple act of voting. Participation in community groups, communal activity, may require even more effort by the individual and produces a qualitatively different form of citizen input. Citizen groups can control both the methods of action and the policy focus of their activities. Finally, some individuals participate for a very particular reason—to have a pothole fixed or to request other government services —that does not address broad policy questions.

This clustering of activities seems to be a common feature of democratic politics. A replication of the American survey found essentially the same participation grouping two decades later (Nie et al. 1988). The British participation study (Parry et al. 1992) added some political activities and found additional modes; but their basic findings are very similar to American research.[1] Thus, our discussion of citizen action focuses on the three most common modes of conventional participation: voting, campaign activity, and communal activity.[2]

TABLE 3.1

DIMENSIONS OF POLITICAL ACTIVITY AND MODES OF ACTIVITY

Mode of activity	Type of influence	Scope of outcome	Conflict	Initiative required	Cooperate with others
Voting	High pressure/low information	Collective	Conflictual	Little	Little
Campaign activity	High pressure/low to high information	Collective	Conflictual	Some	Some or much
Communal activity	Low to high pressure/ high information	Collective	Maybe yes/ maybe no	Some or much	Some or much
Contacting officials on personal matters	Low pressure/high information	Particular	Nonconflictual	Much	Little
Protest	High pressure/high information	Collective	Very conflictual	Some or much	Some or much

SOURCE: Verba et al. (1978, 55) with modifications.

Voting

The history of modern democracies has followed a pattern of almost ever-expanding citizen involvement in elections (Rokkan 1970). The voting franchise in most nations initially was restricted to property owners, and long residency requirements existed. The United States was one of the first nations to begin liberalizing suffrage laws. By 1850 virtually the entire white adult male population in the United States was enfranchised. The extension of voting rights proceeded more slowly in Western Europe. These societies lacked the populist tradition that existed in the United States. In addition, social cleavages were polarized more sharply than in America; many European conservatives were hesitant to enfranchise a working class that might vote them out of office. An emerging socialist movement in the 1800s pressed for the political equality of the working class, but mass suffrage often was delayed until war or revolution disrupted the conservative political order. Voting rights were granted to French adult males with the formation of the Third Republic in 1870. Britain limited election rolls until early in the twentieth century by placing significant residency and financial restrictions on voting and by allowing multiple votes for business owners and university graduates. Electoral reforms followed World War I and granted the vote to virtually all British males. Germany, too, had limited the franchise and allowed for multiple votes during the Wilhelmine Empire. True democratic elections with mass suffrage began with the creation of the Weimar Republic in 1919.

During the twentieth century, suffrage rights were gradually extended to the rest of the adult population. Women's right to vote was acknowledged first in Britain (1918); Germany (1919) and the United States (1920) quickly followed. France lagged most of Western Europe in this instance; French women were enfranchised only in 1944. The Voting Rights Act of 1965 removed most of the remaining formal restrictions on the voting participation of American blacks. Finally, in the 1970s all four nations lowered the voting age to eighteen years of age.

In contemporary democracies the right to vote now extends to virtually the entire adult population. There are, however, distinct national differences in the rate at which citizens actually turn out to vote. Table 3.2 presents the rates of voting turnout for twenty-four industrialized democracies from the 1950s to the 1990s. These data display sharp cross-national differences in participation levels across democratic polities. In the United States and Switzerland, for instance, national elections involve barely half of the eligible adults. Voting rates are consistently higher in most European nations, especially in Germany, where close to 80 percent of the electorate cast a ballot in Bundestag elections. Turnout ranges between 70 and 90 percent in most British House of Commons elections and French National Assembly elections.

The other significant pattern in table 3.2 is the trend in participation rates over time. Comparing the two end points for the twenty-one nations with a complete time series, thirteen (including France, Germany, and the United States) have experienced turnout declines of more than 2 percent six have had stable turnout levels (plus or minus 2 percent), and two saw a turnout increase of more than 2 percent. The drop-off in voting rates was exceptionally marked in the first elections of the 1990s. Thus, voting participation is generally decreasing across national boundaries.

Compared to most other nations, voting levels in the United States appear significantly lower; moreover, the marked decrease in American turnout over the past forty years has exacerbated this pattern. Some analysts cite these statistics as evidences of the American electorate's limited political involvement (and by implication limited political abilities). But a more complex set of factors is at work (Verba et al. 1978; Rosenstone and Hansen 1993; Flickinger and Studlar 1992; Teixeira 1992, chap. 1). Voter registration systems and other electoral procedures strongly influence transatlantic differences in turnout. Most Europeans are automatically included on the roster of registered voters, and these electoral registers are updated by the government. Thus, a much larger percentage of the European public is registered to participate in elections. In contrast, most Americans must take the initiative to register themselves to vote, and many eligible voters fail to do so. By many estimates, participation in American elections would increase by at least ten percentage points if the European system of registration were adopted (Wolfinger and Rosenstone 1980). The scheduling of most European elections on weekends also encourages turnout, because more voters can find the time to visit the polls. In addition, most European electoral systems are based on proportional representation (PR) rather than plurality-based single-member districts, as in the United States. Proportional representation stimulates turnout because any party, large or small, can increase its representation in the legislature as a direct function of its share of the popular vote.

G. Bingham Powell (1980, 1986) and Markus Crepaz (1990) show that political competition is another strong influence on turnout rates. Sharp social or ideological cleavages between parties stimulate turnout. The more polarized European party systems generally encourage higher voting rates than those found in the United States. When European voters go to the polls, they are deciding whether their country will be run by parties with socialist, green, conservative, ethnic, or even religious programs. Most European elections have a greater potential to make significant politi-

TABLE 3.2

LEVELS OF TURNOUT FROM THE 1950S TO THE 1990S
(PERCENTAGE VOTING)

	1950s	1960s	1970s	1980s	1990s
Australia	90	93	93	91	94
Austria	94	93	93	90	84
Belgium	88	86	86	87	85
Canada	74	77	73	73	69
Denmark	82	87	86	86	83
Finland	86	85	78	75	72
France	75	75	81	70	69
Germany (West)	84	85	90	86	77
Greece	—	—	78	80	80
Iceland	89	90	89	88	88
Ireland	74	74	76	74	66
Israel	78	80	78	78	77
Italy	90	90	89	84	87
Japan	76	80	78	78	73
Luxembourg	88	84	84	83	87
Netherlands	93	93	83	84	78
New Zealand	91	88	85	89	80
Norway	78	83	82	83	76
Portugal	—	—	88	78	68
Spain	—	—	73	75	76
Sweden	78	86	90	90	87
Switzerland	68	63	53	47	46
Great Britain	80	76	75	74	78
United States	61	62	54	52	53
21-nation average	82	82	81	79	76

SOURCES: Mackie and Rose (1990) and data collected by the author.

cal choices than do American elections. Robert Jackman (1987) has shown that the structural incentives for voting also strongly affect turnout rates. He finds that the number of party choices and the structure of legislative power in a system are direct predictors of turnout.

The United States also differs from most other democracies because the American government asks its citizens to vote on far more matters. While the typical European voter may cast two or three ballots in a four-year period, many Americans face a dozen or more separate elections in the space of four years. Furthermore, Americans are expected to vote for a much wider range of political offices. Only one house of the bicameral national legislature is directly elected in Britain, Germany, and France; the French president is one of the few directly elected European heads of state. Local, regional, and even national elections in Europe normally consist of casting a single ballot for a single office; the extensive list of elected offices and long ballots common to American elections are unknown in Western Europe. Finally, direct democracy techniques such as the referendum and initiative are used only sparingly in France and Britain and not at all in German national politics.

Thus the American political system places unusual demands on the voters to decide on an array of political offices, government bond and tax proposals, and other policy initiatives. Voting in low-information contests, such as voting for local nonpartisan offices, is a real challenge for American voters. It is probably no coincidence that the one European country that has a comparable turnout level to the United States—Switzerland—also presents its citizens with extensive voting opportunities, calling eighty-nine national elections in the period between 1947 and 1975 (for other reasons why Swiss turnout is so low, see Powell 1982, 119).

Rather than count only the number of people who vote in national elections, an alternative measure of participation focuses on the *amount of electing* being done by the public (Crewe 1981). When the context of American elections is considered, the amount of electing is actually quite high:

> No country can approach the United States in the frequency and variety of elections, and thus in the amount of electing. No other country elects its lower house as often as every two years, or its president as frequently as every four years. No other country popularly elects its state governors and town mayors, or has as wide a variety of nonrepresentative offices (judges, sheriffs, attorneys general, city treasurers, and so on) subject to election. Only one other country (Switzerland) can compete in the number and variety of local referendums, and only two (Belgium and Turkey) hold party "primaries" in most parts of the country. Even if differences in turnout rates are taken into account, American citizens do not necessarily vote less often than other nationalities; most probably, they do more voting. (Crewe 1981, 262)

A simple comparison of the electoral experiences of a typical European and American voter highlights this difference in the amount of voting. For example, between 1985 and 1990 a resident of Cambridge, England, could have voted about four times; a resident of Irvine, California, could have cast forty-four votes in just the single year of 1992.[3]

Turnout rates in national elections thus provide a poor indicator of the overall political involvement of the public. In addition, the simple quantity of voting is less important than the quality of this participation mode. Verba and his colleagues (1978, chap. 3) describe voting as an activity of high pressure because leaders are being chosen, but there is limited specific policy information or influence because elections involve a diverse range of factors. Therefore, the infrequent opportunity of most Europeans to cast a single vote for a prepackaged party is a limited tool of political influence. This influence may increase when elections extend to a wide range of political offices and include referendums, as in the United States. Still it is difficult to treat elections as policy mandates because they assess relative support for broad programs and not specific policies. Even a sophisticated policy-oriented electorate cannot be assured that important policy options are represented in an election or that the government will follow these policies in the period between elections. Consequently, research shows that many people vote because of a sense of civic duty, involvement in a campaign, or as an expression of political or partisan support, rather than to influence policy (Verba and Nie 1972; Conway 1991a).

The limits of voting have led some critics to claim that by focusing mass participation on voting, parties and political elites are seeking to protect their privileged position in the policy process and actually limit citizen influence. Even if this skepticism is deserved, voting will remain an important aspect of democratic politics, as much for its symbolic value as for its instrumental influence on policy. Voting is the one activity that binds the individual to the political system and legitimizes the rest of the democratic process.

Campaign Activity
Participation in campaign activities represents an extension of electoral participation beyond the act of voting. This mode includes a variety of political acts: working for a party or candidate, attending campaign meetings, persuading others how to vote, membership in a party or political organization, and other forms of party activity during and between elections. Fewer citizens are routinely active in campaigns because this is more demanding than merely casting a vote. Campaign work requires more initiative, and there is greater need to coordinate participation with others (see table 3.1, p. 42). As a result of the additional effort, campaign activity can provide more political influence to the individual citizen and convey more information than voting. Campaign activities are important to parties and

candidates, and candidates generally are more sensitive to, and aware of, the policy interests of activists (Verba and Nie 1972, chaps. 17–19).

Campaign activities can take many forms, depending on the context of electioneering in the nation. In the United States, for example, campaigns are now largely media events. Popular involvement in organized campaign activities is limited (table 3.3). Few Americans attend party meetings, work for a party or candidate, or belong to a party or political club. Steven Rosenstone and John Hansen (1993, chap. 3) present additional poll data that indicate a decreased attendance at political meetings over the past decade. The most frequent campaign activities are individualistic forms of political involvement: giving money to a campaign or trying to persuade others. Personal involvement in campaign discussions has held steady or even increased slightly over the past thirty years. The stimulus of the tight presidential election and the Perot candidacy actually pushed political discussion in 1992 to its highest level ever.

The structure of British campaigns differs in important ways from American elections. British elections do not follow a regular time schedule; the prime minister may dissolve Parliament and call for new elections at almost any time during a legislative term. Therefore, elections are often quickly organized and brief, averaging little more than a month. In addition, British parties depend on a pool of formal party members for the bulk of campaign work. Party members attend political rallies, canvass the constituency during the campaign, and go door-to-door contacting potential voters on election day. Beyond the core of party members, there is limited participation in most campaign activities (table 3.4). Moreover, with declines in the percentage of party members has come a general decrease in organized campaign activities.

Germany's development of a democratic political system during the past thirty years has increased citizen involvement in campaigns and most other aspects of the political process (Ühlinger 1989). Membership in political parties has remained stable or even increased, and participation in campaign activities has grown. For example, 11 percent of the public attended a campaign meeting in the 1961 election; by 1976 this figure had nearly doubled (20 percent). Similarly, beginning in the 1970s, popular displays of party support became a more visible aspect of campaigns. Citizen groups display electoral support independent of the party-run campaigns, so campaign activity now extends beyond formal party members to include a significant proportion of the public. In the 1989 European Parliament (EP) election, for instance, German voters closely followed the campaign in the media and nearly one out of ten spoke with a party worker during the campaign—although the EP elections attract much less attention than

TABLE 3.3
CAMPAIGN ACTIVITY IN THE UNITED STATES
(IN PERCENTAGES)

Activity	1952	1956	1960	1964	1968	1972	1976	1980	1984	1988	1992
Belong to a club or political organization	2	3	3	4	3	—[a]	—[a]	3	—[a]	—[a]	—[a]
Work for a party or candidate	3	3	6	5	6	5	4	4	4	3	3
Go to meetings	7	7	8	8	9	9	6	8	8	7	8
Give money	4	10	12	11	9	10	16	8	12	6	6
Wear a button or have a bumper sticker	—[a]	16	21	17	15	14	8	7	9	9	11
Persuade others how to vote	28	28	34	31	33	32	37	36	32	29	38

SOURCE: American National Election Studies.

a. Data are not available.

TABLE 3.4
CAMPAIGN ACTIVITY IN GREAT BRITAIN, 1964–87
(IN PERCENT)

Activity	1964	1966	1970	1974	1974	1979	1983	1987
Canvass	3	2	1	2	2	2	2	2
Work for a party or candidate	8	2	2	2	3	2	2	2
Attend meeting (indoors)	8	7	5	5	6	4	3	4
Attend meeting (outdoors)	8	3	6	4	3	2	—[a]	—[a]
Display poster	—[a]	—[a]	10	9	11	8	12	10
Party member	14	—[a]	10	—[a]	8	—[a]	7	9
Read electoral address	46	49	53	51	43	56	49	49

SOURCE: 1964–75, Gallup (1976a); 1983–87, Hastings and Hastings (1989, 312); participation data for 1979 and party membership data for all years from British Election Studies.

a. Data are not available.

Bundestag elections (see table 3.5). Indeed, German involvement in the 1989 EP election was generally higher than that of British or French electors. Thus past stereotypes of an unconcerned and uninvolved German electorate no longer apply.[4]

The available evidence on party and campaign activity in France is less extensive. Formal party membership has increased during the Fifth Republic, first as a result of the consolidation of a Gaullist majority and then because of Mitterrand's development of the socialist Left. At the same time, there are ongoing debates about the general depoliticization of French politics (Boy and Mayer 1993). Attendance at campaign meetings, public displays of party support, and other campaign activities probably have decreased during the past two decades, though firm empirical evidence is limited. Data from the 1989 EP election show that many French voters followed the campaign, but campaign involvement lagged slightly behind British and German levels (table 3.5).

It is difficult to abstract a general pattern of campaign activity from these diverse national experiences. Overall involvement in campaigns apparently has increased in Germany, held steady in the United States, and declined in Britain and France. Nevertheless, several common trends are at work in each nation. The expanding electoral role of the mass media is lessening the importance of party-organized activities designed to inform the public: campaign rallies, canvassing, and formal party meetings. The media's growing importance has also encouraged the spread of American-style electioneering to Western Europe. British candidates orchestrate "walkabouts" to generate stories for the evening television news, campaigns focus more attention on candidate personalities than in the past, and televised preelection debates are the norm in Germany and France.

In addition to these institutional changes, the public's increasing sophistication and interest in politics spurs campaign involvement. Many individuals are still drawn to the excitement and competition of elections, but now campaign participation is more often individualistic, such as a display of party support or discussing the elections with friends. The *level* of campaign activity may be changing less than the *nature* of the public's involvement.

Communal Activity

Communal activity is a third participation mode. Communal participation can take a wide variety of forms; this is one of the positive characteristics of this kind of activity. Much communal activity involves group efforts to deal with social or community problems, ranging from issues of schools or roads to protecting the local environment. In addition, participation in citi-

TABLE 3.5

PARTICIPATION IN VARIOUS ACTIVITIES FOR EUROPEAN
PARLIAMENT ELECTION (IN PERCENTAGES)

	Great Britain	Germany	France
Followed campaign			
Watched TV program on election	50	61	51
Read newspaper report on election	30	32	26
Read a party poster	11	35	25
Listened to radio on election	18	19	19
Read party materials	32	16	18
Read advertisement about election	15	23	14
Active in campaign			
Talked to people about election	32	40	39
Spoke to a party worker	4	9	5
Tried to persuade someone on vote	7	3	8
Attended a public meeting	1	7	3

SOURCE: Eurobarometer 31A (June 1989).

zen groups can include involvement in public interest groups with broad policy concerns, such as environmental interest groups, women's groups, or consumer protection (Berry 1989; Dalton and Kuechler 1990).

This mode is distinct from campaign activity because communal participation takes place largely outside the electoral setting and lacks a partisan focus. Because participation is not structured by an election, a relatively high level of political sophistication and initiative is required of communal activists (table 3.1, p. 42). Citizens define their own issue agenda, the methods of influencing policymakers, and the timing of influence. The issues might be as broad as nuclear disarmament or as narrow as the policies of the local school district—citizens, not elites, decide. This control over the framework of participation means that communal activities can convey more information and exert more political pressure than the public's restricted participation in campaigns. In short, the communal mode shifts control of participation to the public and thereby increases the citizenry's political influence.

The unstructured nature of communal activities makes it difficult to measure participation levels accurately or to compare levels across nations. Still, general impressions of national differences exist. Americans are noted for their group-based approach to political participation. This trait is embedded in the American political culture as far back as the nineteenth century, when Tocqueville commented on the American proclivity to form groups to address community problems:

> The political activity that pervades the United States must be seen to be understood. No sooner do you set foot upon American ground than you are stunned by a kind of tumult; ... here the people of one quarter of a town are meeting to decide upon the building of a church; there the election of a representative is going on; a little farther, the delegates of a district are hastening to the town in order to consult upon some local improvements; in another place, the laborers of a village quit their plows to deliberate upon a project of a road or a public school.... To take a hand in the regulation of society and to discuss it is (the) biggest concern and, so to speak, the only pleasure an American knows. (Tocqueville 1966, 249–50)

Recent studies find that many Americans still favor organized groups for dealing with political problems. And in addition to traditional community-based involvement, a variety of new political movements and single-issue groups have developed in recent years: the environmental lobby, the women's movement, disarmament groups, moral/religious groups, and other organizations. Sidney Verba and his colleagues find that 30 percent of Americans participated in community groups in 1967, and this increased to 34 percent by 1987 (Verba, Schlozman, and Brady 1995; Verba et al. 1978).

European political norms traditionally placed less emphasis on group activities (Almond and Verba 1963, chap. 7), and the structure of European political systems did not encourage direct citizen contact with elected representatives. Nevertheless, communal activities have also grown in Europe in recent years (Westle 1992). In the early 1970s individuals with similar issue concerns organized into citizen-action groups (*Bürgerinitiativen*) in Germany; participation in these groups expanded rapidly during the 1980s. In 1980, 6 percent of Germans had participated in a citizen-action group; by 1985 membership had increased to 13 percent; it remained at 12 percent in 1989 (Dalton 1993a, chap. 6; Ühlinger 1989). Membership in British citizen groups has also grown markedly. The British Participation Study found that 10–14 percent of Britons were involved in group actions (Parry et al. 1992, 44–45). By most accounts, communal activity is more limited in France. Tocqueville, for example, contrasted American social cooperation with the individualism of the French political culture. The French tradition of individualism continues to the present (Hoffmann 1974; Ehrmann and Schain 1992, chaps. 1 and 3). The average French citizen is somewhat hesitant to cooperate with others and thereby submerge individual interests in those of the group.

The 1990–91 World Values Study gives a glimpse of cross-national differences in the public's involvement in citizen groups. The survey asked whether individuals were members of a local community-action group, an environmental group, or a women's group. Involvement was greatest among Americans (18 percent); Britons (11 percent) and western Germans (11 percent) displayed slightly lower levels of activity, and French participation (8 percent) fell further behind. Furthermore, in most nations membership in these citizens groups exceeded formal membership in a political party. In sum, this form of political involvement is becoming a more common aspect of political action in contemporary democracies.

The Predictors of Participation

The question of who participates in politics is as important as the question of how many people participate. First, the characteristics of participants help us to interpret the meaning of political activism. For example, policy dissatisfaction might either increase or decrease the likelihood of political action. In one instance, dissatisfaction might stimulate individuals to participate in order to redress their grievances; in another instance, dissatisfaction might lead to alienation and a withdrawal from politics. These two alternatives cast a much different light on the significance of participation. Second, if citizen participation influences policy results, then the pattern of participation suggests which citizens are making their voices heard by policymakers and which interests are not represented. Finally, comparing the correlates of participation across nations and participation modes provides insights into the political process in each nation and the distinct aspects of each mode.

We can organize potential predictors of participation into three groupings: *personal characteristics, group effects,* and *political attitudes.* Under the first heading, political scientists stress social status as the personal characteristic that is most strongly related to political action. Following politics requires the time to stay informed and the conceptual abilities to understand complex political issues; social status is often a surrogate for these traits (Brady et al. 1995). Higher-status individuals, especially the better educated, are more likely to have the time, the money, the access to political information, the knowledge, and the ability to become politically involved. So widespread is this notion that Sidney Verba and Norman Nie refer to social status as the "standard model" of political participation (Verba and Nie 1972, chap. 8; Verba et al. 1978; Parry et al. 1992, chap.

4). Therefore, social status is the first variable to add to our inventory of the potential causes of participation.

Another personal characteristic is the individual's position in the life cycle (Strate et al. 1989; Parry et al. 1992, chap. 7). For many young people, politics is a remote world. As individuals age, however, they take on social responsibilities that increase their motivation to develop political interests. People become taxpayers and homeowners, their children enter public schools, and they may begin to draw benefits from government programs. Most studies thus find that political involvement increases with age.

Gender is another personal characteristic that might affect political activism. Men are often more politically active than women in democracies (M. Inglehart 1981; Lovenduski 1986). Differences in political resources, such as educational level, income, and employment patterns, explain a large part of this gap (Schlozman, Burns, and Verba 1994). In addition, early life socialization often portrays politics as inappropriate to the female role; this undoubtedly restrains the motivation of women to participate and the willingness of the male world to accept female participation. In an age of changing sex roles, we can determine whether gender is still an important predictor of participation.

Our second group of potential predictors reflect group-based forces. Some group influences may be psychological, such as attachments to one's preferred political party. Because campaigns and elections are largely partisan contests, party attachments can stimulate individuals to action (Verba et al. 1978, chap. 6). A sense of party identification motivates individuals to vote or participate in campaigns as a display of party support; they are concerned that their party win. Conversely, individuals with weak or nonexistent party bonds are less concerned with election results and are less likely to participate.

Participation in social and voluntary groups provides another potential stimulant to political participation. Theorists argue that experience in the participatory decision making of a social club or volunteer organization develops skills and orientations that carry over to the world of politics (Verba, Schlozman, and Brady 1995). Groups also provide a useful reference structure for judging whether participation is a worthwhile activity in stimulating action (Uhlaner 1989). In addition, certain social groups actively mobilize the involvement of their members. Therefore, participation in nonpolitical groups may also stimulate political involvement.

Finally, the citizen's political values represents a third possible influence on participation. For example, political dissatisfaction might influence participation patterns (Farah et al. 1979). The causal role of political dissatisfaction is debated by researchers. On the one hand, policy satisfaction might increase support for the political process and thereby political participation. In these terms, high turnout rates show the public's basic support of the government. On the other hand, dissatisfaction might stimulate efforts to change policy. From this perspective, high turnout rates show widespread public dissatisfaction with the government. While scholars may disagree on the causal direction of policy dissatisfaction, they regard this as an important potential influence on participation levels.

In a somewhat different vein, scholars are also concerned about the policy or ideology differences across participants (Verba and Nie 1978; Wolfinger and Rosenstone 1980; Verba, Schlozman, and Brady 1995). If participation has an influence on policymakers and the government, then the question whether activists are drawn equally across political camps has important implications for the representativeness of the democratic process. Political participation that is heavily concentrated among liberals or conservatives might distort the policy process. Therefore, it is important to consider the political orientations (and policy preferences) of participants.

Another set of political attitudes includes the cluster of beliefs about the citizen's role and the nature of political action. Beliefs that citizens should participate in politics and that participation makes a difference should stimulate involvement (Nie et al. 1979; Parry et al. 1992, chap. 8).[5] This belief is described as a sense of political efficacy, the feeling that one's political action can affect the political process (Abramson 1983, chap. 8). Conversely, a feeling of political cynicism can lead to political apathy and withdrawal. If one cannot affect the political process, why bother to try?

Among these three groups of potential predictors, the surveys available for analysis include the following factors identified by prior research:

- Educational level
- Age
- Gender
- Political party attachments
- Union membership
- Satisfaction with democratic process
- Left/Right position

It also should be clear that the effects of these variables tend to overlap. Age, for example, should independently influence participation rates; but age is related to the strength of partisanship and socioeconomic status. To assess the actual influence of each variable, we combined them in a summary model predicting political participation. This model provides a measure of the causal importance of each factor on political activism, independent of the effects of the other variables. We separately calculated the model for voting, campaign activity, and communal activity to compare the causal patterns across participation modes.

Voting

The possible influences on voting were used to predict turnout in the 1992 U.S. presidential election and in the 1989 European Parliament elections (figure 3.1).[6] The thickness of the arrows in the figure illustrates the strength of the causal influence of each factor.

The thick arrows connecting age and voting show that turnout increases significantly with age, especially in the United States (β = .21), Britain (β = .24), and France (β = .33). The figure expresses these causal effects as statistical coefficients, where the effects of age are estimated independent of the effects of the other predictors in the model. If the simple relationship is expressed in percentage terms, about 80 percent of Americans in their fifties claim to have voted, compared to about 60 percent among twenty year olds. Voting turnout follows this life-cycle pattern in all three nations.

The second major influence on turnout rates is the strength of party identification. Because elections are partisan contests, those who identify strongly with a party are more likely to show up at the polls (and presumably cast a ballot for their party). Strong party attachments heighten the motivation to participate in elections. Another organizational influence, union membership, shows a weak influence in stimulating turnout.

The other variables in the model exert some influence on voting turnout, but their effects are weak. Voting rates are slightly higher among the better educated in all three European publics, although educational differences are much more pronounced among Americans. Political values—satisfaction with democracy and Left/Right position—have a negligible impact on turnout.[7] In this most common of political activities, the political bias in participation is minimal.

Campaign Activity

Because the characteristics of campaign activity differ from the simple act of casting a ballot, we might expect that the correlates of campaign activity also differ. We combined several measures of campaign activism into a single index.[8] Then we used our standard set of predictors to explain campaign activism.

Figure 3.2 shows that partisan attachments are strongly related to campaign activity in each of our four nations. Because campaign work is an intensely partisan activity, partisan ties exert an even stronger force than for voting turnout. In percentage terms, for example, 54 percent of the

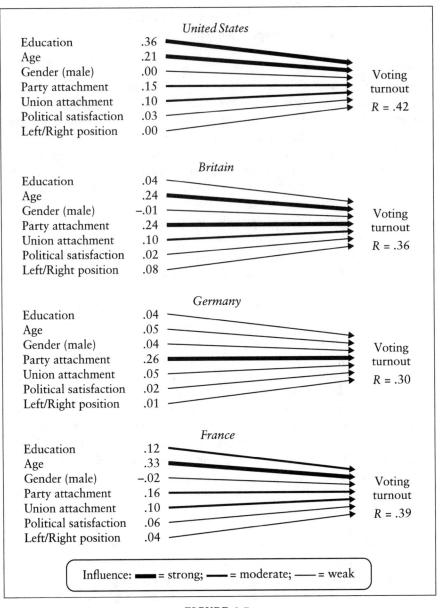

FIGURE 3.1

PREDICTORS OF VOTING TURNOUT

SOURCES: American National Election Study, 1992; Eurobarometer 31A.

NOTE: Analyses are based on individuals aged 18 and older in the United States and 19 or older in the Eurobarometer study.

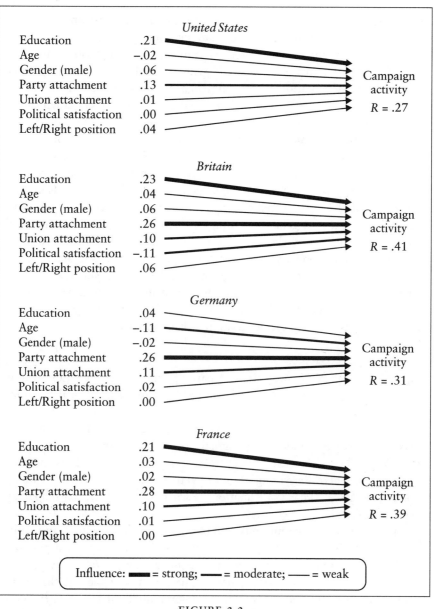

FIGURE 3.2

PREDICTORS OF CAMPAIGN ACTIVITY

SOURCES: American National Election Study, 1992; Eurobarometer 31A.

NOTE: Analyses are based on individuals aged 18 and older in the United States and 19 or older in the Eurobarometer study.

strong partisans in the United States participated in at least one campaign activity, compared to only 33 percent among nonpartisans.

The greater initiative required by campaign activity also means that the political skills and resources represented by education have a greater influence on participation rates. Campaign activists in the United States, Britain, and France are disproportionately drawn from the better educated. At the same time, union involvement also stimulates campaign activity among Europeans, indicating that unions are mobilizing this sector into the political process.

For both voting and campaign activity, gender differences in participation are small and inconsistent. Males vote at a higher rate in Germany and the United States, females are more frequent voters in Britain and France. The effects of gender on campaign activity are equally limited and varied across nations. Earlier research found a clear tendency for men to be more active than women (Verba and Nie 1978; Dalton 1988, chap. 3). Although we are analyzing only a single survey, the findings suggest that gender differences in participation may be decreasing (Inglehart 1990, chap. 10). The gender image of politics may be lessening as more women enter the political process and gender roles in society narrow.

Communal Activity

Figure 3.3 presents the predictors of participation in citizen-action groups for our three European nations.[9] This mode requires a great deal of initiative and sophistication from the participant. As a result, education is the strongest predictor of political action. The better educated are significantly more likely to participate in communal activities. The other personal factors—age and gender—generally exert little influence. The one exception is in Germany, where the young are more active in citizen groups. This may reflect younger Germans' inclination toward more direct, participatory styles of political action.

Working with a community group is distinct from voting and campaign activity because communal participation is generally not a partisan activity. In fact, in many instances participants are drawn to public interest groups because they lack strict party allegiances. Consequently, the figure shows that party ties have less impact on communal participation than on voting or campaign activities. We also find that union membership is less influential than for the other two participation modes because citizen-action groups lie outside the normal domain of union-based politics.

Broad political orientations exert only a limited influence on communal activity. In Britain ($\beta = -.18$) and France ($\beta = -.10$) satisfaction with the functioning of democracy diminishes communal participation; but in Ger-

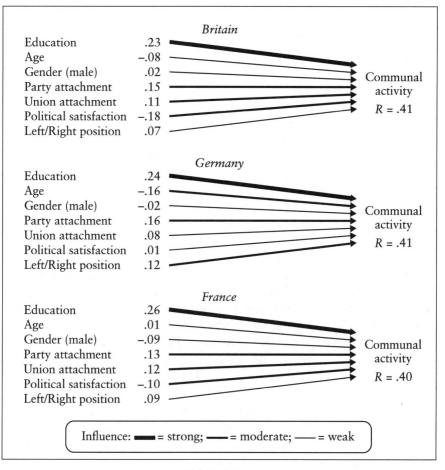

FIGURE 3.3

PREDICTORS OF COMMUNAL ACTIVITY

SOURCE: Eurobarometer 31.

many this variable has little influence. There is a slight tendency for Leftists to be more involved in citizen groups, but again these differences are modest in each nation.

The causal relationships for the three participation modes are fairly similar across nations. Two national deviations deserve attention, however. For all three participation modes, social status has a much stronger influence on political activity in the United States than in the other nations. American differences in voting by education ($\beta = .36$), for instance, are far greater than in Britain ($\beta = .04$), Germany ($\beta = .04$), or France ($\beta = .08$).

Moreover, Ruy Teixeira (1992) has shown that educational differences in turnout are increasing in America. We expect some differences in participation rates between social strata, but too large a gap implies that certain groups are excluded from the democratic process.

Most European democracies have avoided the problem of large social-status differences in voting turnout. Strong labor unions and working-class parties mobilize the working class and the less educated and equalize participation rates across social strata. Indeed, union membership is more strongly related to participation among European electorates, and the extent of union membership is much greater among the European working class. The weakness of these organizations in the United States, when coupled with the restrictive registration requirements of the American electoral system, has created a serious participation gap between social groups. In a provocative book, Frances Fox Piven and Richard Cloward (1989) argue that this class bias was an intentional consequence of the U.S. system of voter registration. Regardless of the intent, this system has limited participation by the poor and the less educated. This large participation gap in the United States shows the need for some method of maximizing the involvement of all social groups in American politics.

A second national difference involves the age variable. In Germany the young participate more than the old in campaign and communal activities, which is a direct reversal of the normal life-cycle pattern.[10] This age relationship reflects German historical conditions. In the 1970s Germany experienced a "participatory revolution" that greatly increased public involvement in politics, and the young were at the forefront of this revolution (Kaase 1982). The persisting tendency for the young to be politically more active reflects the continuation of this process and the ability of alternative groups, such as the Green Party, to attract the young into the political process.

Changing Publics and Political Participation

This chapter has provided an overview of conventional political participation in the United States, Britain, Germany, and France. Voting turnout in these nations and other Western democracies is high, averaging more than 70 percent in most electorates. In addition, a sizable proportion of the populace is involved in more demanding political activities, such as campaigns or communal participation.

From the participation levels for specific modes, one can describe the overall patterns of involvement across nations. Americans come closest to the pattern of multidimensional participants. Turnout in elections is low, but Americans are active in campaigns and community activities at relatively high levels. Germans also are a relatively participatory public. Turnout rates are much higher than in the United States, and Germans are involved in campaign and communal activities. The British patterns of participation focus on voting, with modest involvement beyond the ballot box. In their more extensive analysis of British participation patterns, Parry and his colleagues (1992, chap. 10) note with some dismay that a quarter of the British public are almost completely inactive, and less than 2 percent are active across several modes. Based on the limited available evidence, we expect the French to display limited involvement in group and campaign activities, focusing their conventional participation on voting.

Our findings show that contemporary electorates are involved in politics. Yet a paradox remains. Measures of political information, interest, and sophistication in chapter 2 display a clear increase over the past few decades. Several scholars have pointed out that rising levels of education, increased media consumption, and changes in the age composition of Western electorates should increase participation (Teixeira 1992; Topf 1996a). In overall terms, conventional participation levels are not increasing significantly; in some areas participation actually has declined. Voting turnout rates have decreased in the United States, Britain, Germany and France. With the exception of Germany, campaign activity has held steady or declined slightly. Richard Brody (1978) refers to this as "the puzzle of political participation." Why are some aspects of political participation decreasing, if the public's political skills and resources are increasing?

Steven Rosenstone and John Hansen (1993) suggest that a major explanation for the decline in turnout in the United States lies in the decreasing ability of political organizations to mobilize individuals into action (also Abramson and Aldrich 1982). The political parties are less active in bringing individuals to the polls and getting the public involved in campaigns. Another argument stresses the disenchantment of voters with the political process, leading to decreased involvement in politics (Burnham 1982; also see chapter 12). Growing social isolation and the decline of community is another explanation (Putnam 1995; Teixeira 1992, chap. 2). Although these arguments carry some weight, they are partially circular in their logic. People are less active in partisan politics because fewer people are actively involving others in politics; people are less active because they doubt the efficacy of action.

We think it is necessary to look beyond the electoral arena and reconsider how political sophistication and participation patterns are interrelated. Increasing political sophistication does not necessarily imply a growth in the level of all forms of political activism; rising sophistication levels may be more important in changing the *nature* of participation. Voting, for example, is an area where elites and political organizations traditionally can mobilize even disinterested citizens to turn out at the polls. High turnout levels often reflect the organizational skills of political groups rather than the public's concern about the election. Moreover, citizen input through this participation mode is limited by the institutionalized structure of elections, which narrows (and blurs) the choice of policy options and limits the frequency of public input. A French environmental group bluntly stated its disdain for elections with a slogan borrowed from the May Revolts of 1968: *Élections—piège à cons* (Elections—trap for idiots). This aversion to partisan politics is shared by environmental groups in general (Dalton 1994, chap. 9). An increasingly sophisticated and cognitively mobilized electorate is not likely to depend on voting and campaign activity as the primary means of expanding its involvement in politics.

The growing political skills and resources of contemporary electorates have had a more noticeable impact on increasing participation in areas where activity is citizen initiated, less structured, and more policy oriented (Dalton 1984; Inglehart 1990, chap. 10). The self-mobilized individual favors referendums over elections and communal activity over campaign work. The use of referendums has, in fact, increased dramatically in Western democracies in recent years (Butler and Ranney 1994; Cronin 1989). Similarly, the activity of citizen lobbies, single-issue groups, and citizen-action movements is increasing in nearly all advanced industrial democracies. Verba, Schlozman, and Brady (1995, chap. 3) similarly find that issue-based contacting of political elites has significantly increased among Americans. Even the electoral arena might be reinvigorated in Europe by expanding the public's decision-making responsibilities to include primaries, preference-ranking mechanisms for party-list voting, or candidate ranking within party lists. Why have the electoral opportunities of European citizens not kept pace with the general expansion of democratic politics?

The new style of citizen politics thus seeks to place more control over political activity in the hands of the citizenry. These changes in participation make greater demands on the participants. At the same time, these activities can increase public pressure on political elites. Citizen participation is becoming more closely linked to citizen influence.

Notes

1. Parry et al. (1992) add items on protest and political violence that form another mode in their study of British participation. Bettina Westle (1992) re-

views the broader European literature on this topic. A study of Buffalo residents by Milbrath and Goel (1977) identifies the same four modes and two additional ones: communication and protest. Their communication mode is a residual category that encompasses the additional items Milbrath and Goel added to their participation list, and the protest mode is studied in the next chapter.

2. Verba and Nie (1972) originally found that only 4 percent of the American public is active primarily through contacting officials on personal matters. These individuals tend to be sophisticated, but also unconcerned with broad political issues. Because of the very small size of this group, we do not include this fourth participation mode. Parry and his colleagues (1992, chap. 3) find that contacting is more common in Britain, especially for the new examples of local contact that they included in their study. Similarly, Verba, Schlozman, and Brady (1995, chap. 3) find that the frequency of issue-based contacting among Americans almost doubled between 1967 and 1987, involving almost a quarter of the public. So this participation mode is exapanding.

3. The British votes include local council, county, the 1987 House of Common election, and the 1989 European Parliament election. The American votes include both primary and general elections: four votes in the primary for federal offices and two for state offices (these six offices were filled in the general election), one vote for a county supervisor, three votes for judges, four for the junior college school district, three for city government, three for the water district, and fourteen state initiatives and referendums.

4. Initial comparisons between eastern and western Germany suggest that citizens in both regions participate at roughly the same levels. Easterners lag a bit behind on measures of party and campaign involvement, but display comparable levels of voting turnout and political interest (Dalton 1993a, chap. 6; Westle 1992).

5. Even though feelings of efficacy are important, a valid measure was not available in the surveys we analyzed, so this is not included in the models that follow. For more on the impact of efficacy, see Dalton (1988, chap. 3), Rosenstone and Hansen (1993, chap. 5), and Parry et al. (1992).

6. The analyses in figures 3.1, 3.2, and 3.3 are based on multiple regression analyses; figure entries are standardized regression coefficients. The European Parliament elections attract less interest than national parliamentary elections, which may affect our findings. Turnout as reported by our respondents is 54 percent for Britain, 75 percent for Germany, and 54 percent for France. We decided to use this election because it was held simultaneously in all three European nations and we have comparable public opinion data from the Eurobarometer survey. In addition, these European turnout rates are fairly comparable to participation in U.S. elections.

7. Political satisfaction in the European samples was measured by a question on the respondent's satisfaction with the way democracy functions in his or her nation. In the United States, satisfaction was measured by a question on trust in government.

8. Campaign activity in the European samples was drawn from Eurobarometer 31A (table 3.5). Activism was measured by a count of participation in the following actions: talked to friends about the campaign, spoke to a party worker, attended a meeting, read party material, or tried to persuade others. Campaign activity in the American survey was measured by a count of the activities listed in table 3.3, p. 49.

9. The measure of communal participation is taken from Eurobarometer 31. Respondents were asked about "taking part in citizen's action groups." We coded these responses: (1) would never do, (2) would do under exceptional circumstances, (3) would do for important matters, and (4) have done. Comparable data are not available for the United States, but see Dalton (1988, 54–56) for analyses of earlier American results.

10. A similar finding was presented in Dalton (1988, chap. 3).

4. Protest Politics

Occasionally, citizen participation bursts beyond the bounds of conventional politics to include demonstrations, protests, and other forms of unconventional activity. Although protesters often go beyond the normal channels of democratic politics, they are nevertheless an essential part of the democratic process. The protests that accompanied the civil rights demonstrations in the United States during the 1960s, the environmental protests of the past decade, and the people-power protests that brought democracy to Eastern Europe illustrate how the public can force political systems to respond, to change, and to grow.

Protest is not new to Western democracies. The United States has experienced political conflict throughout its history (Tilly 1969). The colonial period saw frequent revolts against taxation, property restrictions, and other government policies. When rural elements allied themselves with the urban poor and the bourgeoisie, an American revolution against British control became inevitable. After independence, political conflict continued with the growth of workers' movements and agrarian/populist movements in the 1800s. Abolitionists, suffragettes, and other political groups used large-scale, nonviolent protests and demonstrations throughout the past century. The early half of this century was a period of often intense and violent industrial conflict.

A revolutionary tradition is even more deeply ingrained in the French political culture (Cerny 1982). Many French Leftists trace the foundations of French democracy to the revolutions of 1789, 1830, and 1848, as well as the Paris Commune of 1871. Between these dramatic political events, French society displayed a high level of protest and collective violence for most of the past century (Tilly et al. 1975, chap. 2). Food riots and similar conflicts were widespread in the mid-1800s, and industrial conflict developed during the second half of the century and the early 1900s. A call to the barricades stirs the hearts of many French citizens, contributing to historically high levels of unconventional political activity. In the words of one expert, protest in France is a national way of life.

Protest and collective have action occurred on a more limited scale in

Germany and Britain, although political conflict still has been fairly common. The German government crushed an incipient democratic revolution in 1848, and intense political violence eventually consumed the Weimar Republic (Tilly et al. 1975, chap. 4). Conflicts over industrial policy during the Wilhelmine Empire and the Weimar Republic often manifested themselves in mass protests. Even Britain, with its tradition of gradual political change, has a history of violence and political conflict that is often overlooked by political scientists (Marsh 1977, chap. 2).

The history of Western democracies is thus marked by repeated episodes of protest and vigorous political dissent by the citizenry. This record has persisted to the present (Kaase 1989, 35–36). For example, the civil rights movement and ghetto riots of the 1960s were a divisive and violent period in America. Similarly, peasant protests—pouring milk onto highways, blocking traffic, symbolic animal slaughters—are an established part of contemporary French politics. The 1980s saw widespread protests over environmental protection and disarmament in virtually all Western democracies. And these nations continue to experience at least modest levels of protest over industrial issues.

Despite the historical roots of unconventional action, many political experts expected protest politics to fade with the spreading affluence of advanced industrial societies. Yet the frequency of protest and other unconventional political activities apparently has increased in recent years (Jennings and van Deth, 1989). Cross-national comparisons also find that protest levels are higher in more affluent nations (Powell 1982, 129–32). These trends have led some analysts to argue that a new style of protest is becoming a regular form of political action in advanced industrial societies.

In historical terms, protest and collective action were often the last desperate acts of the public, arising from feelings of frustration and deprivation. Protest was concentrated among the socially disadvantaged, repressed minorities, or groups alienated from the established political order. Unconventional action was an outlet for groups that lacked access to politics through conventional channels.

Protest remains a political resource of minorities and repressed groups, and demonstrations by racial minorities (foreign workers in Europe), the economically disadvantaged, and similar groups will continue. Perhaps the most graphic illustrations of this form of protest were the democratic revolution that spread through Eastern Europe in the late 1989 and the "people power" protests in the Philippines, South Africa, and other democratizing nations. When citizens are blocked from exercising political influence through legitimate participation channels, protest politics stands as an option.

Within advanced industrial societies, however, the use of protest has broadened from the disadvantaged to include a wider spectrum of political groups. A wave of student protests swept through Western societies in the late 1960s, making protest an accepted form of political action by the better educated. Political protest is now common among the middle class and the politically sophisticated. The sources of protest have shifted from ghettos and slums toward the Ivy League, Oxbridge, and the Grand Ecoles.

With the changing locus of protest came a shift in the focus of unconventional political action. Protest historically was an extreme political act. Protests and demonstrations frequently were indicators of revolutionary ferment and often challenged the basic legitimacy of political institutions. Food riots, tax revolts, and socialist worker uprisings exemplify this anti-governmental activity. The new forms of protest in advanced industrial societies are seldom directed at overthrowing the established political order—the affluent and well-educated participants are some of the primary beneficiaries of this order. Reformism has replaced revolutionary fervor.

Finally, before modern times, collective political action was often a spontaneous event, such as an unorganized crowd attacking a tax collector or staging a food riot. Modern protest behavior is a planned and organized activity. Political groups consciously plan protests when these activities will benefit their cause. Modern protests are often orchestrated events, with participants arriving in chartered buses to planned staging areas complete with demonstration coordinators, Port-o-potties, and facilities for the media. Protest is simply another political resource for mobilizing public opinion and influencing policymakers (Tilly 1975).

The first, and perhaps clearest, example of this new style of protest politics was the flowering of the student protest movement in the 1960s. In the United States, student activism in the free speech movement and civil rights movement evolved into opposition to the Vietnam war and governmental priorities in general. We recently celebrated the twenty-fifth anniversary of Woodstock, and the period of social protest and unrest that it represented. Similar student protest spread to Europe and challenged traditional social values. The May Revolts in France dramatized this development (Brown 1974). The conflict in France was the most intense, yet student protests in America and the rest of Europe followed this same course. Whether in Berlin, London, or Washington, this was a time of social upheaval.

The environmental movement provided another focal point for spreading protest activity (Dunlap and Mertig 1992; Dalton 1994). Environmental groups in the United States and Western Europe mobilized in opposition to nuclear power and in support of environmental protection.

American environmentalists staged repeated demonstrations and blockades at target facilities such as Seabrook (New Hampshire), Barnwell (South Carolina), and Diablo Canyon (California). Gradually there was a broadening of public concern and increasing sensitivity to how environmental problems could threaten local communities (such as Love Canal, New York) or the health of the planet (e.g., the widening ozone hole and global warming).

This pattern was repeated in Western Europe. Environmentalists organized protests in opposition to domestic nuclear facilities. Massive demonstrations at Creys-Malville in France and Brokdorf in Germany led to armed clashes between the police and protesters. The catastrophe at Chernobyl added more fuel to the antinuclear movement. Green groups brought attention to issues of wildlife protection, acid rain, and other environmental problems of contemporary societies. Even more common were the variety of local groups and local protests that addressed local environmental concerns. Environmental groups also developed an imaginative array of protest activities that captured the public's interest and, more importantly, media coverage to their cause. Environmentalists climbed polluting smokestacks, dyed the effluents of polluters, staged mock die-ins, and risked their own lives to save whales and harp seals.

The spread of environmentalism was paralleled by increased citizen activity on other issues. A movement for women's rights developed during the 1970s in virtually all Western democracies (Katzenstein and Mueller 1987). In the early 1980s, protest groups demonstrated for nuclear disarmament and nuclear freeze proposals—until these issues diminished in salience with the collapse of the Soviet Union (Rochon 1988; Klandermans 1991). The consumer protection movement and other self-help groups became prominent actors in the politics of many Western democracies. Max Kaase (1989) has shown that the context for protest politics reached into many policy areas.

Thus old forms of protest politics have been joined by a new style of protest in advanced industrial democracies. It began with the student protests of the 1960s and 1970s and now has spread to a broad spectrum of society. Gray Panthers protest for senior citizen rights, consumers are active monitors of industry, environmentalists call attention to ecological problems, and citizen groups of all kinds are proliferating. Clearly, these are not revolutionary groups. This participation mode is used whether the issue is a relatively mundane one, such as zoning regulations, or a basic issue, such as nuclear war (Jennings and van Deth 1989). Political protest has become less unconventional: it is a continuation of conventional participation by other means.

Many people claim that this period of protest is passing; just the opposite is true. As protest becomes less unconventional, it also becomes less noticeable and newsworthy. The growing use of protests in European societies and the spread of single-issue groups in the United States should convince us that protest politics will continue. Furthermore, there is now an infrastructure for continued protest activities for other issues. The creation of citizen lobbies, environmental groups, consumer activists, and other groups provides a basis for organizing future protests. The existence of these new opposition groups may be crucial in permanently changing the style of citizen politics.

The spread of protest politics not only expands the repertoire of political participation, it also represents a style of political action that differs markedly from conventional politics (see table 3.1, p. 42). Protest can focus on specific issues or policy goals—from protecting whales to protesting the policies of a local government—and can convey a high level of political information with real political force. Voting and campaign work seldom can focus on a single issue because parties represent a package of policies. Instead of participating within a framework defined by elites, protest gives participants control over the action. The public controls the timing and location of protest activities. Sustained and effective protest is a demanding participation mode that requires initiative and cooperation with others. Thus the advocates of protest have argued that the public can strengthen its political influence by adopting a strategy of direct action.

Measuring Protest

Although protest and other forms of collective action are regular features of democratic politics, these activities were absent from early empirical studies of political participation. This omission reflected the low level of protest that existed in the 1950s and early 1960s, as well as the unconventional nature of these activities. The growing wave of protest in recent years stimulated several studies to fill this void in our knowledge (Muller 1979; Marsh 1977; Barnes, Kaase, et al. 1979; Jennings and van Deth 1989).

The first task was to measure unconventional political participation. Edward Muller (1972) and Alan Marsh (1974) developed a model of this participation mode. They ordered the various forms of unconventional participation along a continuum from least to most extreme. This continuum is marked by several thresholds (figure 4.1). The first threshold indicates a transitional phase between conventional and unconventional politics. Signing petitions and participating in lawful demonstrations are unorthodox political activities but are still within the bounds of accepted democratic norms.

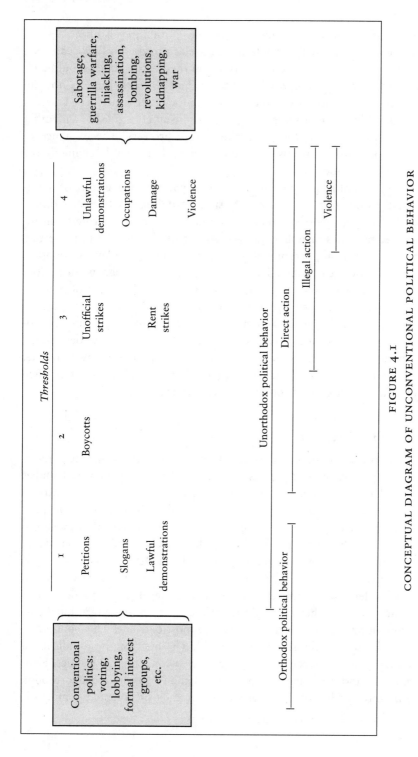

FIGURE 4.1

CONCEPTUAL DIAGRAM OF UNCONVENTIONAL POLITICAL BEHAVIOR

SOURCE: Marsh (1977, 42), with modifications.

Ian McAllister (1992, 63–69) emphasizes the importance of the second threshold because it marks the change to techniques that involve direct action and are only semilegal, such as boycotts (also see Westle 1992). Activities at this level or beyond exceed the boundaries of conventional, institutionalized political action. A third level of political activities involves illegal, but nonviolent, acts. Unofficial strikes or peaceful occupation of a building typify this step. Finally, a fourth threshold includes violent activities such as personal injury or physical damage. At this fourth level, political action exceeds what is accepted or tolerable in a democracy. Research shows that unconventional political action is cumulative. Individuals active at any one threshold also generally participate in milder forms of protest.

To provide a first overview of unconventional political activity, table 4.1 describes cross-national levels of action. The column on the left ranks nations according to the percentage of citizens who have signed a petition —the most modest and most common form of unconventional action. The column on the right ranks nations by public involvement in one of four more challenging types of unconventional action: attending a lawful demonstration, joining in boycotts, joining unofficial strikes, or occupying buildings.

Signing a petition is a very mild form of unconventional action that involves a large share of the citizenry in most Western democracies. The petition has a long and venerable heritage in British and American politics, and political groups of every color use it (Parry et al. 1992). One can hardly enter a Marks & Spencer or a Kmart without being asked to sign a petition. Thus most Britons (75 percent) and Americans (70 percent) have signed a petition. This form of political action also is commonplace in most other Western democracies. Indeed the breadth of usage is so wide that one might question whether this form of political activity should be considered unconventional at all.

A more telling test of the public's willingness to exceed conventional political bounds is participation in the four challenging acts in the right column of the table. The French have a very high level of unconventional political action, exceeded only by the Italians and eastern Germans. More than one-third of the French public has participated in at least one of the four unconventional activities, and there is a widespread willingness to engage in these activities (Ashford and Timms 1992, chap. 7). This verifies our earlier description of the French as disdaining conventional politics and relishing protest. In a much earlier work, William Kornhauser (1959) argued that the very weakness of social groups and conventional participation channels in France encourages support for protest. Michel Crozier (1964) described a French aversion to interpersonal interaction that also restricts political participation. Indeed the French rank relatively low in the

TABLE 4.1

CROSS-NATIONAL LEVELS OF UNCONVENTIONAL

POLITICAL PARTICIPATION

(PERCENTAGE OF CITIZENS ACTIVE)

Signed a petition		Participated in a challenging act	
Canada	77	Germany (East)	52
Great Britain	75	Italy	37
Sweden	70	France	36
United States	70	Denmark	35
Germany (East)	67	Norway	34
Norway	59	Iceland	33
Germany (West)	55	Canada	32
Japan	52	Sweden	30
Denmark	51	Netherlands	27
France	51	Belgium	25
Netherlands	49	Great Britain	25
Belgium	47	United States	25
Iceland	47	Germany (West)	23
Austria	46	Finland	22
Italy	42	Spain	22
Ireland	41	Ireland	20
Finland	34	Austria	13
Spain	18	Japan	12

SOURCE: 1990–91 World Values Survey.

NOTE: Entries under "Participated in a challenging act" are the percentage who have engaged in at least one of the following acts: a lawful demonstration, a boycott, an unofficial strike, or occupying a building.

signing of petitions, a political activity that requires face-to-face contact. To this is added a cultural tradition that enshrines France's revolutionary tradition. In just the single year following the 1990 French survey there were large-scale protest actions by farmers opposed to meat imports, royalists clashed with police, youths protested in Narbonne, Arab minority groups protested in Paris, environmentalists demonstrated about Chernobyl, the police staged their own protest, and state employees called a general strike. French protest knows few social bounds.

Most other European democracies display a modest level of unconventional political action, involving 20 to 30 percent of the public in at least one of these activities (also Westle 1992; Topf 1996b). Mediterranean and Scandinavian nations are found at the top of this ranking, and the Japanese display a marked aversion to these political activities. It is surprising to find that few Britons and Americans engage in challenging activities, although they often sign petitions. We return to this point shortly.

Many western Germans have participated in one of these activities, as protest has become an accepted form of action by groups ranging from neighborhood associations to the environmental movement. More striking, however, is the frequency of protest activities in eastern Germany. Most residents of the former German Democratic Republic (GDR) have signed a petition (67 percent) and participated in at least one challenging action (52 percent). These high levels of activity occur because the Germans' "peaceful revolution" in 1989 was not so peaceful; it required massive public demonstrations to topple the old regime. In addition, the politics of the East has been in tumult since unification. To an extent, the high participation rates in eastern Germany may be similar to the pattern in other Eastern European states.

On the whole, most citizens participate in some form of unconventional political action, even if only in the most mild form of signing a petition. Participation in higher forms of unconventional politics—such as participating in a lawful demonstration or joining a boycott—actually rivals activity in conventional activities (see chapter 3).

A longitudinal series of public opinion surveys enables us to track the development of unconventional activities for our four core nations (table 4.2). In every nation, unconventional political activities are more common at the end of the survey period than at the first time point. Ronald Inglehart (forthcoming, chap. 8) has used the additional nations included in the 1981 and 1990–91 World Values Survey to document the general increase in protest activities for the larger set of advanced industrial societies. This growth of protest probably results from a general increase in small demonstrations over highways, schools, neighborhood issues, and other specific concerns, rather than a few large-scale movements. Protest is becoming a more common political activity in advanced industrial democracies. The era of protest politics is not passing.

Time trends might explain why the United States ranks so low in recent cross-national comparisons (table 4.1) despite its reputation for a high level of protest activity. The American public had high levels of protest in the first systematic studies of unconventional political action (Barnes, Kaase, et al. 1979; Muller 1979). These activities have gradually increased in the United States, but their use has spread even more rapidly in Britain, Germany, and other Western democracies. American participation has not declined; participation in other nations has grown at a faster rate and thus has overtaken American activity levels.

TABLE 4.2
UNCONVENTIONAL POLITICAL PARTICIPATION
(IN PERCENTAGES)

	United States			Great Britain			Germany			France	
	1975	1981	1990	1974	1981	1990	1974	1981	1990	1981	1990
Sign a petition	58	61	70	22	63	75	30	46	55	44	51
Participate in lawful demonstration	11	12	15	6	10	13	9	14	25	26	31
Join in boycott	14	14	17	5	7	14	4	7	9	11	11
Participate in unofficial strike	2	3	4	5	7	8	1	2	2	10	9
Occupy building	2	2	2	1	2	2	*	1	1	7	7
Damage property	1	1	N.A.	1	2	N.A.	*	1	N.A.	1	N.A.
Personal violence	1	2	N.A.	*	1	N.A.	*	1	N.A.	1	N.A.

SOURCES: 1974–75 Political Action Study; 1981 World Values Survey; 1990–91 World Values Survey.

NOTE: Table entries are the percentages who say they have participated in the activity. An asterisk denotes less than 1 percent; N.A. denotes the question was not asked in this study.

Although we have generally spoken about protest in positive terms, the dark side of unconventional politics occurs when citizens pass the fourth threshold and engage in violent behavior. The abortion clinic bombers or the terrorist activities of the Irish Republican Army go far beyond the tolerable bounds of politics. These actions are fundamentally different from the protest behavior of most citizens. Table 4.2 contains evidence on the extent of violent political action in our four nations. Although protest politics is widely accepted, the number who participate in violent activities is minimal. In 1981, for example, 44 percent of the French public had signed a petition and 26 percent had participated in a lawful demonstration, but only 1 percent had damaged property or engaged in personal violence. Citizens want to protest the actions of the democratic political process, not destroy it.

Predictors of Protest

Why do citizens protest? Every protester has an individual explanation for his or her participation. Some people are stimulated by commitment to an issue or ideology. Other protesters are motivated by a general opposition to the government and political system and search for opportunities to display their feelings. Still others are caught up in the excitement and sense of comradeship that protests produce or simply accompany a friend to be where the action is. Social scientists have tried to systematize these individual motivations to explain the general sources of protest activity.

The *deprivation approach* maintains that protest is primarily based on feelings of frustration and political alienation. Analysts since Aristotle have seen personal dissatisfaction and the striving for better conditions as the root causes of political violence. For Aristotle, the principal causes of revolution were the aspirations for economic or political equality on the part of the common people who lack it or the aspirations of oligarchs for greater inequality than they have. Much later, Tocqueville linked the violence of the 1789 French Revolution to unfulfilled aspirations expanding more rapidly than objective conditions, thereby increasing dissatisfaction and the pressure for change. Karl Marx similarly posited personal dissatisfaction and the competition between the haves and have-nots as the driving force of history and the ultimate source of political revolt.

Modern social scientists have echoed and quantified these themes. The theory has a psychological base: frustration leads to aggression. Therefore, dissatisfaction with society and politics can lead to political violence. The seminal study in the area is the work of Ted Robert Gurr (1970). He states that "the primary causal sequence in political violence is first the development of discontent, second the politicization of discontent, and finally its actualization in violent political action against political objects and actors" (pp. 12–13). Gurr bases his conclusions on analyses of cross-national levels of political violence. Analyses of public opinion data also show that policy dissatisfaction increases the likelihood of participation in protest activities (Farah et al. 1979; Muller 1979).

This model implies that political dissatisfaction and alienation should be major predictors of protest. Indirectly, this theory suggests that unconventional political activity should be more common among lower-status individuals, minorities, and other groups who have reasons to feel deprived or dissatisfied.

A second general explanation of protest is termed a *resource model* (Tilly 1975; Lipsky 1968). This model does not view protest and collective action as emotional outbursts by a frustrated public. Instead, protest is another political resource (like voting, campaign activity, or communal activity) that individuals may use in pursuing their goals. Unconventional action is seen as a normal part of the political process as competing groups vie for political power. Excluding voting, modest forms of unconventional action are among the most common forms of mass political participation.

The resource model provides some guidance in predicting who will resort to protest behavior. The model implies that protest should be viewed as simply another participation mode. Consequently, protest activity should be higher among the better educated and politically sophisticated, who have the political skills and resources to engage in these demanding forms of activity. One also might view participation in other social groups as providing resources and experiences that would encourage activities across other participation modes (Verba, Schlozman, and Brady 1995). In addition, a belief that protest will be effective should significantly increase the likelihood the individuals will participate (Muller 1979; Barnes, Kaase, et al. 1979, chap. 3). Indeed, one of the most interesting studies of protest found that participants in the American ghetto riots in the 1960s were actually more efficacious than nonparticipants (Aberbach and Walker 1970).

In addition to these broad theories of protest politics, several personal characteristics might be linked to unconventional action. Research has shown a strong tendency toward higher levels of protest among the young. Gender is another factor that might influence unconventional political participation (Schlozman et al. 1994). The confrontational style of protest politics attracts male participants in disproportionate numbers, although there is evidence that this pattern is changing with a narrowing of gender roles.

Finally, we are interested in the political orientations of protesters. Unconventional political action is often seen as a tool for liberals and progressives who want to challenge the political establishment and who feel the need to go beyond conventional politics to make their views heard. At the same time, there has been a broadening of protest activity across the political spectrum, and protest may no longer be the primary domain of the Left. For every pro-choice protest, there is now a pro-life demonstration. Thus we should consider whether there remains a political bias in the use of unconventional political action.

We used the six predictors of conventional political participation from chapter 3 to tap these various models of protest behavior: education, age, gender, union attachments, political satisfaction, and Left/Right position (figure 4.2).[1] To a large degree, the correlates of unconventional political activity are similar to the patterns found in analyses from surveys in the mid-1970s (Dalton 1988, chap. 4).

Political dissatisfaction has a stronger impact on the willingness to engage in protest behavior than on most forms of conventional participation (see figures 3.1 to 3.3, pp. 58–61). Yet dissatisfied citizens are only slightly more willing to protest than citizens who are satisfied with government policy performance. Furthermore, the pattern of other variables tends to undercut the dissatisfaction model. For example, the willingness to protest is more common among males and the better educated than among women and the less educated.[2]

In short, protest in advanced industrial democracies is not simply an outlet for the alienated and deprived; often, just the opposite appears. Protest is better described by the resource model. Protesters are individuals who have the ability to organize and participate in political activities of all forms, including protest. The clearest evidence of this is the strong positive relationship between educational level and willingness to protest in all four nations.[3] Protest is more common among the better educated.

In one important area, however, the correlates of protest distinguish it from conventional political activity. Conventional political participation routinely increases with age, as family and social responsibilities heighten the relevance of politics. In contrast, protest is the domain of the young. In the United States, for example, two-thirds of those in their twenties have participated in at least one protest activity, compared to less than half of those in their sixties. Age is the among the strongest predictors of unconventional activity in each of the four nations.

Political scientists differ in their interpretations of this age relationship. On the one hand, this relationship may reflect life-cycle differences in protest activity. Youth is a period of enthusiasm and rebellion, which may encourage participation in protests and other unconventional activities. Young people also may be more accessible to protest because of their free

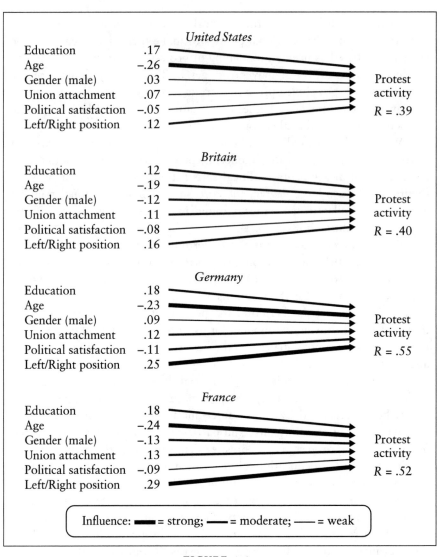

FIGURE 4.2
PREDICTORS OF PROTEST ACTIVITY

SOURCE: 1990–91 World Values Survey.

time and concentration in university settings. This explanation would pre-dict that an individual's protest activity should decline with age.

On the other hand, age differences in protest may represent a genera-tional pattern of changing participation styles. That is, today's young people protest, not because of their youth, but because their generation has adopted a new style of political participation. The increasing educational levels, political sophistication, and participation norms among younger generations are producing support for direct-action techniques. If this is true, age differences in protest represent a historical change in participation patterns. Thus youthful protesters should gradually mature into middle-age activists and not fade with the passage of time.[4]

Age differences in protest probably represent a combination of life-cycle and generational effects. Attempts to assess the relative importance of either explanation stress the primacy of generational effects (Barnes, Kaase, et al. 1979, 524; Jennings 1987). Protest levels among the younger generations may decrease as these individuals move through the life cycle; but younger generations probably will remain more involved in direct action than their elders. Moreover, this pattern of progressive generational change should continue among later generations. In the long run this process implies an inevitable increase in citizen action and a broadening of participation to include unconventional political activities.

Another important correlate of unconventional action is Left/Right position. Although protest politics has spread throughout the political process and is used by groups on the Left and Right, the willingness to engage in these activities is more common among Leftists in each nation. These effects are stronger than the ideological biases in conventional forms of political action and is consistent even though one nation was headed by a Leftist government (France) and the other three by conservative governments. Protest politics is still disproportionately the domain of the Left.

Participation and Contemporary Democracies

The nature of political participation in advanced industrial societies is changing. Participation in citizen-initiated and policy-oriented forms of political activity is increasing. The last chapter discussed the growth of citizen-action groups, communal participation, and direct democracy methods. This chapter documents the expansion of protest politics.

Protest politics can take many forms. The most dramatic examples are the attention-getting events of large groups that draw public attention to an issue or organization. Greenpeace, for instance, has become famous for using rubber boats to disrupt whaling, protecting harp seals from hunters, and other spectacular actions. These tactics have been adopted and expanded by other environmental groups. But the larger significance of protest politics lies in its adoption by a wide variety of other citizen groups. The use of protests has broadened to include consumer groups dissatisfied with a company's product, taxpayers dissatisfied with the action of local government, and students dissatisfied with university policies. The general acceptance of protest politics is what has transformed the style of citizen politics.

Increases in these activities are especially significant because they place greater control over the locus and focus of participation in the hands of the citizenry. Political input is not limited to the issues and institutionalized channels determined by elites. A group of citizens organized around a specific issue or a single individual can select the timing and method of influencing policymakers. These direct-action techniques also are high-information and high-pressure activities. They therefore match some of the participation demands of an increasingly educated and politically sophisticated public far better than conventional participation in voting and campaign activities.

A major goal of democratic societies is to expand citizen participation in the political process and thereby increase popular control of political elites. Therefore, increases in communal participation, protest, and other citizen-initiated activities are generally welcomed. This changing pattern of political participation is an important element of the new style of citizen politics in advanced industrial democracies.

In addition, however, these changing participation patterns are creating some new problems for modern democracies. The growing complexity and technical nature of contemporary issues requires that citizens have substantial political sophistication to cope with the world of politics. Moreover, participation in citizen-initiated activities is more demanding of the individual than voting or campaign activity. Electoral participation of the less sophisticated is often mobilized by political groups (such as unions or religious/ethic associations). Communal activity and unconventional politics require greater personal initiative. Consequently, involvement in politics is becoming even more dependent on the skills and resources represented by social status.

This situation may increase the participation gap between lower-status groups and higher-status individuals. As the better educated expand their political influence through direct-action methods, less-educated citizens may be unable to compete on the same terms. The politically active may become even more influential, while the less active may see their influence wane. Ironically, overall increases in political involvement may mask a growing social-status bias in citizen participation and influence, which runs counter to democratic ideals.

Some evidence of this problem can be seen in the relationship between educational level and political activity. Differences in voting turnout by education, for example, are modest. Differences in communal participation and protest by educational level are substantial; the better educated are the benefactors of these new participation opportunities. The solution to this problem is to raise the participation levels of lower-status groups, not limit the activity of the better educated. Political leaders must facilitate participation by a broader spectrum of the public and lower the remaining barriers to participation. The dictum of "maximum feasible citizen participation" needs to be followed more closely.[5]

Direct-action methods pose another challenge to contemporary democracies. By their very nature, direct-action techniques disrupt the status quo. These participation forms occasionally challenge the established institutions and procedures of contemporary democracies. This has led some critics to question whether rapidly expanding citizen participation, especially in protest activities, is placing too many demands on already overburdened political systems (Huntington 1974, 1981; Crozier et al. 1975). Policy cannot be made in the streets, they argue. Efficient and effective policymaking requires a deliberative process, where political elites have some latitude in their decisions. A politicized public with intense policy minorities lobbying for their special interests would strain the political consensus that is a requisite of democratic politics.

In short, these analysts argue that it is possible to have too much of a good thing—political participation. Indeed, they cite the empirical evidence of mass politics, and the accompanying elitist theory of democracy, in taking this position (chapter 2). Citizen activism must be balanced against the needs for government efficiency and rational policy planning. Hence they believe that the expansion of participation in recent years may have upset this balance, leading to problems of governability in Western democracies. These arguments were commonplace in the 1980s, and even with the democratization wave of the 1990s there are still too many who would limit the rights of others.

Cautions about the excess of participation display a disregard for the democratic goals their spokesmen profess to defend; such warnings have more in common with the former regimes of Eastern Europe than with real democratic principles. In a recent review article, the associate editor of *The Economist* noted the irony of worrying about the excesses of democracy as we simultaneously celebrate the fall of communism:

> The democracies must therefore apply to themselves the argument they used to direct against the communists. As people get richer and better educated, a democrat would admonishly tell a communist, they will no longer be willing to let a handful of men in the Politburo take all the decisions

that govern a country's life. The same must now be said, with adjustment for scale, about the workings of democracy. As the old differences of wealth, education and social condition blur, it will be increasingly hard to go on persuading people that most of them are fit only to put a tick on a ballot paper every few years, and that the handful of men and women they thereby send to parliament must be left to take all the other decisions. (Beedham 1993, 6)

Contemporary protest and calls for direct citizen input are not antidemocratic behavior. Indeed they are often attempts by ordinary citizens to pressure the political system to become more democratic. More often than not, the protesters are pressing political elites to open the political process and be responsive to new issue interests. Furthermore, very few citizens subscribe to the extreme forms of violent political action that actually might threaten the political system.

I favor a more Jeffersonian view of the democratic process. The logic of democratic politics is that expanding political involvement can also expand citizens' understanding of the political process. Citizens learn about the responsibilities of governing and the choices facing society by becoming involved—and that makes them better citizens. Geraint Parry and his colleagues (1992, chap. 13), for instance, provide empirical evidence that participation increases the public's knowledge about politics. A recent comparative study of environmental groups similarly stressed the educational role of citizen-action groups (Pierce et al. 1992). In the long run, involving the public can make better citizens and better politics.

Ironically, there is some evidence from Britain that active citizens also become more critical of politicians and the political process (Parry et al. 1992, chap. 13). Thus the educational role of participation can lead to further challenges to the political status quo. These demands can introduce new strains on the democratic process. But one would hope that a responsive political system could build positive experiences with the democratic process. Moreover, it is in addressing the demands of a critical public that the democratization process makes progress.

Contemporary democracies clearly face important challenges, and their future depends on the nature of the response. The response should not be to push back the clock, to re-create the halcyon politics of a bygone age. Democracies must adapt to survive, maximizing the advantages of increasing citizen participation while minimizing the disadvantages. The experience of the past several years suggests that this is the course we are following. Institutions are changing to accommodate increased citizen participation. German administrative regulations now require consultation with citizen groups as part of the political process. Public access and advice have become much more open in the United States. Citizen-action groups are winning legal standing to bring lawsuits to protect the public interest. Politicians and bureaucrats are becoming more comfortable with an expanded form of democracy. Democracy is threatened when we fail to take the democratic creed literally and reject these challenges.

Notes

1. The protest measure is a simple additive scale of the respondent's willingness to participate in the four challenging activities of table 4.1 (p. 74). The model differs slightly from those in chapter 3 because the World Values Survey lacked a measure of party attachments and had a different measure of political satisfaction (support for radical social change). The analyses in figure 4.2 (p. 80) are based on multiple regression; figure entries are standardized regression coefficients.

2. We conducted comparable analyses with Eurobarometer 31, which allowed us to match the predictors of chapter 3 but without data for the United States. Our measure of unconventional action is willingness to engage in the same four activities as in figure 4.2 (p. 80). The results are generally consistent with those from the World Values Survey:

Predictor	Britain	Germany	France
Education	.15	.22	.21
Age	−.08	−.17	−.14
Gender (male)	.04	.06	.11
Party attachment	.14	.05	.20
Union attachment	.15	.08	.17
Political satisfaction	−.14	.00	−.03
Left/Right position	.18	.11	.19
R	.44	.39	.49

3. Union activity is also related to unconventional political action. This relationship is, however, generally less than for conventional action. In addition, the different union measure in the World Values Survey produces very few union activists (about 10 percent) and thus might accentuate the influence of this factor.

4. For interesting evidence on the endurance of this new style of protest politics see Jennings's (1987) national study of youth and Fendrich's (1993) longitudinal tracking of student protestors from the 1960s.

5. This term is identified with the Great Society programs initiated by the Johnson administration to increase the participation of minorities and low-income groups. These institutionalized participation channels have been adopted by a range of citizen groups and governments in the United States and other democracies.

PART TWO

Political Orientations

5. Values in Change

Human values define the essence of our lives. Our values tell us what is important, to ourselves and society, and provide the reference standard for making our decisions. We structure our lives around our beliefs about what is important to us: whether it is the choice of careers, a marriage partner, or a movie on Saturday night.

Politics often involves human values. Values identify what people feel are, or should be, the goals of society and the political system. Shared values help define the norms of a political and social system. The clash between alternative values creates a basis for political competition over which values should shape public policy. For instance, are welfare programs constructed in terms of values of economic efficiency or empathy for the life conditions of families in need? Are issues of criminal justice based on concerns about protecting the security of the populace or protecting the rights of the accused? In a real sense, all of politics involves conflicts over values.

I believe that the new style of citizen politics includes a fundamental shift in the basic political values of many people. A comparison of contemporary societies to those of a generation ago would uncover strong evidence of changing social norms. Hierarchical relationships and deference toward authority are giving way to decentralization, quality circles, and participatory decision making. People demand more control over the decisions affecting their lives. Previous chapters describe how participatory norms are stimulating greater political involvement, but the consequences of value change are much broader. The new values are affecting attitudes toward work, lifestyles, and the individual's role in society.

The definition of societal goals and the meaning of "success" are also changing. Until recently, many Americans measured success almost solely in economic terms: a large house, two cars in the garage, and other signs of affluence. The late Malcolm Forbes said that life was a contest, and the winner was the person who accumulated the most possessions before he or she died. In Europe the threshold for economic success might have been lower, but material concerns were equally important.

Once affluence became widespread, however, many people realized that bigger is not necessarily better and that small could be beautiful (Schumacher 1973). The consensus for economic growth was tempered by a concern for environmental protection. Environmental sensitivities spread throughout society, as well as green consumerism (McCormick 1991). Social relations and acceptance of diversity are additional examples of values in change. Progress on racial, sexual, and religious equality are transforming American and European societies. Moreover, social norms involving sex, social relations, and the choice of lifestyles have changed dramatically in a few short decades. Basic value priorities are being transformed in advanced industrial societies.

Evidence of value change is all around us, if we look. We think in the present, and so the magnitude of these changes is not always appreciated. One can get a sense of these changes by comparing the diversity of contemporary American lifestyles to the images of American life depicted on vintage television reruns from the 1950s. Series such as *Ozzie and Harriet, Father Knows Best,* and *Leave It to Beaver* reflect many values of a bygone era. How well would the Nelsons or the Cleavers adjust to a world with women's liberation, the new morality, racial desegregation, rap music, and alternative lifestyles? Imagine the Cleavers and the Bundys as next-door neighbors.

This chapter examines the public's value priorities and the evidence that values are systematically changing in advanced industrial societies. Then we consider some of the implications of this process of value change for democratic politics.

The Nature of Value Change

We study citizen values because they provide the standards that guide the attitudes and behaviors of the public. Values signify a preference for certain personal and social goals, as well as the methods to obtain these goals. One individual may place a high priority on freedom, equality, and social harmony—and favor policies that strengthen these values. Others may stress independence, social recognition, and ambition in guiding their actions.

Many personal and political decisions involve a choice between several valued goals. One situation may force a choice between behaving independently and obediently or between behaving politely and sincerely. A national policy may present contrasts between the goals of world peace and national security or between economic well-being and protection of nature. People develop a general framework for making these decisions by organizing values into a value system, which organizes values by their importance to the individual. Citizen behavior may appear inconsistent and illogical (see chapter 2) unless the researcher considers the values of each individual and how people apply these values in specific situations. To one citizen, busing is an issue of social equality and civil rights; to another, it is an issue of freedom and providing for one's family. Both perspectives are correct, and attitudes toward busing are determined by how individuals weigh these conflicting values.

Value systems should include the salient goals that guide human behavior. Milton Rokeach (1973) developed an inventory of eighteen instrumental values focusing on the methods of achieving desired goals and eighteen terminal values defining preferred end-state goals. A complete list of important human goals should be much longer, and a complete list would be necessary to explain individual behavior fully.

Social scientists focused their attention on questions of value change as the evidence of the public's changing priorities became apparent in several areas. In reaction to the individualization of society, David Riesman and others stressed the shift from group solidarity and other-directed values to self-actualizing and inner-directed goals (Riesman 1950; Sennett 1978). Alex Inkeles and David Smith (1974) described a more general process of value change, linking developed and modern societies. More recently, Scott Flanagan (1982) emphasized the shift from authoritarian values to libertarian values as a characteristic of advanced industrial societies. Many observers have noted the decline in the traditional work ethic; others have observed a general decrease in concern for economic security as Western societies entered an age of affluence.

Ronald Inglehart has developed the most systematic attempt to describe and explain the process of value change for advanced industrial societies (Inglehart 1977, 1981, 1990; Abramson and Inglehart 1995). Inglehart bases his theory of value change on two premises. First, he suggests that basic value priorities are determined by a scarcity hypothesis: individuals "place the greatest value on those things that are in relatively short supply" (Inglehart 1981, 881). That is, when some valued object is difficult to obtain, its worth is magnified. If the supply increases to match the demand, then the object is taken for granted and attention shifts to objects that are still scarce. For example, water is a precious commodity during a drought, but when the rains return to normal, the concern over water evaporates. Similarly, the recent concern for clean water arose when pollution became widespread and the availability of clean water became uncertain. This general argument can be applied to other items valued by society.

The second premise of Inglehart's theory is a socialization hypothesis:

"to a large extent, one's value priorities reflect the conditions that prevailed during one's preadult years" (Inglehart 1981, 881). These formative conditions include both the immediate situation in one's own family and the broader political and economic conditions of society. Value change may continue after this formative period as individuals move through the life cycle or are exposed to new stimuli. Nevertheless, Inglehart assumes that latter learning must overcome the inertia of preexisting orientations.

The combination of both hypotheses—scarcity and socialization—produces a general model of value change. An individual's basic value priorities are initially formed early in life in reaction to the conditions of this formative period. Once these values develop, they tend to endure in the face of later changes in social conditions.

The introductory chapter describes how advanced industrial societies are now characterized by unprecedented affluence, greatly increased educational levels, expanding information opportunities, an extensive social welfare system, and other related characteristics. These societies have experienced dramatic changes in these features over a brief time. We have linked these social trends to the growing sophistication, cognitive mobilization, and participation of modern electorates. In addition, Inglehart maintains that these social forces are important in changing the public's basic value priorities because these trends are altering the socioeconomic structure of these nations. Hence the relative scarcity of valued goals is changing.

To generalize the scarcity hypothesis into a broader theoretical model, Inglehart draws on the work of Abraham Maslow (1954).[1] Maslow suggests a hierarchical ordering of human goals. Individuals first seek to fulfill basic subsistence needs: water, food, and shelter. When these needs are met, the search continues until enough material goods are acquired to attain a comfortable margin of economic security. Having accomplished this, individuals may turn to higher-order needs, such as a sense of belonging, self-esteem, participation, self-actualization, and the fulfillment of aesthetic and intellectual potential. Thus, goal seeking can be predicted by this ordering of values.

Inglehart applied the logic of Maslow's value hierarchy to political issues (figure 5.1). Many political issues, such as economic security, law and order, and national defense, tap underlying sustenance and safety needs. Inglehart describes these goals as *material* values. In a time of depression or civil unrest, for example, security and sustenance needs undoubtedly receive great attention. If a society can make significant progress in addressing these goals, then attention can shift toward higher-order values. These higher-order goals are reflected in issues such as individual freedom, self-expression, and participation. Inglehart labels these goals as *postmaterial* values.

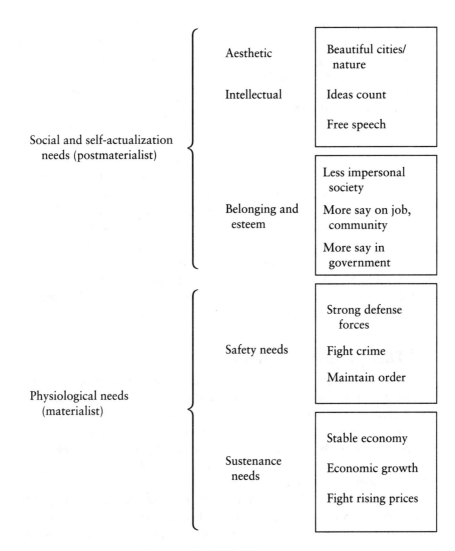

FIGURE 5.1

THE MASLOVIAN VALUE HIERARCHY

SOURCE: Inglehart (1977, 42).

Inglehart contends that this material/postmaterial continuum provides a general framework for understanding the primary value changes now occurring in advanced industrial democracies. One measure of the significance of this concept is the large number of other studies that have examined the logic and method of the postmaterial theory (see the extensive literature cited in Inglehart 1990). Some of these researchers note the broad nature of value change and describe the process as a transition from "Old Politics" values of economic growth, security, and traditional lifestyles to "New Politics" values of individual freedoms, social equality, and the quality of life (Baker et al. 1981; Miller and Levitin 1976).

The major challenge to Inglehart's conceptualization of value change has come from Scott Flanagan (1982, 1987). Flanagan has argued that instead of a single dimension of value change, public values in advanced industrial societies are shifting along at least two dimensions. One dimension involves a shift from material to noneconomic values; a second dimension involves a shift from authoritarian to libertarian values. Flanagan's theoretical distinction is useful, but the empirical evidence suggests that these two value dimensions overlap and that both value shifts are occurring simultaneously in most advanced industrial democracies. Thus Flanagan's two dimensions can be seen as subelements of Inglehart's broader framework. Regardless of how we conceptualize this process, however, there is general agreement that the value priorities of modern publics have been changing.

The Distribution of Values

When we measure citizen values, we must realize that most people attach a positive worth to both material and postmaterial goals. The average individual prefers both economic growth and a clean environment, social stability and individual freedom. Politics, however, often involves a conflict between valued goals. Therefore, rather than study one set of values in isolation from another, we must identify which goals take priority in the public's mind when values come in conflict.

Survey researchers have used a variety of methods to measure public values. Indeed, because values are deeply held and relatively pure feelings, it is complicated to tap them with a simple public opinion survey question. In addition, researchers have debated whether we should measure values in terms of personal life conditions or phrased as political goals that are linked to political behaviors. This measurement debate is ongoing (Marsh 1977; Inglehart 1990; Flanagan 1982; van Deth and Scarbrough 1996).

Following the model of Inglehart's research, the 1990–91 World Values Survey assessed value priorities by asking respondents to rank the importance of twelve possible political goals. Table 5.1 presents the top priorities of Americans, Britons, Germans, and the French across these items. The selection of items was guided by the Maslovian value hierarchy presented in figure 5.1.

TABLE 5.1

DISTRIBUTION OF VALUE PRIORITIES

(IN PERCENTAGES)

	United States	Great Britain	West Germany	France
High level of economic growth (M)[a]	76	67	65	72
More say in work/community (PM)[b]	55	69	59	68
A stable economy (M)	71	62	66	47
Fight against crime (M)	65	64	49	55
Protect free speech (PM)	48	45	61	63
Maintain order in nation (M)	57	46	55	44
More say in government (PM)	55	51	50	38
More humane society (PM)	33	43	55	57
Fight rising prices (M)	44	52	28	50
Make cities/country beautiful (PM)	23	36	42	38
Ideas count more than money (PM)	27	27	25	35
A strong defense (M)	38	19	12	12
N	1,839	1,484	2,101	1,002

SOURCE: 1990–91 World Values Survey.

NOTE: Table entries are the percentage listing item as first or second choice among items presented in sets of four. Missing data were included in the calculation of percentages.

a. (M) = materialist.
b. (PM) = postmaterialist.

Most citizens on both sides of the Atlantic cite material goals as their first priority. Americans most often emphasize economic growth, a stable economy, and crime prevention. Europeans stress the same material needs. At the same time, Europeans and Americans also give high rankings to the postmaterial goals of participating in job-related and political decision making, as well as protection of free speech. A majority of Germans and French greatly value progress toward a more humane society. Defense concerns were once quite salient; they attract much less public concern in the new post–Cold War world. In short, a significant proportion of these publics now gives priority to postmaterial goals.

Using the choices made among these twelve items, we created a single index that scores individuals by the relative weight they attach to postmaterial goals.[2] Materialists place high priority on the six economic and security goals (marked "M"), while postmaterialists stress participation and higher order goals (marked "PM"). Table 5.2 displays the distribution of value groups on this twelve-item index for a set of nations over time.[3]

TABLE 5.2

THE SHIFT IN POSTMATERIAL VALUES OVER TIME
(PERCENTAGE POSTMATERIAL
ON 12-ITEM INDEX)

	1973	*1990*
Netherlands	35	39
Belgium	38	38
Spain	—	37
Germany (West)	13	36
Italy	16	33
Denmark	19	32
Sweden	—	31
Japan	—	31
Canada	—	29
France	33	27
Germany (East)	—	23
Ireland	15	23
United States	—	21
Great Britain	18	19
Norway	—	17
Eight-nation average	23	31

SOURCES: 1973 European Communities Study; 1990–91 World Values Survey.

NOTE: Entries are the percentage in each nation that place a higher priority on postmaterial goals based on an index created from the twelve items in table 5.1.

In the early 1970s, the number of materialists exceeded the number of postmaterialists in every nation. Using the twelve-item index, only 13 percent of Germans and 18 percent of the British scored high on the postmaterial scale. The proportion of materialists was even more pronounced with Inglehart's four-item index (Inglehart 1977, 1990). The excess of materialists was not surprising. The conditions fostering value change should take several generations to accumulate, and in historical perspective the development of advanced industrialism is a relatively recent phenomenon.

By the early 1990s, the proportion of postmaterialists had increased in almost every nation for which 1973 data are available. Paul Abramson and Ronald Inglehart (1995) describe a similar pattern of value change for an even larger set of nations covered by the 1980 and 1990–91 World Values Survey. Using the four-item index, for example, the proportion of postmaterialists in Germany increases from 10 percent in 1970–71 to 16 percent in 1982 and 28 percent in 1990.

Data from other sources underscore this value shift among Western publics. For instance, there has been a dramatic long-term reversal between 1949 and 1975 in the priority Germans attach to two freedoms: freedom from want and freedom of speech (Dalton 1989, 118). In the insecure climate of the immediate postwar period, 35 percent of the public emphasized freedom from want and 26 percent gave priority to free speech. After the Economic Miracle had transformed German lifestyles, only 23 percent stressed freedom from want and 54 percent emphasized free speech. Similar trends are apparent in the values parents say they would emphasize in raising their children.

Even if one is uncertain about the exact proportion of postmaterialists because of debates over how to measure these values, the trend toward postmaterial goals is clear. Now, larger proportions of the public—often a third—espouse a priority for postmaterial goals in most advanced industrial democracies. Because many of the remaining individuals favor an equal mix of both value types, the number of people exclusively preferring material goals is less than half in every nation except Norway and the United States.[4] Thus citizen priorities in these societies are now characterized by a mix of material and postmaterial objectives.

For more than two decades I have heard repeated arguments that postmaterialism is a "sunshine" issue that will fade with the next economic downturn or period of political uncertainty. In the 1970s, the OPEC increases in oil prices stimulated global recessions that some claimed would end the liberalism of the 1960s. The 1980s were heralded as the "me" decade. Neither claim was correct.[5] The public opinion surveys presented above and later in this chapter document the slow and steady growth of postmaterial values in advanced industrial democracies. An evolutionary change in values is transforming the nature of citizen politics.

Modeling the Process of Value Change

How do we know expressed support for postmaterial goals really reflects an ongoing process of societal value change? At first, the evidence was tentative. With time, however, the evidence in support of postmaterial value change has accumulated. The longitudinal data cited above provide one sort of evidence. Inglehart's theory would predict an evolutionary shift toward postmaterial priorities.

The most telling evidence supporting the postmaterial thesis comes from analyses that test the two hypotheses underlying Inglehart's theory. Inglehart's scarcity hypothesis predicts that the socioeconomic conditions of a nation are related to the priorities of its citizens. In addition, the socialization hypothesis predicts that values become crystallized early in life; thus the overall values of a society reflect the conditions decades or more earlier, when values were being formed.

We can test these hypotheses by comparing national levels of post-material values to the socioeconomic conditions of each nation. If scarcity breeds a concern for materialist values, then these concerns should be more common in nations with lower living standards. Conversely, the affluence of advanced industrial societies should increase support for postmaterial goals among these publics. Moreover, according to the socialization hypothesis, these effects should occur with some time lag. Thus the best predictor of values should be national conditions a generation ago, when values were forming.

Figure 5.2 documents a clear relationship between national affluence (gross national product per capita in 1965) and the distribution of material/postmaterial values in 1990–91 for thirty-three nations.[6] In general, postmaterialists are most common in nations (including the four core nations in this book) that had high living standards during the formative years of the average adult surveyed in 1990. In contrast, there are low levels of postmaterialism in less affluent nations, such as Nigeria, India, China, and other less developed nations (including several nations in Eastern Europe). Moreover, this is not simply a correlation between contemporaneous measures, as Abramson and Inglehart have presented (1995, 128); we are comparing economic conditions a generation ago with value priorities in the 1990s.

Prior research has noted the curvilinear nature of the relationship between economic condition and value change (Dalton 1977; Abramson and Inglehart 1995).[7] As can be seen in the figure, the greatest shift in values occurs during the transition from a subsistence economy to an advanced industrial society, such as that found in postwar Western Europe. Once this level of affluence is achieved, further increases in well-being produce progressively smaller changes in values. This implies that the process of value change will continue at a slower rate in the future, but a gradual shift in values should continue.

Another test of the postmaterial theory involves generational patterns in the distribution of values within Western nations. Inglehart's scarcity hypothesis predicts sharp generational differences in value priorities. Older generations, reared in the years before World War II, grew up in a period of widespread uncertainty. These individuals suffered through the Great Depression in the 1930s and endured two world wars and the social and economic traumas that accompanied these events. Given these circumstances, older generations in most Western democracies should have been

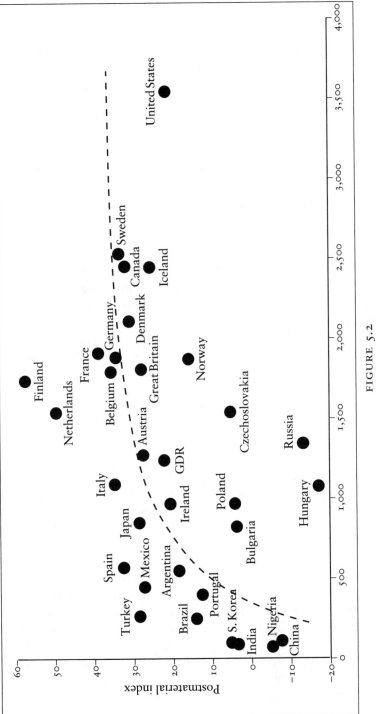

FIGURE 5.2

FORMATIVE ECONOMIC CONDITIONS AND POSTMATERIAL VALUES

SOURCES: Taylor and Hudson (1972, 314–21); Abramson and Inglehart (1995, 124–25).

socialized into a greater concern with material goals: economic growth, economic security, domestic order, and social and military security.

Conversely, younger generations in Europe and North America were raised in a period of unprecedented affluence and security. Present-day living standards are often several times higher than those experienced before World War II. The rapid growth of the welfare state now protects most citizens from even major economic problems. Postwar generations also have a broader worldview, reflecting their higher educational levels, greater exposure to political information, and more diverse cultural experiences. Furthermore, the past five decades are one of the longest periods of international peace in modern European history. Under these conditions, the material concerns that preoccupied prewar generations should have diminished in urgency. Growing up in a period when material and security needs seem assured, postwar generations should shift their attention toward postmaterial goals.

Furthermore, Inglehart's socialization hypothesis predicts that initial value differences across generations should resist later life change. That is, if values are enduring, different age groups should retain the mark of their formative generational experiences even if their later life experiences change. Older Europeans should still stress security concerns even if their present lifestyles include a high level of affluence. Generations socialized in the affluence of the postwar economic miracle should retain their greater concern for postmaterial values even as they age and assume greater family and economic responsibilities.

Thus a crucial test of the value-change thesis involves tracking the value priorities of generations over time. Figure 5.3 describes the value priorities of several European generations from 1970 until 1992 using Inglehart's four-item value index.[8] The oldest cohort, age 65–85 in 1970 (born between 1886 and 1905), is located near the bottom of the figure. In 1970 the proportion of materialists in this cohort outweighs postmaterialists by nearly 50 percent. In contrast, the youngest cohort in 1970 (born between 1946 and 1955) is almost evenly balanced between material and postmaterial values.

Not only is the relative ranking of generations an important bit of evidence in support of Inglehart's theory, but so is the persistence of this pattern over time. The level of values fluctuates over time in response to random sampling variation and the sensitivity of the four-item values index to inflation levels (which I consider a methodological imperfection in the four-item measure).[9] Most important, the generational gaps in value orientations remain fairly constant over time—seen in the parallel movement of each generation—although all cohorts are moving through the life cycle.

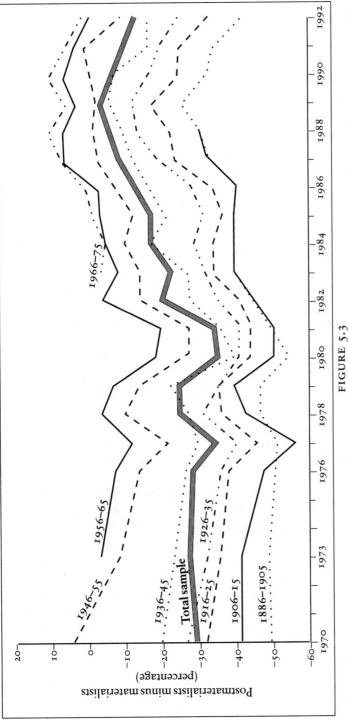

FIGURE 5.3

DISTRIBUTION BY AGE COHORT OF EUROPEAN VALUE PRIORITIES OVER TIME

SOURCE: Redrawn from Inglehart and Abramson (1994, 340). Used by permission of the authors and publisher.

NOTE: The data represented are based on a combined weighted sample of European Community surveys carried out (in the years indicated along the x axis) in West Germany, France, Britain, Italy, the Netherlands, and Belgium, using the four-item materialist/postmaterialist values index. The total sample size was 222,699. The values plotted are the percentage of postmaterialist minus percentage of materialist aggregated scores for eight cohorts defined by their birth years and for the total six-nation sample.

The youngest age group from 1970, for example, is approaching middle age by the end of the survey series (ages 37–46). Yet their postmaterial value orientations do not lessen significantly between 1970 and 1992. Life-cycle experiences can modify, but do not replace, the early learning of value priorities.

The size of the generational differences in values across nations pro-vide supplemental support for the value-change thesis. Germany, for ex-ample, experienced tremendous socioeconomic change during the past few generations. Consequently, the value differences between the youngest and oldest German cohorts are larger than for many other nations. Conversely, for a nation that experienced little socioeconomic change over the past generation, age groups should display smaller generational differences in their values. Inglehart and Abramson (1995, 134) demonstrate that across a wide set of developed and less developed nations there is a strong rela-tionship between rates of economic growth and the size of the age gap in value priorities. Large social changes produce large changes in values.

The most serious challenge to the postmaterial theory has come from Ray Duch and Michael Taylor's (1993) extensive multivariate analysis of value differences across age groups. They claim that formative conditions do not influence current value priorities. Abramson and Inglehart (1995) have challenged this interpretation, arguing the Duch and Taylor have dis-torted the results by their selection of time points and misinterpret the meaning of educational effects. This debate involves complex statistical and methodological issues (Duch and Taylor 1994). My own view is that generational differences in value priorities are strong and enduring, as seen in figure 5.3, and a correctly specified statistical analysis will find this re-sult. Nevertheless, the debate over the nature and extent of value change will continue.

The effects of educational level on value priorities illustrate the com-plexity of the value-change process. The effects of education obviously over-lap with those of generation; the young are better educated than the old. Ed-ucation also is an indirect measure of an individual's economic circumstances during adolescence, when value priorities were being formed, because access to higher education often reflects the family's social status during an individ-ual's youth. Education also may affect value priorities because of the content of instruction. Contemporary Western educational systems generally stress the values of participation, self-expression, intellectual understanding, and other postmaterial goals. Moreover, the diversity of the modern university milieu may encourage a broadening of social perspectives.

Figure 5.4 presents the differences across educational groups in the percentage scoring high on postmaterial values on the twelve-item index.

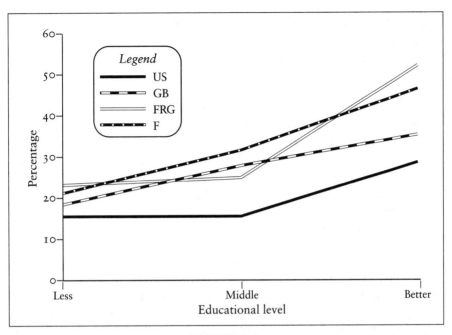

FIGURE 5.4
POSTMATERIALISTS BY EDUCATIONAL LEVEL

SOURCE: 1990–91 World Values Survey.

In every nation, there is a strong positive relationship between educational level and support for postmaterial goals. In France, for instance, only 21 percent of the lesser educated are postmaterialists, compared to nearly half of those with higher education (48 percent). These educational differences are greater in Europe, reflecting the greater class polarization in access to education and hence the stronger link between educational level and early life conditions.

The concentration of postmaterial values among the young and better educated gives added significance to these orientations. If Inglehart's theory is correct, the percentage of postmaterialists should gradually increase over time, as older materialist cohorts are replaced by younger, more postmaterialist generations (Inglehart and Abramson 1995, chap. 4).[10] Similarly, if expanding educational opportunities continue to increase the public's educational level, support for postmaterial values should grow. Furthermore, because postmaterialists are more active in politics, their political influence is greater than their numbers imply. Indeed, among the group of future elites—university educated youth—postmaterial values predominate.[11] As these individuals advance into positions of economic, social, and political leadership, the impact of changing values should strengthen. Value change thus has the appearance of an ongoing process.

The Consequences of Value Change

Although postmaterialists now constitute only a minority of the population in most advanced industrial democracies, the impact of these values is already apparent, extending beyond politics to all aspects of society. Indeed, one of the most impressive aspects of Inglehart's book *Culture Shift in Advanced Industrial Society* is the range of political phenomena he links to postmaterialism.

At the workplace, for example, these new value orientations are fueling demands for a more flexible and individually oriented work environment. Rigid, hierarchical, assembly-line systems of production are being challenged by worker participation (codetermination), quality circles, and flexible working hours. Postmaterial values prompt a shift from materialist occupational goals (security and a good salary) to qualitative goals (a feeling of accomplishment and sense of responsibility). Many business analysts bemoan the decline of the work ethic, but it is more accurate to say that the work ethic is becoming motivated by a new set of goals.

Social relations are changing in reaction to the public's new value orientations. Deference to authority of all forms is declining, as individuals are more willing to challenge elites. Bosses, army officers, university professors, and political leaders all decry the decline in deference to their authority. But the postmaterial credo is that an individual earns authority, it is not bestowed by a position. Similarly, many citizens are placing less reliance on social norms—class, religion, or community—as a guide for behavior. The public's behavior in all aspects of social and political life is becoming more self-directed. This shows in the declining brand-name loyalty among consumers, and the decline of political party loyalty among voters. In short, contemporary lifestyles reflect a demand for greater freedom and individuality, which appears in fashions, consumer tastes, social behavior, and interpersonal relations.

This broader process of value change includes religious values and sexual mores (Harding 1986; Inglehart, forthcoming). Materialists are significantly more likely to hold restrictive attitudes on sexually related issues, such as extramarital sex, abortion, or homosexuality. National levels of postmaterialism are linked to declining fertility rates. In short, materialists are not just concerned with economic matters; these values tap a broader collection of traditional social norms.

Focusing our attention on the realm of politics, postmaterial values are often linked to the new social movements of advanced industrial societies (Dalton and Kuechler 1990). Postmaterialists champion a new set of political issues—environmental quality, nuclear energy, women's rights, and consumerism—that the political establishment often overlooked. Debates in Washington about acid rain, the safety of nuclear plants, and gender equality have close parallels in the capitals of Europe. Proponents of these issues have similar characteristics: they are young, better educated, and postmaterialists.

Table 5.3 displays the relationship between values and support for new social movements. In each of our four nations, support for groups opposing nuclear power and groups supporting women's rights is significantly higher among postmaterialists. Postmaterialists are roughly twice as supportive as materialists, and this gap widens if we examine participation in movement activities (Dalton 1994, chap. 3; Inglehart 1990). Postmaterialists have revived many other issues—disarmament, codetermination, and social equality—and reinterpreted them in terms of new value perspectives. These new issues have been added to the political agenda of contemporary democracies. Perhaps even more important, a new set of public interest groups and political movements advocating these issues is part of the contemporary political process.

Value change also affects patterns of political participation. Postmaterial values stimulate direct participation in the decisions affecting one's life—whether at school, the workplace, or in the political process. Postmaterialists are more interested in politics than are materialists and more likely to translate this interest into political action (Dalton 1988, chap. 5; Inglehart 1990).[12]

The participatory orientation of postmaterialists adds to the puzzle of participation noted in chapter 2: if factors stimulating participation are increasing, why are voting and some other forms of action declining? The answer to this puzzle reinforces our contention that the pattern of political action is changing in advanced industrial societies. The participatory orientation of postmaterialists has not affected all participation modes equally (Inglehart 1979). Postmaterial values are not related to electoral participation, and in some nations voting turnout is actually lower among postmaterialists.[13] This is partially because the establishment parties have responded ambiguously to new issue demands. In addition, postmaterialists are skeptical of established hierarchical organizations, such as most political parties.

Instead, postmaterial values stimulate participation in citizen initiatives, protests, and other forms of unconventional political activity. In the

TABLE 5.3

SUPPORT FOR SOCIAL MOVEMENTS BY VALUE TYPE

(IN PERCENTAGES)

	Value type				
	Material-ist	—	—	Postmaterial-ist	Correla-tion
Strongly approve of antinuclear groups					
United States	18	22	24	37	.12
Great Britain	14	14	18	30	.16
Federal Republic	19	25	29	55	.26
France	19	23	29	29	.09
Strongly approve of women's groups					
United States	24	30	28	46	.12
Great Britain	15	17	17	23	.05
Federal Republic	11	11	16	31	.21
France	16	22	23	21	.06

SOURCE: 1990–91 World Values Survey.

NOTE: Table entries are the percentage expressing strong approval for each group. Correlations are tau-b coefficients; each is statistically significant at .05 level or better.

1990 World Values Survey, for instance, postmaterialists are more than twice as likely as materialists to participate in protests (figure 5.5). These nonpartisan participation opportunities provide postmaterialists with a more direct influence on politics, which matches their value orientations. Most postmaterialists also possess the political skills to carry out these more demanding forms of political action. As chapters 3 and 4 noted, along with increasing levels of citizen involvement has come a change in the form of political participation.

Value Change and Value Stability

This chapter has emphasized the changing values of Western publics, but a more accurate description would stress the increasing diversity of the public's value priorities. Most people still give primary attention to material goals, and the socioeconomic issues deriving from these values will continue to dominate political debates for decades to come. The persistence of traditional values should not be overlooked.

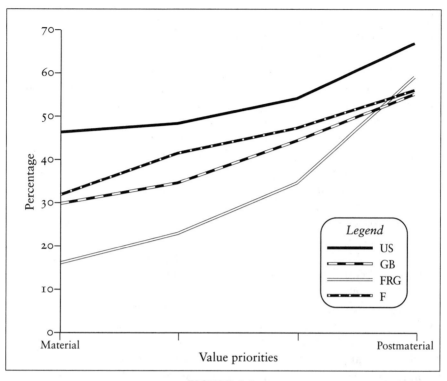

FIGURE 5.5
PROTEST POTENTIAL BY VALUE PRIORITIES

SOURCE: 1990–91 World Values Survey.

NOTE: On the vertical dimension are plotted the percentages of respondents willing to perform two or more unconventional activities.

At the same time, postmaterial values are spreading within advanced industrial societies. A sizable proportion of the public will sacrifice further economic growth for a clean environment. Many people value the opportunity to participate in the decisions affecting their lives more than they value institutions and procedures that ensure stability and order at the possible cost of citizen input. Public values are changing.

The current mix of values sometimes makes it difficult for political analysts and politicians to know what the public wants. For nearly every example of the persistence of traditional material value patterns, there is now a counterexample reflecting postmaterial values. For every citizen lobbying a local town council to stimulate the economy, there is another who worries that growth will mean a loss in green space or a loss in the quality of life. The diversity of values marks a major change in the nature of citizen politics: political debates again involve questions of goals and not just means to reach consensual goals.

The mix of values also makes it difficult for journalists and political analysts to discern the public's priorities when ultimate goals are being debated. At times, such as during the 1960s, media reports made it seem that every young person was joining the counterculture. In the 1980s, images of the Yuppie in pursuit of an MBA and a BMW were equally common. Now, Generation X is defined, in part, by the lack of either identity. The strength of empirical research is that we can track the values of the public in a more scientific manner. And what we find is a slow evolution toward greater priority for postmaterial goals.

This process of value change should have several consequences for contemporary politics. Value change is shifting the issues of contemporary political debate. Concerns for environmental protection, individual freedom, social equality, participation, and the quality of life have been *added* to the traditional political agenda of economic and security issues. For now and the foreseeable future, politics in most advanced industrial societies will be marked by a mix of material and postmaterial issues.

Inevitably, changes in the value priorities carry over to the institutions of the political process. No longer are political parties the sole or even the primary agents of political representation in modern democracies. Recent decades have seen a proliferation of citizen interest groups in the United States and Europe (Walker 1991; Berry 1989). The public's participatory demands have led to reforms within established political parties to increase the role of members, such as the convention reforms of the U.S. Democratic Party or the increased role for constituency associations in the British Labour Party. Postmaterialists have promoted the institutional reforms we discussed in the conclusion to chapter 4: greater use of initiatives and referendums, the opening up of administrative processes, and the expansion of the legal rights of citizen groups. Public interest groups are now widely involved in the American policymaking process, from the national government down to local governments and administrative boards (Ingram and Smith 1993). These institutional reforms increase the political influence of these groups, as well as producing even more fundamental changes in the process itself that affect all participants. Postmaterial groups have been agents for expanding the democratization process in advanced industrial democracies.

One other question involves the impact of these new values on the political parties and citizen voting behavior. Most of the established political parties are still oriented to traditional social divisions, and they have repeatedly resisted attempts to incorporate postmaterial issues into a partisan framework. Since the first edition of this book, several of the established political parties have begun to cater to these interests. Later chapters show that postmaterial values and issue concerns are injecting new volatility into Western party systems, often leading to the fragmentation of the established parties or the creation of new parties. A decade ago, few politicians claimed to speak for the environment; in 1992 both Bush and Clinton staked their claims to be the environmental president. A similar commitment is apparent among European politicians, at least at the rhetorical level.

Only a few skeptics still doubt that value priorities are changing among Western publics; the evidence of change is obvious. It is more difficult to anticipate the many consequences of this process of value change. By monitoring these trends, however, we may get a preview of the nature of citizen politics in advanced industrial democracies.

Notes

1. Inglehart's early work was closely linked to the Maslovian value hierarchy, but this is less prominent in his more recent research. As Inglehart has broadened his interests and empirical evidence beyond advanced industrial societies, he has become more sensitive to how cultural forces and local conditions can shape what values are considered scarce, and thus valued by the public.

2. Inglehart normally uses a four-item subset of the twelve items to construct a single index of material/postmaterial values (Inglehart 1990, chap. 2; 1977). The disadvantage of this index is that it is based on only four items, and this provides a narrow basis for tapping a broad dimension of human values. For instance, several analysts, including Inglehart, have shown that the four-item index is sensitive to current inflation levels because one item deals with the "fight against rising prices." The advantage of the four-item measure is that it has been used over more than two decades in European opinion surveys and on a limited basis in several dozen other nations. The analyses in this chapter primarily rely on the more robust twelve-item index that is available in the World Values Survey.

3. The twelve items were presented to respondents in groups of four. We counted the number of material items and postmaterial items selected as first or second priorities in each set of four. Our index is the difference between the number of material and postmaterial choices.

4. The twelve-item index in 1990 tends to understate the position of the United States relative to other nations. The four-item index in both the American National Election Studies and the 1990–91 World Values Survey finds a higher level of postmaterialism among Americans (Abramson and Inglehart 1995, 19, 135).

5. For example, membership in environmental groups grew dramatically on both sides of the Atlantic during the 1980s (Dunlap and Mertig 1992; Dalton 1994). Despite the apparent selfishness of the 1980s in the United States, volunteerism actually increased during the decade (Quigley 1991). Chapter 6 documents the specific issue opinions of these publics in more detail.

6. We use 1965 GNP/capita because this is roughly when values were being formed for many of the adults surveyed in 1990. In addition, we used Abramson and Inglehart's (1995, 124–25) summary index of values in order to be directly comparable to their analysis of the relationship between current GNP/capita and values.

7. There is a strong relationship ($R = .44$) between GNP/capita in 1965 and values in 1990, and this correlation is even stronger if modeled as a curvilinear relationship ($R = .49$).

8. Figure 5.3 is based on the combined results of samples from six nations: Britain, West Germany, France, Italy, Belgium, and The Netherlands. The nations were combined to produce age-group samples large enough to estimate values precisely. For a full discussion of these data, see Inglehart and Abramson (1995).

9. One weakness of the Inglehart measure is that it attempts to measure basic values with items dealing with specific political issues. Thus it is not surprising that the four-item index is sensitive to inflation rates because one of the items taps concern about rising prices (Clarke and Dutt 1991). A broader measure of values, such as Inglehart's twelve-item index or the social priorities question of Flanagan (1982), would be less susceptible to these measurement problems because these measures would come closer to tapping basic values.

10. Even during this relatively brief time span, generational turnover contributed to a postmaterial trend (Abramson and Inglehart 1995). For instance, in 1970 the pre–World War I generation constituted about 16 percent of the West German public; by 1980, this group constituted about 5 percent and by 1990 they had essentially left the electorate. In the place of these older citizens, young Germans, socialized in the affluent post–World War II era, had entered the electorate.

11. Inglehart (1981) finds that European political elites (candidates for the European Parliament) are nearly three times more postmaterialist than the total public. Postmaterialists are also more common among younger elites.

12. In the 1990–91 World Values Survey, for example, postmaterialists are more likely than materialists to say they discuss politics and follow political matters.

13. Markus Crepaz (1990) shows that the presence of a green or New Left party increases voting rates, presumably by encouraging postmaterialists to turn out at the polls.

6. Issues and Ideological Orientations

Issues are the currency of politics. The public's issue opinions identify their priorities for government action and their expectations for the political process. Political parties are largely defined by their issue positions, and elections provide the public with a means of selecting between competing issue programs offered by the candidates and parties. As citizens become more sophisticated and involved in the political process, issue beliefs are an increasingly important influence on voting choice and the policy process. Moreover, researchers find a significant relationship between the public's issue preferences and policy outcomes at the state and federal levels (Erikson et al. 1994; Shapiro and Jacobs 1989). Issues are what politics is about.

Issue opinions also represent the translation of broad value orientations into specific political concerns. Issues are partially determined by the values examined in the last chapter, as well as by factors external to the individual: the cues provided by political elites, the flow of political events, and the application of abstract values to specific situations. For example, a person may favor the principle of equal rights for all citizens; but attitudes toward voting rights, job discrimination, school busing, open housing, and other civil rights legislation represent different mixes of values and practical concerns. Consequently, issue opinions are more changeable and varied than broad value orientations.

Another important characteristic of issues is that people focus their attention on a few areas—they are members of one or more *issue publics* (see chapter 2). Some people are especially concerned with education policy; others are more interested in foreign affairs, civil rights, environmental protection, or another issue. In general, only a minority of the public is interested and informed on any specific issue, although most people are members of at least one issue public. Members of an issue public are relatively well informed about the issue at stake and follow the actions of politicians and the political parties on the issue. The salient issue for an individual has a strong impact on his or her political behavior.

The size of an issue public is influenced by several factors. People generally devote attention to the issues that are most relevant to their everyday lives. Economic and tax policies, for instance, generate substantial interest, while policies with a narrower scope are frequently less salient. Similarly, the issue publics for domestic policies generally are larger than for foreign policy, except for the war-and-peace issue. In addition, a sophisticated study of the American public's changing issue interests indicates that the visibility of an issue in the media often affects popular interest (MacKuen 1981). For example, as media attention to the crime problem grows, so too does public interest in the crime issue.

Issue opinions are a dynamic aspect of politics, and the theme of changing popular values can be carried over to the study of issues. In some areas, contemporary publics are obviously more liberal than their predecessors. The issues of women's rights, environmental protection, social equality, and individual lifestyles were unknown or highly divisive a generation ago; a growing consensus now exists on many of these issues. In other areas, people remain divided on the goals of government. Discussions of tax revolts, the neoconservative revival, and supply-side economics suggest that conservative issues have not lost their appeal for many people. This chapter describes the present issue opinions of Western publics and highlights, where possible, the trends in these opinions.

Domestic Policy Opinions

At one time, domestic policy was synonymous with concern over economic matters, and economic issues still rank at the top of the public's political agenda for most elections. More recently, however, the number of salient domestic issues has proliferated. Many people are now concerned with noneconomic issues such as social equality, environmental protection, and citizen participation. This section provides an overview of the wide-ranging domestic policy concerns of the citizenry.

Socioeconomic Issues and the State

For most of the century, the political conflicts that emerged from industrialization and the Great Depression dominated politics in democratic party systems. This debate revolved around the question of the government's role in society and the economy, especially the provision of basic social needs.

A prime example of this policy area is the set of government-backed social insurance programs that most governments introduced early in the twentieth century; comparable American programs flowed from Roosevelt's New Deal in the 1930s. These social insurance programs protected individuals from economic calamities caused by illness, unemployment, disability, or other hardships. In some nations the government's involvement in the economy also included public ownership of major industries and active efforts to manage the economy.

Labor unions favored the extension of government involvement as a way to improve the life chances of the average person. Business leaders and members of the middle class frequently opposed these policies as an unnecessary government intrusion into private affairs. At stake was not only the question of government involvement in society but also the desirability of certain social goals and the distribution of political influence between labor and business. To a large extent, the terms *liberal* and *conservative* were synonymous with one's position on these questions. Attitudes toward these issues provided the major source of political competition in most elections. Class-based opinions on socioeconomic issues were the primary policy concerns of many voters.

This policy area initially involved the government's implementation of basic social programs such as old-age security, unemployment compensation, sickness insurance, or health-care programs. Nearly every advanced industrial democracy except the United States developed a full range of social programs that eventually were accepted by liberals and conservatives alike. There also developed a general consensus that the government should actively guide economic development and ensure the basic well-being of the citizenry. With these expanded responsibilities, the size of government steadily grew.

Despite this long-term expansion in the role of government, or perhaps because of it, new questions about the scope of governmental activity were revived in the 1980s. Conservative politicians on both sides of the Atlantic championed a populist revolt against big government (Pierson 1994). Margaret Thatcher, Ronald Reagan, and Helmut Kohl attempted to turn back the growth of government, privatizing government-owned businesses or government-run programs and reducing government social programs. Political observers interpreted their electoral successes as evidence of a new conservative trend in public attitudes toward government.

There is abundant evidence that support for the principle of big government has lessened in recent years. For instance, between 1964 and 1980, the number of Americans who believed that the federal government was too powerful rose from 30 to 49 percent. The American public also became more critical of taxation levels and the use of their tax money. The Gallup surveys show that in 1950s less than half of the American public felt they were paying an unfair amount of taxes; by the late 1970s, more than three-quarters believed their share of taxes was too high. Similarly, the American National Election Study finds an increase in the proportion believing that government "wastes a lot" of tax dollars, from 47 percent in 1964 to 69 percent in 1992. These opinions fueled popular support for the tax revolt that spread across America in the 1980s. Concerns about taxes diminished slightly following the 1981 tax reform act, although most Americans still believe their taxes are too high (Page and Shapiro 1992, 160–63; Niemi et al. 1989, chap. 3). Perhaps the strongest indicator of these opinions has been the Republican Party's success in appealing to the antitax sentiments of many voters.

Some signs of a growing cynicism about big government also appear among Europeans. Longitudinal British public opinion trends uncover increasing criticism of big government beginning in the late 1970s (Dalton 1988, 102–3; Heath and McMahon 1992). British desires for the denationalization of some industries grew during the early Thatcher years. Building on these sentiments, the Thatcher government privatized British Petroleum, British Gas, British Airways, and British Telecom, and sold off government-owned shares in a host of enterprises during the 1980s.[1] Thatcher also advocated a cutback in social programs, tax cuts, and a general reduction in the scope of British government that challenged the collectivist consensus of the postwar era. Similar doubts about government also were visible in German political attitudes. Helmut Kohl's administration reduced the scope of government activity by selling off shares of government-owned firms and reducing the benefits of Germany's generous welfare state. The French government expanded governmental activity under a new socialist government at the beginning of the 1980s, but by the end of the decade there had been a retrenchment in French governmental activity also.

Despite this neoconservative policy activity, recent public opinion surveys show that many people still believe the government is responsibile for promoting individual well-being and guaranteeing the quality of life for its citizens. Table 6.1 displays the percentage of citizens who think the government is "definitely responsible" for dealing with specific social problems. Britons have very high expectations of government: half believe the government is definitely responsible for providing for health care, providing a decent standard of living for the elderly, keeping inflation in check, helping needy students, lessening unemployment, and helping industry to grow. Other studies show equally high support for environmental protection, fighting crime, ensuring access to education, and other social programs (Roller 1996; Borre and Scarbrough 1996). Eastern Germans, who were conditioned by the GDR to expect big government, are very similar to Britons in their reliance on the government to guarantee basic social needs. Many western Germans also believe the government is responsible in these

TABLE 6.I

GOVERNMENT RESPONSIBILITY FOR DEALING
WITH PROBLEMS (IN PERCENTAGES)

	United States	Great Britain	Western Germany	Eastern Germany
Provide health care	40	85	57	82
Provide a decent living standard for the elderly	40	79	54	85
Give aid to needy college students	55	49	31	59
Provide housing for those who need it	21	47	24	49
Keep prices under control	25	48	20	50
Provide industry with help to grow	19	41	12	35
Provide a decent living standard for the unemployed	14	32	19	52
Reduce income differences between rich and poor	17	42	22	48
Provides a job for everyone who wants one	16	24	30	63
Average	27	50	30	58
N	1,217	1,197	2,812	1,028

SOURCE: 1990 International Social Survey Program.

NOTE: Table entries are the percentage who say that each area should definitely be the government's responsibility. Missing data were excluded in the calculation of percentages.

policy areas, though to a lesser degree than easterners.[2] Data from the other European nations in this survey show that support for government action to resolve social needs is a core element of the European political culture (Taylor-Gooby 1993).

In comparison to most Europeans, Americans are more reserved in their acceptance of government action. Even in areas where the government is a primary actor, such as care of the elderly and unemployment, only a minority of Americans view these problems as definite government responsibilities (table 6.1). The United States is a major exception among Western democracies in its limited support for activist government (Heidenheimer et al. 1990, chap. 12). Public ownership of a significant portion of the economy was never attempted, and most Americans oppose nationalization on even a limited scale (Niemi et al. 1989, chap. 1; Taylor-Gooby

1993). Popular support for basic social programs remains underdeveloped by European standards. These conservative socioeconomic attitudes of Americans are often explained by the individualist nature of American society and the absence of a socialist working-class party (Lipset 1981a).

Another measure of citizen expectations of government involves preferences for government spending. One of the great paradoxes of public opinion is that even as people have grown more critical about taxes and the overall size of government, support for increased spending on specific policy programs remains widespread. Table 6.2 displays the differences between the percentage of Americans who favor more government spending in various policy areas minus those who want to spend less. These data describe a long-term consensus for increased government spending on education, crime prevention, health care, and environmental protection. Only welfare, the space program, and foreign aid are consistently identified as candidates for budget cuts. Additional items included in the 1994 survey showed that Americans wanted to spend more on programs to deal with drug addiction, assistance to the poor, highways, social security, mass transport, and parks. Moreover, although specific spending priorities change over time, the average preference for increased government spending listed across the bottom of the table has varied surprisingly little across six administrations.

Americans' priorities for spending on specific programs do, however, respond to changes in the federal budget and the political context in a manner consistent with Benjamin Page and Robert Shapiro's (1992) description of a rational public. For instance, the perceived military weakness of the Carter administration was reflected in calls for greater defense spending; 56 percent of Americans thought the government was spending too little on defense in the spring of 1980. This attitude supported the large defense expenditures of the early Reagan administration. Then, as examples of Pentagon waste became commonplace (accounts of $500 hammers and $7,000 coffeepots), popular support for defense spending was replaced by endorsement of the status quo or even a cut in defense budgets. Similarly, limitations on social spending enacted by the Reagan administration exceeded the wishes of many Americans. Between 1980 and 1991, support increased for *more* spending in the areas of health care, environmental protection, education, urban problems, and minority aid. The Clinton administration entered office with a public that supported more spending on health care and other social programs.

Cross-national opinion polls indicate that budgetary support for specific policy programs such as health care, environmental protection, education, housing, and social services is widespread among Europeans (table 6.3). Britons favor increased spending in most areas, especially on policies

TABLE 6.2

BUDGET PRIORITIES OF THE AMERICAN PUBLIC

(IN PERCENTAGES)

Priority	1973	1976	1980	1984	1988	1991	1994
Halting rising crime rate	60	57	63	62	64	59	71
Protecting the nation's health	56	55	47	51	63	66	55
Dealing with drug addiction	59	51	52	57	64	50	54
Protecting the environment	53	45	32	54	60	63	54
Improving the educational system	40	41	42	59	60	62	68
Solving problems of big cities	36	23	19	31	36	35	47
Improving the condition of blacks	11	2	0	19	19	20	12
The military and defense	−27	−3	45	−21	−22	−13	−16
Welfare	−31	−46	−43	−16	−19	−15	−49
Space exploration program	−51	−51	−21	−27	−16	−26	−39
Foreign aid	−66	−72	−64	−65	−63	−68	−71
Average	13	9	16	19	22	21	17

SOURCE: NORC General Social Survey.

NOTE: Table entries are the percentages saying "too little" being spent on the problem minus the percentage saying "too much."

TABLE 6.3

BUDGET PRIORITIES OF THE AMERICAN, BRITISH, AND
GERMAN PUBLICS (PERCENTAGE DIFFERENCES)

	United States	Great Britain	Western Germany
The environment	51	60	90
Health	69	90	70
Police and law enforcement	50	46	29
Education	71	77	52
The military and defense	−35	−39	−78
Retirement benefits	39	83	53
Unemployment benefits	6	19	23
Culture and arts	−27	−32	−8
Average	28	43	29
N	1,217	1,197	2,812

SOURCE: 1990 International Social Survey Program.

NOTE: Table entries are the percentage who say that the government should "spend less" on each problem minus the percentage who say the government should "spend more." Missing data were excluded in the calculation of percentages.

identified with the welfare state. Western Germans display modest support for increased spending, but this is in the context of already large public expenditures and the economic uncertainties accompanying German unification. The other European nations in this survey display general support for increased government spending (Taylor-Gooby 1993, 90–92). Americans also favor increased government spending on these programs, although their support is relatively modest in comparison to other advanced industrial nations.

Public opinion data thus present a picture of contemporary politics that is somewhat at odds with the recent electoral success of neoconservatives in all four nations. For instance, the American public did not want to slash domestic spending in many of the areas targeted by the Reagan and Bush administrations. In fact, American preferences for spending on social needs increased during the Reagan/Bush administrations, which partially paved the way for Clinton's emphasis on the need for change in 1992. Even the Republicans' victory in the fall 1994 elections was paralleled by public opinion polls indicating popular support for many of the policy areas that the Republicans had targeted for cuts. Similarly, the continued electoral success of the Conservative Party in Britain runs counter to public opinion trends that show broad support for government-provided social programs —even at the cost of new taxes (Heath and McMahon 1992).[3]

This paradox of the public's general skepticism about government and simultaneous endorsement of increased spending on specific areas reflects a common contradiction in public opinion. The motto for government is clear: tax less, and spend more. Seymour Lipset and Everett Ladd (1980) describe this paradox as the combination of "ideological conservatism" and "programmatic liberalism." The attitudes of Americans and Europeans remain an ambiguous mix of support and denial of government action.

The most accurate description of popular attitudes toward government might be that citizens are now critical of "big" government, but they also are accustomed to, and depend on, the policies of the modern state. When people confront the choice between cutting taxes and maintaining government services, many surveys find that a plurality prefer the services option even during the midst of the so-called tax revolt. If this interpretation is correct, the Republican majority in the 104th Congress should face difficulties if they attempt to reduce government programs significantly. People believe that government should grow no larger—and neither should it shrink from its responsibilities.

Race and Equality

In recent years many people have developed a greater concern for social equality issues. After generations of dormancy, the issues of civil rights and racial equality inflamed American politics in the mid-1960s. For most of the decade the civil rights issue preoccupied the attention of many Americans and was a major source of political conflict. The importance of the racial issues has continued to the present (Sniderman and Piazza 1993; Carmines and Stimson 1989). In addition, the success of the civil rights movement among African Americans encouraged similar activity among Latinos, Asian Americans, and other minorities.

European experience with ethnic and racial equality is more limited because most of these nations were homogeneous in their ethnic composition. This situation began to change in the 1960s (Hollifield 1993). Decolonialization by Britain and France led to a steady inflow of black and brown immigrants from former colonies. Labor-force shortages led the West Germans to invite "guestworkers" from less developed Mediterranean countries to work in German factories. Nonwhites now account for 5–10 percent of the population in these three nations, and as much as a quarter of the workforce in some cities. During the last decade European societies have experienced some of the same social divisions based on race and ethnic origin that exist in the United States. Governments usually addressed

these problems responsibly, but a public backlash against minorities frequently surfaced. For example, Britain experienced several race riots and
other racially related political conflicts. Tensions between French and
North Africans erupted into violence in southern France, and the National
Front Party has espoused antiforeigner policies. German unification was
accompanied by a surge of violence against foreigners and the emergence
of the xenophobic Republikaner Party.

Although racial and ethnic conflicts are still a part of contemporary
politics, the trends in racial attitudes over the past generation document a
massive change in the beliefs of Americans. In the 1940s a majority of
white Americans openly endorsed racial segregation of education, housing,
transportation, and employment (figure 6.1). The values of freedom, equality, and justice that constitute the American creed did not apply to blacks.
A phenomenal growth in support for racial integration occurred over the
next four decades. Integration of housing, education, and employment won
widespread endorsement. Until he withdrew from the campaign, Colin

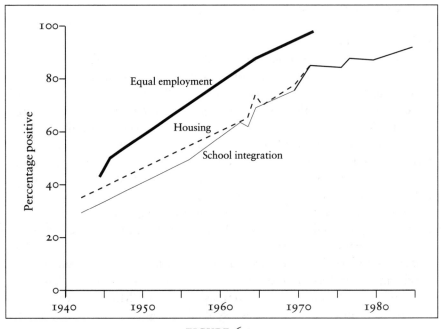

FIGURE 6.1

SUPPORT FOR RACIAL INTEGRATION IN AMERICA

SOURCE: Adapted from Smith and Sheatsley (1984).

Powell was the preferred candidate in trial heats for the 1996 presidential election. Powell's potential candidacy signaled a fundamental transformation of the American political culture over the past generation.

In a recent provocative book on public opinion, Paul Sniderman and Thomas Piazza (1993) examine racial attitudes in contemporary America. They show that as racial integration became accepted, the politics of race broadened to include a new set of issues: affirmative action, government social programs, and equity principles. The American public remains divided on many of these new racial issues. Some of the actions aimed at redressing racial inequality—affirmative action policies (such as school busing and preferential treatment) and racial quotas—are opposed by most Americans (Schuman et al. 1985; Smith and Sheatsley 1984). The spreading controversy over affirmative action programs illustrate this discontent. Many political analysts claim that these divided opinions are signs of a new racism in America. Based on an innovative set of survey experiments, Sniderman and Piazza conclude that although a minority of Americans still harbor racial prejudice, the contemporary clash over racial policies is more attributable to broader ideological conflicts over the scope of government, beliefs about equality, and other political values.

European attitudes toward racial issues are still evolving. Racial policy was once considered the unique American dilemma, but no longer. The British Election Studies indicate that since the early 1960s more than 80 percent of Britons felt that too many immigrants were allowed into the country; similar results emerge from the British Social Attitudes survey. A recent Eurobarometer found that a majority of Europeans feel that too many foreigners reside in their country (Eurobarometer 39).

Although concerns about immigration are widespread in all of Europe, these worries are not translated into equal hostility toward minorities. The majority of Britons endorse legislation that bans racial discrimination; Britons have also become more optimistic about the future of race relations in their nation (Young 1992). The French appear slightly more negative toward foreigners than the European average, and the Germans are slightly more tolerant (Eurobarometer 39). There are several reasons why German attitudes toward foreigners are more restrained. The foreigners who come to Germany ostensibly are visitors, without the rights or expectations of citizenship found among ex-colonial émigrés in Britain and France. In addition, Germans are still sensitive to the past horrors that resulted from racist attitudes toward the Jews during the Third Reich. Thus, when sporadic violence against foreigners occurred in the wake of German union, these acts were followed by mass marches condemning them. Public opinion polls find that many Germans are concerned about the problems of immigration, but few express or condone explicitly prejudicial views (Hoskin 1991).

Although the climate of opinion now endorses racial equality, one must be cautious not to overlook the real racial problems that still exist in many nations. Support for the principle of equality coexists with the remnants of segregation in the United States; racial conflict can still flare up in Brixton, Liverpool, or Marseilles. Problems of housing segregation, unequal education, and job discrimination are real. Public opinion alone is not sufficient to resolve these problems, and undoubtedly some survey respondents overstate their racial tolerance. And yet the shift of social norms in support of racial equality makes these problems more solvable than when discrimination was openly acclaimed.

Gender Issues

Another social dimension concerns equality between men and women. A short generation ago, traditional gender roles were deeply entrenched on both sides of the Atlantic. American women faced limited career opportunities and German housewives were expected to devote their efforts to *Kinder, Kirche, und Küche* (children, church, and kitchen). The status of women in Britain, France, and other advanced industrial societies was equally constrained.

Over the past two decades these traditional attitudes have come under increasing challenge. The women's movement grew most rapidly in the United States, and a parallel growth of women's groups has occurred in Europe (Katzenstein and Mueller 1987; Gelb 1989). Political action led to legislation equalizing the rights of both sexes. The public at large also became more sensitive to gender issues, and social norms have gradually changed.

Most people now express belief in equal opportunities for men and women. The 1992 American National Election Study found that only 15 percent of the public believe a woman's place is in the home; this percentage has decreased in each survey since it was first asked in 1972. Gallup data show a striking increase in the number of Americans who say they would vote for a woman as president. In 1936 only 31 percent expressed this view; by 1988, this figure reached 86 percent. Most Europeans also endorse gender equality as a general principle (Wilcox 1991; Scott et al. 1993). Nevertheless, the true measure of support for gender equality is when abstract principles are applied to specific instances.

Table 6.4 provides evidence on how contemporary publics think about gender-related issues. The top panel in the table displays opinions on the balance between career and family life for women. Most people believe that working women can establish close ties with their children and that a job can establish a woman's independence. Yet there are also common doubts about a woman's undertaking a career; most people feel that a young child will suffer if the mother works. A large number in each nation—including a significant minority of women—believe that women are primarily oriented toward family life over a career. Even in eastern Germany, where the state made exceptional efforts to involve women in the workforce and politics on equal terms, the same mixed attitudes toward the role of women appears.

These findings initially suggest that gender norms have not changed as much as we sometimes assume. Evidence from European surveys indicates that most men feel that women are primarily responsible for housework and a man has more right to a job. Other survey data indicate that most European working women feel their situation is worse that men's regarding wages, promotion prospects, job opportunities, and job security (Eurobarometer 19). Traditional images of the role of women still exist in the minds of many people.

Still there has been a longitudinal decline in the belief that women are limited to a traditional role (Page and Shapiro 1992, 100–104; M. Inglehart 1991; Klein 1987). Further evidence points to a sharp decrease in traditional norms across generations (Scott et al. 1993). Indeed, the cultural legacy of the women's movement might be the creation of a choice for women—both work and family are now accepted options—instead of limiting choice to a single role.

The last panel of table 6.4 displays broad support for the political equality of women. Most Europeans approve of the women's movement; this reflects an increase in support over the prior decade. Large majorities also reject the notion that politics is better left to men, and most express equal confidence in male and female politicians. If comparable data were available from American surveys, we would expect similar results. Although women remain underrepresented within the top stratum of political officials, old stereotypes of politics as an exclusively male domain have eroded.

Environmental Protection

Nearly two decades ago, the issue of environmental protection began attracting attention in advanced industrial democracies. Environmentalism was initially stimulated by a few very visible ecological crises; these concerns persisted and expanded. Separate issues were linked together into environmental programs, and citizen groups mobilized in support of environmental issues (Dalton 1994; Dunlap and Mertig 1992).

TABLE 6.4
ATTITUDES TOWARD GENDER EQUALITY
(IN PERCENTAGES)

	United States	Great Britain	Western Germany	France	Eastern Germany
Work and family					
Working/nonworking mothers can establish same relationship with children	70*	68	39*	73	56
Having a job is best way for woman to be independent	55*	65*	67*	76*	70*
Preschoolers suffer if mother works (*Disagree*)	47	45	15	33	21
A job is all right, but women really want home/children (*D*)	40*	49*	42*	29*	46
Being a housewife is as fulfilling as a job (*D*)	24*	35*	39*	35*	60*
Average	47	52	40	49	51*
Political attitudes					
Approve of women's movement	81	63	62*	62	76
Politics should be left to men (*D*)	—	87	64	81	—
Equal confidence in man/woman as politician	—	75	64	68	—

SOURCES: 1990–91 World Values Survey; last two items are from Eurobarometer 27 (1987).

NOTE: Table entries are the percentage who agree (or *disagree*) with each statement. An asterisk indicates that there are substantial differences between male and female respondents (Cramer's V greater than .10).

The broadest measure of environmentalism is an interest in environmental issues. The first row in table 6.5 indicates that concern about the environment is common among Americans (85 percent), Britons (83 percent), and Germans (63 percent). Even when phrased in negative terms like the second item in the table, most people disagree with the statement that protecting the environment is *not* an urgent problem. Other research finds that interest in environmental issues has grown over the past two decades (Dalton 1994, chap. 3). Environmental policy has become a priority issue for many citizens.

Widespread interest in environmental policy also translates into public support for environmental protection. Contemporary public opinion nearly unanimously endorses stronger measures to protect the environment (table 6.5). In a survey conducted by Gallup before the 1992 environmental summit at Rio de Janiero, more than 90 percent of the public in these nations favor stronger environmental protection laws for business and industry. Nearly equal numbers favor laws requiring that all citizens conserve resources and reduce pollution (also see Dunlap et al. 1992). Significantly, there is also strong support for environmental action among eastern Germans, where years of environmental neglect have caused severe damage to human health and the environment.

Many political analysts discount these environmental opinions because such popular views can be expressed in a survey without concern for the actual costs of a policy. Thus survey researchers have asked people to balance their environmental beliefs against the potential economic costs of environmental protection. The data in the middle panel of table 6.5 indicate that most people say they would give up part of their income or pay higher taxes to prevent pollution. On another question, 58 percent of the American public favor protection of the environment even if it risks holding back economic growth; majorities in Europe agree.

Another sign of public support for environmental reform is environmentally friendly behavior. The Gallup Health of the Planet study found that a majority of Americans (57 percent) say they have avoided products that might harm the environment. The percentage of green consumers is much higher in Europe, where waste problems and recycling efforts are more common (McCormick 1991; Dalton 1994). Even more striking, these publics almost unanimously support ecology and nature conservation groups, with approval ratings above 90 percent in each nation.

Environmental attitudes indicate how citizens are now interested in new political issues, especially issues tapping the noneconomic concerns typical of postmaterial values. In earlier periods, economic needs superseded concerns about the environment. Today, many people say they are

TABLE 6.5
ENVIRONMENTAL ATTITUDES (IN PERCENTAGES)

	United States	Great Britain	Western Germany	France	Eastern Germany
Concerned about the environment*	85	83	63	—	—
Protecting the environment is not urgent problem (*Disagree*)	68	73	82	76	86
Policy Support					
Favor stronger laws for business and industry*	90	93	94	—	—
Favor stronger laws for citizens*	82	83	86	—	—
Tradeoff questions					
Would give up part of income to prevent pollution	72	64	46	59	60
Would pay more taxes to prevent pollution	61	65	46	52	61
Protecting environment has priority over the economy*	58	56	73	—	—
Have to accept pollution to solve unemployment (*D*)	66	61	73	52	64
Government has to reduce pollution but it shouldn't cost money	52	56	75	71	45
Action					
Avoided products that harm the environment*	57	75	81	—	—
Approve of environmental movement	91	91	97	91	98

SOURCES: 1990–91 World Values Survey and 1992 Gallup Health of the Planet Survey; items from the Gallup survey are denoted by an asterisk.

NOTE: Table entries are the percentage who agree (or *disagree*) with each statement. Missing data were included in the calculation of percentages.

willing to sacrifice financially to improve the environment. These concerns reflect more than just a growing awareness of the hidden health and economic costs of pollution. In a broad cross-national study of attitudes toward the environment, Ronald Inglehart (1995) notes that the citizens in prosperous countries with relatively cleaner environments are most willing to make sacrifices for the environment. Material success has allowed these nations to shift attention to the quality of their lives.[4] Similarly, support for environmental protection is more common among the young, better educated, and postmaterial sectors of society (Dalton 1994, chap. 3). Environmentalism thus reflects the processes of value change that are part of the new style of citizen politics.

Social Issues

A final set of domestic issues involves the turbulent debate over social norms that involve interpersonal relations and life choices. In the late 1960s and early 1970s, young people began to question traditional values with symbolic statements, such as the use of drugs or the choice of hairstyles, clothing, and music. This progressive movement tested the extent of individual freedom on matters such as abortion, divorce, homosexuality, and pornography. Thus these issues entered the political debate in a variety of ways.

Social issues differ from most other issues because of their moral content. The critic of abortion or homosexuality views the issue in terms of moral right and wrong; unlike the negotiable monetary benefits of economic issues, principles are at stake. Several consequences follow from the moral base of social issues. People find it is difficult to compromise on social issues because political views are intensely felt, and the issue public for social issues is often larger than might otherwise be expected. In addition, the active interest groups on social issues are religious organizations and Christian Democratic parties, not labor unions and business groups. Religious values are an important determinant of opinions on social issues.

Table 6.6 presents public opinion on several social issues. Until recently, traditional value orientations led many people to be highly critical of divorce. Scandal, dishonor, and religious isolation often accompanied the divorce decree. The table indicates that attitudes have changed dramatically; nearly everyone now believes that divorce is sometimes justified. As attitudes toward divorce have become more tolerant, legislation has removed the stigma of divorce and provisions discriminating against women.

Sexual relations are another social issue. The French are the most liberal toward extramarital sex and sexual relations generally; Americans are the most conservative. Attitudes toward homosexuality are surprisingly tol-

TABLE 6.6
ATTITUDES ON SOCIAL AND MORAL ISSUES
(IN PERCENTAGES)

	United States	Great Britain	Western Germany	France	Eastern Germany
Divorce sometimes justified	81	87	93	89	87
Extramarital sex sometimes justified	30	46	61	67	45
Homosexuality sometimes justified	47	59	71	62	59
Abortion attitudes					
Abortion sometimes justified	66	80	84	82	81
Approve of abortion					
When mother's health in danger	85	92	96	94	96
If child may be handicapped	53	75	80	91	84
When mother unmarried	28	31	21	43	19
Parents don't want child	25	38	31	56	49
Religious attitudes					
Consider self religious	81	55	54	48	33
Believe in God	94	72	63	57	33
Believe in life after death	70	44	38	38	19
Believe in devil	65	30	15	19	10
Importance of God in life[a]	8.06	5.37	5.30	4.44	3.73

SOURCE: 1990–91 World Values Survey. Missing data were included in the calculation of percentages.

a. Importance of God in life measured on ten-point scale ranging from 1 = not at all to 10 = very important; the table presents the mean score.

erant across all four nations. A majority of the public in each European nation feels that homosexuality is sometimes justified, and opinions have become more liberal since the 1980 World Values Study (Ashford and Timms 1992, chap. 5; Inglehart, forthcoming). Americans were more openly critical of homosexuals just a decade earlier, but now opinions are divided almost evenly.

Abortion has been a divisive social issue in several nations. Proponents and opponents of the issue are intense in their issue beliefs and oriented toward political action. Furthermore, this issue has periodically been the subject of major legislative or judicial action in all four nations. Contemporary publics believe that abortion is sometimes justified, although additional questions indicate the conditional nature of this endorsement. There is broad support for abortion when the health of the mother is endangered. Many fewer people approve of abortion when the mother is unmarried or the parents do not want a child. Despite the dramatic ebbs and flows in public events on this issue, attitudes have changed only slightly over the past two decades (Page and Shapiro 1992; Ashford and Timms 1992).

The findings in table 6.6 lead to two broad conclusions. First, Americans are generally more conservative than Europeans on social issues. This pattern is likely the result of national differences in religious feelings, as seen in the bottom panel in the table. Despite the affluence, high mobility rates, and social diversity of Americans, the United States is among the most religious of Western societies. American church attendance and religious feelings are among the highest in the world. A full 81 percent of Americans consider themselves religious, compared to barely half of Europeans. Even more striking are the patterns on other religious beliefs: two-thirds of Americans believe in the existence of the devil, compared to only a third of Britons and less than a fifth of Germans and French. The secular policies of the GDR created an even more secular society in the eastern Germany.

Second, public opinion has generally become more tolerant on social issues as the processes of modernization and secularization have transformed Western societies. Long-term opinion series for the United States and Germany indicate a gradual liberalization of attitudes toward homosexuals over the past generation (Noelle-Neumann and Piel 1984; Page and Shapiro 1992). Conditional acceptance of abortion has also increased in all four nations between the 1980–81 and 1990–91 World Values Surveys (Inglehart, forthcoming).

Underlying these longitudinal changes has been the diminishment of religious values in these nations. Figure 6.2 graphically displays the change in religiosity over just the past decade. In 1980 nearly half of the public in

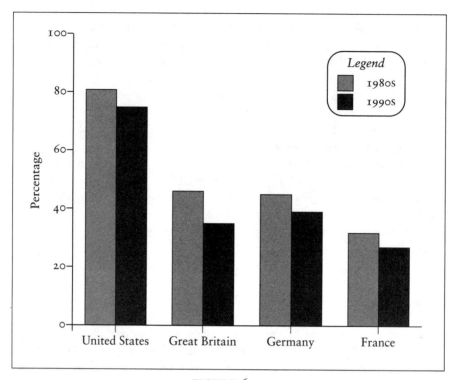

FIGURE 6.2

CHANGE IN RELIGIOUS FEELINGS, 1980–90

SOURCES: 1980–81 World Values Survey; 1990–91 World Values Survey.

NOTE: The values plotted are the percentages of respondents rating the importance of God in their lives "high" (7–10) on a ten-point scale.

each European nation said that God played an important part in their lives; over 80 percent of Americans expressed the same opinion. Even in the short span of ten years, such feelings of religiosity have dropped off markedly in each nation. If comparable data were available for the 1950s or 1960s, the value shift would be markedly greater.[5]

This change in values has had mixed effects on advanced industrial societies. The decline in religiosity may prompt greater tolerance of different lifestyle choices, especially involving abortion rights and alternative lifestyles. At the same time, weakening religious attachments are probably linked to declining respect and acceptance for authority, as well an erosion in moral and ethical standards. A more secular public sees humankind in a different light.

Foreign Policy Opinions

Foreign policy has probably undergone the most dramatic political changes in the few years between the two editions of this book. After a generation of silent conflict during the Cold War, the collapse of the Soviet Union dramatically reshaped the international order. Similarly, the democratic revolution that spread throughout Eastern Europe altered the international distribution of power and values in a fundamental way. There is a new world order, even if governments are unsure about its content and people are unsure about their opinions. This section traces some of these changes.

National Images

Foreign policy is based on the actions of nation-states, and national images therefore play an important role in structuring foreign policy attitudes. The most salient actors for Europeans have long been the two superpowers. Opinions about the United States were generally positive because of the unifying experiences of the postwar period and the benevolence of *Pax Americana* (Dalton 1988, chap. 6; Inglehart 1991). Americans also were positive about their European allies. These mutual images have ebbed and flowed over the past half century, as America foreign policy took courses that Europeans agreed with or criticized. But always, even in the depths of American-European relations, this was an alliance based on mutual trust and approval.

Counterbalancing the positive affinities within the Western alliance, Americans and Europeans were consistently more critical of the Soviet Union. Western publics almost uniformly disliked the Soviet Union in the early postwar period; its image improved during the détente in the 1970s and then deteriorated again with the chilling of East-West relations in the early 1980s. The first edition of this book bluntly concluded that "few Europeans hold positive illusions about the Soviet Union."

This Soviet Union no longer exists. Mikhail Gorbachev created a more positive and personal image of the Soviet Union with his reform policies of the mid-1980s and his international visits. The collapse of communism and the dismemberment of the Soviet Union dramatically changed the bipolar imagery of international politics. This is reflected in public opinion.

Figure 6.3 displays the dramatic shift in Western images of the Soviet Union between the 1980s and early 1990s. For example, in the mid-1980s barely a quarter of Americans held a positive image of the Soviet Union. After *glasnost, perestroika,* and the creation of a new Russian state, nearly three-quarters of Americans are positive about Russia in the 1993 General Social Survey. British and German attitudes show a similar shift in sentiments between 1986 and 1991, though French opinions of Russia dimin-

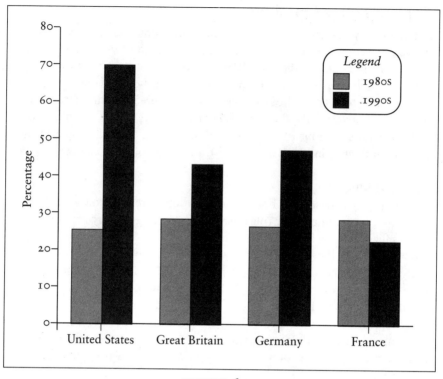

FIGURE 6.3

ATTITUDES TOWARD RUSSIA, 1980–90

SOURCES: *United States,* General Social Survey 1983–87; 1993 surveys. *European nations,* Eurobarometer 25 (May 1986); Eurobarometer 35 (May 1991).

ished slightly. It is likely that surveys after the failed coup in August 1991 and Boris Yeltsin's assumption of power would be more favorable, though opinions may have receded as continuing political stability has diminished the external image of Russian democracy.[6]

Findings from the Times/Mirror Center's Pulse of Europe Survey reinforce these changing national images (Times/Mirror 1991). When Europeans in the East and West were asked who was their nation's most likely ally, a plurality mentioned the United States. When western Germans were asked which nation posed the greatest threat to their country, barely a tenth mentioned Russia or the former Soviet Union. Although there are still real political and social divisions between East and West, and the depth of democracy in Eastern Europe remains uncertain, the psychological wall between citizens of these two worlds has changed dramatically.

Conflict and Cooperation

Although the Cold War is over, the world can still be a brutish place. Regional and local conflicts—such as in the Persian Gulf War, Somalia, and Bosnia—threaten individual and international security. Yet the end of the Cold War has transformed peace and conflict issues in the world. Potential conflict between the superpowers no longer is the central theme of international relations; public attention has shifted toward other sources of international conflict. In a cross-national survey conducted in early 1994, a majority of Americans, Germans, and Britons felt the world had become a *more dangerous* place since the end of the Cold War (*New York Times, 2 April 1994*).

The changing nature of citizen orientations toward military and security issues is apparent in perceptions of the North Atlantic Treaty Organization (NATO). NATO was once the bulwark of Western defense and was roundly supported by the public in most member states (Smith and Wertman 1992; Flynn and Rattinger 1985; Wittkopf 1990). Today, NATO's main threat from the East has largely vanished, and NATO has even given associate status to several East European nations.

Surveys conducted by the U.S. Information Agency find that most Europeans express a continuing need for NATO (McIntosh and MacIver 1994). At the same time, Europeans also seem to be distancing themselves slightly from the alliance with the United States. Roughly a third of the public in Britain, Germany, and France feel that U.S. involvement is no longer needed in the defense of Europe. Continuing their previous tendencies, the French are often openly skeptical about American involvement in Europe and the foreign policy goals of the United States.

The cooperative thrust of contemporary foreign policy is seen in other areas. For instance, the *New York Times* poll found what it described as resounding support for the United Nations and for sending UN troops to enforce peace in the world's trouble spots. Because of the past criticism the United Nations received from many Americans, this support may be an indicator of a new internationalism.

Another example of internationalism is the process of economic, social, and political integration of Europe that has occurred within the institutional framework of the European Union (EU). Longitudinal data indicate that most of the French and German publics supported the process of integration from the outset (Eichenberg and Dalton 1993; Reif and Inglehart 1991). Approval of the EU has been less certain among the British but gradually expanded in the 1980s. Table 6.7 indicates that most Europeans support the principle of European unification; those who think the EU is a

TABLE 6.7
ATTITUDES ON FOREIGN POLICY ISSUES
(IN PERCENTAGES)

	United States	Great Britain	Germany	France
European unification				
EU membership a good thing (net approval)	—	21	39	37
Favor a European government	—	52	57	65
Favor a common foreign policy	—	55	71	73
Favor a European bank	—	48	59	72
Favor single currency	—	35	34	65
Other attitudes				
Favor nation contributing to international environmental agency	74	89	82	—
Favor nation granting authority to international environmental agency	63	73	78	—

SOURCES: European Union items are from Eurobarometer 41 (Spring 1994); international environmental items are from Dunlap et al. (1992).

NOTE: Missing data were included in the calculation of percentages.

"good thing" outnumber those who say it is a "bad thing" by a sizable margin. Europeans are also willing to see the Union expand its policy role in foreign policy and in the creation of a single European bank. Other aspects of unification, such as a common currency, are more contentious. On the whole, however, Europeans are increasingly likely to think of the EU as a forum for European policymaking.

Similarly, the last rows in table 6.7 indicate widespread public support for international action on environmental issues. A majority favor funding an international environmental agency and the transfer of policy responsibilities to this agency.

We are still in a period when international politics are in flux, and new threats to world order have emerged with the ending of the Cold War. Although it is too early to discern the exact shape that foreign policy opinions will take in this new context, it appears that Western publics are broadening their perspectives and thinking about foreign policy in more cooperative and international terms.

Left/Right Orientations

We have presented evidence of how people are changing their opinions on many issues. Opinions on equality issues display a dramatic shift over the past generation; overt discrimination against racial minorities, women, and other minority groups is no longer condoned by most people. Tolerance of nonconformity is also more common, whether the objects of tolerance are political or social minorities (Nunn et al. 1978; Sullivan et al. 1982). Liberal attitudes toward new issues such as environmental quality and alternative lifestyles are also commonplace. Moreover, there is a broad consensus in support of the basic social programs provided by the modern state, although voters do not endorse a further growth in these programs and would welcome a restriction in the size of government.

Still it is difficult to use specific issue opinions to make sweeping generalizations about the changing political orientations of the public. Citizens are now interested in a wider range of issues than just socioeconomic concerns, and so a general assessment of overall political tendencies must weigh several different issues. The rate of social change across various issue interests is uneven. Support for environmental protection has grown rapidly over time, while attitudes toward abortion have been more stable. Finally, the content of ongoing political controversies also changes over time. For instance, the racial issues that were intensely fought over in the 1960s —school desegregation, open housing, and public accommodations—now register overwhelmingly liberal responses; but new racial issues—quotas and affirmative action programs—divide the American public. This represents progress in the development of racial tolerance, but racial policy remains politically contentious. One of the major points we have (re)learned from recent political trends is that new issues of conflict inevitably replace old, now consensual issues.

One way to generalize about the overall political orientations of Western publics is to examine broad ideological orientations that extend beyond specific issues. Political scientists frequently measure such broad orientations in terms of Left/Right attitudes (Klingemann 1979; Fuchs and Klingemann 1989). Political issues are often discussed or summarized in terms of Left/Right or liberal/conservative philosophies. Republicans attack what they call the "loony Left," while Democrats rail against the "reactionary Right." These labels provide the reference points that help voters interpret and evaluate political activities. The ability to think of oneself in Left/Right terms does not imply that citizens possess a sophisticated conceptual framework or theoretical dogma. For many individuals, Left/Right attitudes are simply a summary of their positions on the political issues of greatest concern.

Figure 6.4 presents the distribution of Left/Right orientations across nations. The survey asked respondents to place themselves on a 10-point scale, labeled from "Left" to "Right." The figure plots the average Left/Right self-placement of electorates from over a dozen Western democracies, comparing results from the 1980–81 and 1990–91 World Values Surveys.

The United States is one of the more conservative nations in overall Left/Right terms; only Ireland and Japan are more Rightist in 1990. This reaffirms an impression derived from many of the specific issue areas examined in this chapter. Britain, western Germany, and most other advanced industrial democracies are clustered around the midpoint of the scale. At the liberal pole are several Mediterranean nations—France, Italy, and Spain —that have significant Leftist traditions. They are now joined by eastern Germans and presumably by other democratizing nations in Eastern Europe that display traces of their socialist past (Inglehart, forthcoming).

Over the past decade there has been a gradual, albeit small, shift toward the Left in most nations. The American electorate, for example, located itself at position 5.94 in 1981, and at 5.74 in 1990. The only significant rightward shifts among the nations in figure 6.4 are found in Italy and Sweden. Generational comparisons provide even stronger indication of political change. The young are consistently more liberal than their elders (Ashford and Timms 1992, appendix). This generation gap suggests that democratic publics are gradually becoming more liberal in their overall political orientations.[7] But even these data tell only a partial story.

As we suggested above, the content of Left and Right reflects the issues of salience to the public, and this is another source of political change. The meaning of Left and Right varies across age and political groups (Inglehart 1984; Fuchs and Klingemann 1989). For older citizens, these terms are largely synonymous with attitudes on socioeconomic issues: *Left* means support for social programs, working-class interests, and the influence of labor unions; *Right* is identified with limited government, support for middle-class interests, and the influence of the business sector. Among the young, the New Politics issues of environmental protection, social equality, and lifestyle freedoms are added to socioeconomic interests. For the young, the term *Left* can mean opposition to nuclear energy, support for sexual equality, a preference for disarmament, or endorsement of social programs.

Therefore, it is difficult to speak in simple terms about whether contemporary publics are becoming more liberal or conservative in an overall sense. It is clear, however, that the overall Left/Right placement of young citizens differs from their elders, and the meaning of Left and Right in political discourse is also changing.

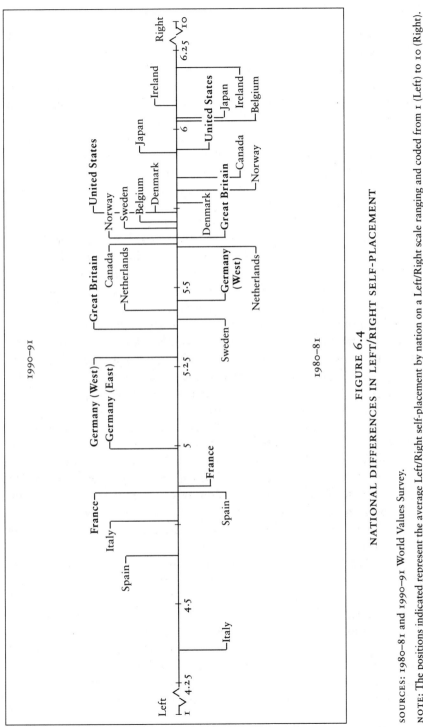

FIGURE 6.4

NATIONAL DIFFERENCES IN LEFT/RIGHT SELF-PLACEMENT

SOURCES: 1980–81 and 1990–91 World Values Survey.

NOTE: The positions indicated represent the average Left/Right self-placement by nation on a Left/Right scale ranging and coded from 1 (Left) to 10 (Right).

Public Opinion and Political Change

A significant feature of contemporary issue opinions is that more people are interested in more issues. Opinions on socioeconomic issues were once the predominant concern of voters and political elites; one could realistically describe political competition in terms of a single overarching policy area, such as the New Deal in the United States or capitalist/socialist conflicts in Europe. In recent years the number of the public's distinct issue interests has diversified. Socioeconomic matters still attract widespread attention. In addition, issues of social equality, environmental protection, social morals, and foreign policy capture the interest of large numbers of citizens.

The expansion of the boundaries of politics to include these new issues has several implications for the nature of contemporary politics. Governments have increased the scope of their activity. Governments are now worried not only about economic policy but also about whether the environment is clean and whether personal life choices are tolerated. This expansion of the government's role has rekindled ongoing debates about the appropriate scope of government, although the policy content of the current debate is much different from prior debates about the economic role of the state.

This proliferation of issue publics also changes the structure of political representation and decision making. Issue publics focus the public's political efforts to maximize their representation on key issues. The proliferation of issue publics probably increases the complexity of the governing process, however. A majority of (differing) voters want government to spend more on (differing) specific programs; a majority also want government to tax them less. Policymakers thus see conflicting signals emanating from the public, without a method (or perhaps motivation) to resolve these conflicts systematically. Government responses to the demands of one issue public may conflict with the demands of another issue group. Policy proliferation can lead to issue-by-issue decisions rather than broad programmatic planning. One of the challenges facing contemporary governments is how to adapt the democratic process to this different pattern of interest representation.

What can we say about the overall political orientations of contemporary publics? Journalists and social commentators frequently refer to a liberal or conservative mood sweeping a nation. The early 1960s and early 1970s supposedly were a time of radical change and liberal ascendance (Stimson 1991). Similarly, discussions of the new conservative mood in Western democracies became commonplace in the 1980s, exemplified by the electoral strength of Reagan, Thatcher, Kohl, and Chirac. Clinton's victory in 1992 was called a signal of a new era, and just two years later the Republican victories supposedly marked another new era.

Tested against actual public opinion data, such generalizations are often difficult to substantiate. The counterculture movement of the 1970s was not as widespread as the media would suggest, and the conservative revival of the 1980s was equally overdrawn. Opinion change does not follow a simple predictable course, and the visible public actions of political groups can distort our images of the broader currents of public opinion.[8] Furthermore, there are many issues of potential interest to the public, and not all of them move in a consistent direction over time.

Still, some general trends emerge from our findings. One apparent trend has been the shift toward what might be termed *libertarian attitudes.* Contemporary publics are becoming more tolerant of individual diversity and more concerned with the protection of individual freedoms. This applies to the rights of minorities and women, as well as to a general acceptance of individual freedom in social relations. These trends are manifested in attitudes toward social equality, moral issues, and the quality of life. Paralleling these changes have been a decline in respect for authority and concern with social order.

The counterevidence is *socioeconomic attitudes.* Concerns about the excessive cost and bureaucracy of government are now commonplace (even if people favor greater government spending on a wide variety of programs). The end of socialism and the retrenchment of the welfare state in the West have made it impossible for the Left to attain its traditional goals of state control of the economy and state guarantees of basic social needs. There has been a conservative shift on these aspects of the socioeconomic issue.

In a period of increasing issue proliferation, such conflicting trends are not surprising. There can be a gradual liberalization of political values on social issues, with a conservative gain on socioeconomic matters. But even this generalization would be difficult to sustain because the meaning of such ideological/programmatic labels has changed as part of this process. No longer does liberalism stand for the creation of social programs, the nationalization of industry, and peaceful coexistence with the communist world. It might just as well mean protection of a clean environment or women's rights legislation. No longer does conservatism represent the prohibition of government social programs or the defeat of the Soviet empire. It might mean advocacy of term limits or supporting family policies.

The content of contemporary political debate is therefore difficult to compare to the political conflicts of the New Deal era of the 1930s or even the Great Society of the 1960s. Perhaps this shift in the content of the political debate is what most directly indicates how advanced industrial societies are modernizing and progressing politically.

139

Notes

1. As the Conservative government sold off public enterprises, the public responded to this changing political context; support for further privatizations decreased over this same time span (Heath and McMahon 1992, 118–19).

2. A majority of Westerners do hold the government responsible for two key provisions of the welfare state: providing health care and a decent living standard for the elderly. For more on East-West contrasts, see Bauer-Kaase (1994).

3. Data from the British Social Survey find that support for greater social spending actually increased under the Thatcher/Major governments, at the same time the conservatives attempted to scale back the welfare state. The following table presents the percentage who think the government should "increase taxes and spend more on health, education and social benefits" (Heath and McMahon 1992, 118):

1983	1984	1985	1986	1987	1989	1990	1991
32	39	45	46	50	56	54	65

4. Support for environmental action also might be stimulated by pressing environmental problems that threaten human health and the ecosystem. Thus we would attribute eastern German support for environmental action to these grievances more than to postmaterial sentiments among the public.

5. Most advanced industrial societies have also experienced a long-term trend toward secularization. Church enrollment, for instance, has dropped off in most nations, as well as other forms of involvement in the churches (Franklin et al. 1992, chap. 1).

6. Eurobarometer 35 found that trust in the Russians was actually lower among eastern Germans (42 percent) than among Westerners (48 percent).

7. These generational differences might be due to life-cycle effects, implying that younger people will become more conservative as they age. We could determine this if we had access to data over a longer time period. The period between the 1980 and 1990 World Values Surveys is too brief for this purpose, and there were few significant changes in national positions. Even if longer-term data were available, however, this would not address questions about the changing content of Left and Right terms as discussed here.

8. Elections provide a poor indicator of ideological trends except in a very long-term perspective. Elections measure the positions of parties and candidates relative to the electorate, but not the overall distribution of opinion on any specific issue. A party that moves too far Left can lose votes, as can one that moves too far Right. Furthermore, the combination of issues in an election makes it difficult to make simple estimations of the voters' intentions on specific policies.

PART THREE

The Electoral Connection

7. Elections and Political Parties

Citizens use a variety of means to influence politics, but the electoral connection through political parties is still the primary basis of public influence in representative democracies. Elections are one of the few available methods that enable a society to reach a collective decision based on individual preferences. The choice between parties aggregates the preferences of individual voters, thereby converting public opinion into specific political decisions. Other forms of citizen participation may exert substantial influence on government, but they lack this representative quality.

Elections are also important because of what they decide. Electoral outcomes determine who will manage the affairs of government and make public policy.[1] The selection of leaders and the ability to "throw the rascals out" at the next election are the public's ultimate power. Political leaders may not always act as they promise, but the selection of a government provides some popular control of policy outcomes.

Elections also attract disproportionate attention from social scientists because they involve the most common form of political action. Voting is a regular activity for most citizens, and thus it provides an opportunity to study the link between political attitudes and actual behavior. Individuals translate their beliefs and opinions into a specific decision. Hence, voting choices are likely to be relatively well thought out, intelligible, and predictable. The electoral connection is thus a useful setting for examining public opinion and political behavior.

In addition, any study of democracy must examine political parties as the foundation of the electoral process. Parties are the primary institutions of representative democracy, especially in Europe (Rose 1984; Beyme 1985; Ziegler 1993). Parties define the structure of electoral competition. Candidates in most European nations are selected by the parties and elected as party representatives, not as individuals. Open primaries and independent legislators are virtually unknown outside the United States. A large proportion of Europeans (including the Germans) vote directly for party lists rather than for individual candidates. Campaign financing in Europe supports the political parties, not individual candidates.

Political parties also can determine the content of election campaigns. Party programs help define which issues are discussed during the campaign (Budge et al. 1987). In many European nations the parties, not individual candidates, control advertising during the campaign. Political parties and party leaders are thus the primary actors in articulating the public's concerns during an election.

Once in government, parties exercise control over the policymaking process. Control of the executive branch and the organization of the legislative branch are decided on the basis of party majorities. The parties' control is often absolute, as in the parliamentary systems of Europe, where representatives from the same party vote as a bloc. American parties are less united and less decisive, but even here parties are the prime factors structuring the legislative process. Because of the centrality of political parties to the democratic process, political scientists describe many European political systems as examples of "responsible party government" (Katz 1987). More generally, E.E. Schattschneider once concluded that "democracy without parties is unthinkable."

Political parties thus provide the focus for our study of the electoral connection. This chapter presents an overview of the history and political bases of contemporary party systems. This discussion furnishes a framework for understanding the party options available to the voters. In addition, we discuss the characteristics of the major parties as political organizations and agents of representative democracy.

An Overview of Four Party Systems

To introduce the party systems in our four core nations, we begin by describing the characteristics of each of the major parties in each nation. Parties vary in their size, structure, and governmental experience, as well as in their political orientations. This section focuses on the basic features of the parties; the next section discusses their political orientations in more detail.

Table 7.1 presents some basic traits of the parties in each nation.[2] The American party system is atypical in many ways. The majoritarian single-member district electoral system encourages the development of a two-party system. The two-party competition between the Democrats and Republicans is unusual, since most democracies have multiparty elections and often require multiparty coalitions to form a government. In congressional elections, the Republicans' dramatic breakthrough in the 1994 elections ended forty years of Democratic rule.[3] Until 1994, the Democrats had won

TABLE 7.1

PARTY CHARACTERISTICS

Party	Year founded	Vote share	Leg. seats	Political structure	Years in government (1970–95)
United States					
Democrats	1832	51.0	258	Decentralized	23
Republicans	1856	45.6	176	Decentralized	2
Great Britain					
Labour	1900	34.4	271	Centralized	9
Liberal Democrats	1987	17.9	20	Decentralized	0
Conservatives	1830	41.9	336	Mixed	16
Germany					
Party of Democatic Socialism (PDS)	1990	4.4	30	Centralized	0
Social Democrats (SPD)	1863	36.4	252	Centralized	12
Greens	1980	7.8	49	Decentralized	0
Free Democrats (FDP)	1948	6.9	47	Decentralized	25
Christian Democrats (CDU)	1950	41.5	294	Mixed	13
Republikaner	1983	1.9	0	Personalistic	0
France					
Communist Party (PC)	1920	9.1	23	Centralized	0
Socialists (PS)	1905	19.1	54	Centralized	10
Greens	1978	7.8	0	Decentralized	0
RPR	1947	20.2	257	Mixed	15
UDF	1978	19.6	215	Mixed	15
National Front	1972	12.7	0	Personalistic	0

SOURCE: Compiled by the author.

every House election since World War II with two exceptions (1946 and 1952). The fluctuations in congressional vote totals are relatively small, however, averaging less than a 3 percent vote change between elections. The results of presidential elections are more varied, ranging from Lyndon Johnson's Democratic landslide in 1964 to Ronald Reagan's Republican majority in 1984. Presidential elections are heavily influenced by the candidate's own attributes, instead of serving as strict partisan contests. Therefore, our cross-national analyses of electoral patterns in subsequent chapters analyze American congressional elections because they are more similar to Western European parliamentary contests.

Another distinctive aspect of the American political system is the decentralized nature of party organizations (Beck and Sorauf 1992). Because of the federal system of American government, instead of one Democratic Party (or Republican Party) there are really fifty: one in each state. National party meetings are like medieval gatherings of feudal states, rather than the actions of a unitary organization. The presidential nominating convention is not controlled and directed by a national party but is taken over every four years by the personnel of the winning candidate. Even in Congress, American legislators are more likely to cross party lines than are parliamentarians in disciplined party systems. This means there is considerably more diversity and fluidity within the American party system. The institutional weakness of the parties is also apparent in their small memberships (chapter 3).

Britain is often described as a two-and-a-half-party system, and it also has a majoritarian electoral system. The Labour Party is the major force on the Left, and the Conservative Party is the representative of the Right. The general stability of this party alignment is seen in the record of postwar election results. The Labour and Conservative parties each routinely receive between 40 and 50 percent of the national vote, while the small Liberal Democrats garner 10–15 percent.[4] Shifting vote margins have led to a regular alternation of government between Labour and Conservatives in the modern era, although the Conservatives have held the majority since 1979.

The British party system has experienced significant volatility during the past two decades. Revived regional movements strengthened the nationalist parties in Scotland (Scottish Nationalist Party) and Wales (Plaid Cymru) in the 1970s. Thatcher's polarized politics of government retrenchment stimulated the creation of a new centrist party, the Social Democratic Party (SDP), in the early 1980s. By the end of the 1980s the SDP had merged with the Liberal Party to form the Liberal Democrats. In the 1989 European Parliament election there was also a temporary surge in support for the British Green Party. Despite these changes in the party system, the competition between Labour and the Conservatives still structures the British electoral process.

The British political parties also are highly organized and centralized in comparison to the American parties. The national parties play an important role in selecting candidates and determining the strategies and activities of election campaigns. Members of Parliament (MPs) generally follow party lines in policy debates and in their voting behavior. The British political system is based on a model of strong party government (Rose 1984).

For a long period of time, analysts also described Germany as a two-

and-a-half-party system. The Christian Democrats (CDU/CSU) are the major conservative party and the Social Democrats are the major Leftist party. The CDU/CSU controlled the government for the first two decades of the Federal Republic, and have done so again since 1982. It has a fairly stable electoral base of 45 percent of the popular vote. The SPD controlled the national government from 1969 until 1982 and averages between 35 and 40 percent of the popular vote. The smaller Free Democratic Party (FDP) captures between 5 and 10 percent of the vote; it has been a junior coalition partner for almost every government since the Federal Republic was formed. From 1961 until 1983, only these three parties were represented in parliament and they accounted for more than 90 percent of the popular vote.

The participants in the German party system began to change in the 1980s. First, the Greens emerged on the partisan stage as representatives of a postmaterial agenda (Frankland and Schoonmaker 1992; Poguntke 1993). The Greens garnered more than 5 percent of the national vote in the 1983, 1987, and 1994 elections.[5] The Greens use their seats in the Bundestag to advocate a variety of New Left causes and to criticize the policies of the established parties.

German unification further changed the political landscape. Unification added millions of new voters from the East. With the expansion of the electorate came the formation of the Party of Democratic Socialism (PDS) as a successor to the communist and socialist values of the German Democratic Republic. In 1994 the PDS won nearly 20 percent of the vote in the territory of the former GDR and gained thirty seats in the Bundestag.[6] The PDS represents another version of the Old Left, with an ambivalent position on many New Left issues. Another new participant in the electoral process is the Republikaner, a right-wing party that advocates nationalist and antiforeigner sentiments. The Republikaner have not won seats in the national parliament, though their presence has affected the climate of political debate in contemporary Germany (Cole 1996). In short, in a relatively short period of time the German party system has been transformed into a multiparty system with great diversity in the political philosophies being represented.

The German system emphasizes the role of political parties to a greater degree than in the United States, Britain, or France. For example, parties control the candidate selection process. In Bundestag elections the voter casts two votes. The first vote (*Erststimme*) is for a candidate from the district. The district candidates are nominated by a small group of official party members or by a committee appointed by the membership. The second vote (*Zweitstimme*) is directly for a party, which leads to the selection of half the Bundestag deputies from lists provided by the parties. In addition, election campaigns are generously financed by the government; and government funding and access to public media are allocated to the parties and not the individual candidates. Government funding for the parties also continues between elections, to help them perform their educational functions as prescribed in the Basic Law. Within the Bundestag, the cohesion of parties is exceptionally high. Parties caucus in advance of major legislation to decide the party position, and most legislative votes follow strict party lines. With the notable exception of the Greens, the German political parties are highly organized and centralized institutions. Therefore, it is not surprising to hear analysts describe Germany as a system of "party government."

France is an example of a highly fragmented multiparty system. Instead of one party on the Left, there are several: the Communist Party (PC), the Socialist Party (PS), and several smaller Left extremist parties. Instead of one major party on the Right, there are several: the Rally for the Republic (RPR) and the Union for French Democracy (UDF). During the 1980s the National Front (FN) emerged as an extreme right-wing party that attracts voters opposed to social changes occurring in France. The party is headed by a former army general with a checkered past. A new environmental party also formed in the early 1980s, then reformed in mid-decade, and reformed again in the early 1990s. Now running under the label of the Green Party, it attracts the support of a small number of young, postmaterial voters. Add to this mix a miscellaneous assortment of small centrist or extremist parties. In the 1993 election, for example, more than ten parties were officially listed on the ballot.

The electoral history of the Fifth Republic depicts a growing polarization of party support. A large bloc of voters supported centrist parties during the 1950s and early 1960s. These voters gradually migrated to parties of the Left or the Right, leaving the center depopulated. The Gaullist Party, now RPR, was the original benefactor of this trend and participated in conservative governments for the first two decades of the Fifth Republic. The tide shifted toward the Left in the 1980s, especially toward the Socialists with their broad program of Old Politics and New Politics reforms. The leader of the Socialist Party, François Mitterrand, was elected president in 1981, and this was followed by a socialist majority in legislative elections. The conservatives temporarily gained control of parliament from 1986 to 1988 and then a Left majority reestablished itself. The conservatives (RPR and UDF) swept the parliamentary elections of 1993 and won the presidency in the 1995 elections. In short, the volatility of the French party system is exceptional.

It is difficult to analyze the French system in terms of a theoretical model of responsible party government. On the one hand, the French party system offers the voter a greater ideological choice than is available to American, British, or German voters. Political parties also play a major role in running political campaigns and directing the activities of parliament. On the other hand, the fragmentation of the party system necessitates coalitional politics where parties are forced to negotiate and compromise on their programs. This weakens the chain of party responsibility found in British or German governments. Moreover, it is often the party leader, rather than the national party organization, who defines a party's goals and strategies. French parties are often highly personalistic, even for a highly centralized party such as the PC. The French party system thus might be characterized as a party system in constant transition.

The History of Party Systems

Discussions of political parties normally focus on the present, on the policy positions and political leaders that define current party images. Nevertheless, historical experiences have deeply etched their features on the framework of party systems. The Democratic tendencies of American Catholics, for example, result from their class position when they first emigrated to America and the history of their integration into society and politics.

The legacy of history is even more evident in Western Europe. Seymour Martin Lipset and Stein Rokkan (1967) described the development of European party systems in terms of the historical conditions of national and socioeconomic development. They maintained that two successive revolutions in the modernization of Western societies—the *National Revolution* and the *Industrial Revolution*—created social divisions that still structure partisan competition today. Although their discussion deals primarily with Western Europe, the approach has relevance to other Western democracies including the United States.

The National Revolution involved the process of nation building that transformed the map of Europe in the eighteenth and nineteenth centuries. The National Revolution spawned two kinds of social cleavage. The *center-periphery* cleavage pitted the dominant national culture against ethnic, linguistic, or religious minorities in the provinces and the peripheral sectors of society. It involved conflicts over values and cultural identities. Were Alsatians to become Germans or French; was Scotland a separate nation or a region within Britain? The westward expansion of the United States during its history generated similar tensions between regional cultures.

This cleavage is visible today in persisting regional differences in political orientations; between the English, Welsh, and Scots; between Bretons and the Parisian center; between the "Free State of Bavaria" and the Federal Republic of Germany; between the "old" Federal Republic and the new German Länder in the East; and between the distinct regional cultures in the United States.

The *church-state* conflict cast the centralizing, standardizing, and mobilizing forces of the national government against the traditional influence of the Catholic church. In the face of a growing secular government, the church sought to protect its established corporate privileges. Furthermore, Protestants often allied themselves with nationalist forces in the struggle for national autonomy. Contemporary divisions between religious denominations and between secular and religious groups are a continuation of these earlier social divisions.

The Industrial Revolution in the nineteenth century also generated two new social cleavages. The *land-industry* cleavage aligned the rural and agrarian interests against the economic concerns of the rising class of industrial entrepreneurs. The Ruhr industrialists challenged the power of the Prussian Junkers; the landed gentry of Britain and the United States were challenged by the barons of industry. We see this cleavage in contemporary conflicts between rural and urban interests.

As the industrial sector became dominant, a second cleavage developed between *owners and workers*. This cleavage furnished the basis of the Marxian class conflict between the working class and the middle class composed of business owners and the self-employed. The struggle for the legitimization and representation of working-class interests by labor unions often generated intense political conflict in the late nineteenth and early twentieth centuries. Today this cleavage is seen in the political competition between business associations and labor unions, and more generally between members of the middle class and working class.

These historical events may seem far removed from contemporary party systems, but Lipset and Rokkan (1967) demonstrated that a linkage exists. These four dimensions of cleavage defined the potential major bases of social conflict. As social groups related to these cleavages developed, they won access to the political process before the extension of the voting franchise. When mass voting rights were granted to most Europeans around the turn of the century, this political structure was already in place. In most instances new voters were mobilized into supporting the party groups that already were represented in the political process. New voters entered the electorate with preexisting partisan tendencies. The Conservative Party in Britain, for example, became the representative of the middle-class establishment, and the Labour Party catered to the interests of the working class. The working class in France and Germany supported the Communist and Socialist parties. The American party system developed more gradually because the voting franchise was granted earlier and social groups were less polarized; still, the modern party system reflects the experiences of the Civil War and class alignments created in the 1930s. The formation of mass political parties thus tended to institutionalize the existing elite coalitions, creating the framework for modern party systems. Once voters formed party loyalties and interest groups established party ties, the potential for dramatic partisan change lessened and the parties became self-perpetuating institutions. In one of the most often cited conclusions of comparative politics, Lipset and Rokkan (1967) stated: "the party systems of the 1960s reflect, with but few significant exceptions, the cleavage structures of the 1920s" (p. 50).

Early electoral research substantiated Lipset and Rokkan's claims. Regional voting patterns from early in this century were mirrored in later election returns (Clubb et al. 1980; Miller 1977, chap. 5). Survey research found that social cleavages, especially class and religious differences, exerted a potent effect on voting. Richard Rose and Derek Urwin's (1969, 1970) comparative studies of postwar party systems found striking stability in electoral results.

As this theme of partisan stability became the conventional wisdom, dramatic changes began to affect these same party systems. The established parties were presented with new demands and challenges, and the evidence of partisan change became obvious (Dalton et al. 1984).[7] At the root of this development was a decreasing relationship between traditional social cleavages and partisan choice. In their comparative study of Western democracies, Mark Franklin (1992) and his colleagues found broad evidence that traditional social divisions were losing their ability to predict voting choices (also see chapter 8). Because of this erosion in traditional social-based voting, party systems became more fractionalized. Fluctuations in voting results increased. Voting is now characterized by higher levels of partisan volatility at the aggregate and individual levels (Crewe and Denver 1985). Popular attachments to political parties weakened and discussions of the crisis of party systems became commonplace (see chapter 9). In sum, the major research question changed from explaining the persistence of contemporary party systems to explaining their instability.

Several unique national circumstances contributed to these patterns: the Vietnam war and Watergate in the United States, regional and economic tensions in Britain, the green movement in Germany. In addition, a similar set of new issues are visible across national boundaries. Party systems derived from the National and Industrial revolutions faced the issues of environmental protection, social equality, nuclear energy, sexual equality, and alternative lifestyles. Citizens demanded more opportunities for participation in the decisions affecting their lives and pressed for a further democratization of society and politics. Once these trends began, they evoked a conservative counterattack that opposed the liberalization of social norms, women's rights, environmentalism, and related issues. These new political conflicts are now an important aspect of contemporary politics.

A major factor in the destabilization of modern party systems was the initial inability or unwillingness of the major parties to respond fully to the new demands. As a result, several new parties formed specifically to represent the new political perspectives. The first wave included environmental parties, such as the green parties in Germany and France or Left-libertarian parties (Müller-Rommel 1989; Kitschelt 1989). This stimulated a counter wave of New Right parties, such as the National Front in France or the Republikaner in Germany (Betz 1994; Ignazi 1992). It is unclear whether these parties reflect temporary adjustments to new issues or a more long-lasting realignment of political conflict. American history is filled with third-party movements eventually incorporated into the established parties. Is the present partisan instability in advanced industrial democracies just another case of this recurring pattern?

Several scholars claim that we are witnessing a permanent restructuring of political alignments as a result of the socioeconomic trends of advanced industrialism. They maintain that advanced industrial democracies are experiencing a third revolution, the *Postindustrial Revolution* (Bell 1973; Inglehart 1977, 1990). Indeed, new issue interests, new styles of participation, and new expectations about the citizen's role in society seem to flow from the value changes discussed in chapter 5.

Party systems are in a state of flux, and it is difficult to determine how fundamental and long lasting these changes will be. It is clear, however, that the new political conflicts of advanced industrial societies have contributed to this situation. While we wait for history to determine the significance of these trends, we can look more closely at the political alignments that now exist in America, Britain, Germany, and France.

The Structure of Political Alignments

Most parties and party systems are still oriented primarily toward the traditional political alignments described by Lipset and Rokkan. We shall refer to these alignments collectively as the *Old Politics* cleavage. The Old Politics cleavage is based on the political conflict between Old Left and Old Right coalitions. Lipset and Rokkan considered the class cleavage to be the primary factor in structuring the Old Politics alignment because class issues were the most salient during the extension of the franchise. The Old Left therefore identifies itself with the working class and labor unions, as well as secular groups and urban interests (also see Lijphart 1981). The Old Right is synonymous with business interests and the middle class; in some nations this conservative coalition also includes religious and rural voters. When political issues tap the concerns of the Old Politics cleavage—for example, wage settlements, employment programs, social security programs, or church-related legislation—party positions reflect their traditional social orientations.

The political conflicts of advanced industrial societies have created a new dimension of cleavage in recent years. This *New Politics* dimension involves conflict over a new set of issues: environmental quality, alternative lifestyles, minority rights, participation, and social equality. This dimension represents the cleavage between proponents of these issues, the New Left, and citizens who feel threatened by these issues, the New Right.

The Old Politics cleavage is likely to remain the primary basis of partisan conflict in most advanced industrial democracies for the immediate future. The New Politics dimension is significantly affecting these party systems, however, because it can cut across the established Old Politics cleavage. Despite their differences, labor unions and business interests occasionally join forces to fight the opponents of nuclear energy. Farmers and students sometimes become allies to oppose industrial development projects that may threaten the environment. Fundamentalist blue-collar and white-collar workers unite to oppose changes in moral codes. An emerging New Left and New Right potentially may restructure social-group alignments and party coalitions. In sum, the simple dichotomy between Old Left and Old Right is no longer adequate to describe present patterns of political competition. The contemporary political space is now better described by at least two dimensions.

In the last edition of this book we mapped the sociopolitical space using cross-national data from the *Political Action* study (Dalton 1988, chap. 7). Contemporary data of this sort are available only for the United States, and we will use the American case to illustrate the Old Politics and New Politics cleavages.

For much of this century, the Old Politics cleavage provided the framework for party competition in the American party system. The New Deal coalitions created by the Great Depression determined the social bases of party support: the Democratic Party and its labor union supporters against the Republicans and big business. Religious differences were muted because of the formal separation of church and state in the United States.

In the 1960s the New Politics began to affect American politics. Student protesters, the women's movement, and the alternative movement challenged the symbols of the political establishment. Herbert Weisberg and Jerrold Rusk (1970) described how this cultural conflict introduced a new dimension of cleavage into American politics, as represented by dissident Democratic candidates in the late 1960s and early 1970s. New Politics issues entered the agenda of subsequent campaigns. Rusk and Weisberg found, however, that the Democrats and Republicans were not clearly divided on New Politics issues; these issues divided parties internally rather than separating them politically.[8] Another study of party cleavages in 1974 found that the Democrats and Republicans were only slightly differentiated on the New Politics dimension (Dalton 1988, chap. 7).

The policies of the Reagan and Bush administrations stimulated a convergence of Old Politics and New Politics alignments over the 1980s and early 1990s. The tax and spending priorities of the Reagan administration sharply favored business and the more affluent sectors of society. This served to reinforce ties between business interests and the Republican Party. Furthermore, the Reagan administration pursued a conservative social agenda and developed strong political links to religious groups such as the Moral Majority and other fundamentalist organizations. To an extent atypical of modern American politics, religion was injected into partisan politics.

The Reagan and Bush administrations also clarified party positions on the New Politics agenda. Environmental protection was an issue that had roots in the Republican Party; Richard Nixon, for example, had established the Environmental Protection Agency during his first presidential term and had introduced a variety of environmental legislation. Yet Ronald Reagan openly speculated that "killer trees" were a major cause of air pollution. The policy initiatives of the Reagan administration demonstrated its hostility toward the environmental movement. Although George Bush claimed to be the environmental president, the assault on environmental protection legislation continued under his administration. Similarly, the Reagan and Bush administrations were openly antagonistic toward feminist organizations. The abortion issue became a litmus test of Republican values in the appointment of federal judges and the selection of candidates.

As the Republicans became critical of the New Politics agenda, the Democrats became advocates of these issues. The Democrats became the partisan supporters of the environmental movement in congressional legislation. The Democrats were the first to nominate a woman and feminist for national political office, Geraldine Ferraro in 1984. Alternative political groups also developed a political base and prominence among the activist core of the Democratic Party.

In short, political cleavage lines seemed to overlap and become more polarized during the 1980s. This pattern of ideological convergence was simplified because only two parties exist in America; if one party adopts a position, the opposition naturally gravitates toward the other party. Furthermore, the Reagan and Bush administrations consciously sought to clarify their position on New Politics issues because they thought this could benefit them electorally. The Democrats were as enthusiastic in embracing these same constituencies.

We can test these expectations with data from the 1992 American National Election Study. The survey asked respondents about their feelings toward a set of sociopolitical groups and the political parties.[9] These data can identify the structuring of major social groups and the political parties in relation to Old Politics and New Politics dimensions. We used a statistical analysis method to represent the interrelationship of group perceptions in graphic terms.[10] This technique maps the political space as defined by Americans. When there is a strong similarity in how two groups are evaluated, they are located near each other in the space. When groups are evaluated in dissimilar terms, they are positioned a distance apart in the space.

The American sociopolitical space in 1992 is depicted in figure 7.1. The traditional Left/Right cleavage of the Old Politics is quite evident. Clinton is located at the left of the horizontal dimension, along with labor unions. Bush is located at the opposite end of this continuum, and the nearest group is big business; fundamentalist religious groups are part of the conservative Republican cluster.

We also find a second dimension of political cleavage, which has Texas billionaire Ross Perot juxtapositioned against minority groups, such as Hispanics, blacks, and the poor. This pattern fits the tone of the Perot campaign in 1992 and the social base of Perot supporters. What is distinctive about the 1992 patterns, however, is the movement toward fusion of the Old Politics and New Politics cleavages. Instead of two dimensions of conflict aligned at right angles, as seen in earlier studies, one sees that New Left groups have apparently moved toward the Democratic Party. The cluster of Clinton support groups includes the unions *and* feminists, gays, and environmentalists. Even if some tensions exist among groups within each cluster, the bipolar nature of contemporary American politics is becoming apparent.[11]

Comparable and current data on the sociopolitical space in Britain, Germany, and France are not available, but another study uses a different method to illustrate party positions on Old Politics and New Politics issues in all four party systems. Michael Laver and W. Ben Hunt (1992) asked experts to position the parties in their respective nations on a set of policy di-

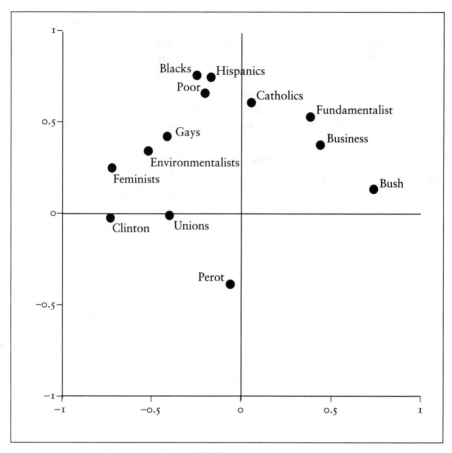

FIGURE 7.1

THE SOCIOPOLITICAL SPACE IN THE UNITED STATES

SOURCE: American National Election Study, 1992.

mensions. Figure 7.2 presents party positions on two issues: taxes versus social spending as a measure of the socioeconomic issues of the Old Politics, and the environment versus economic growth as a measure of New Politics priorities.

The top panel of the figure locates parties on the spending/taxes issue. Here we find a traditional Left/Right party alignment in each nation. The Democratic Party in the United States is located at the left end of this continuum, following the pattern found above in mapping the sociopolitical space. At the opposite end of the Old Politics dimension are the Republicans. Even before the present "Contract with America," the Reagan admin-

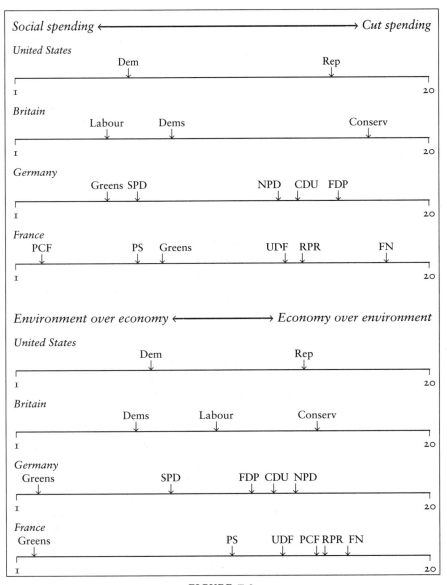

FIGURE 7.2

PARTY POSITIONS ON TWO POLICY DIMENSIONS

SOURCE: Laver and Hunt (1992, appendix).

istration had developed a strong commitment to cutting public services and cutting taxes. This is now ingrained in the Republican policy image.

In Britain, the Labour Party has been the representative of the working class and the advocate for socialist policy. The party's working-class orientation is institutionalized through formal ties to the labor unions. Normally, membership in a union automatically includes a dues-paying membership in the Labour Party; union leaders also control this large bloc of votes at Labour Party conventions. Past Labour governments have nationalized several major industrial sectors, expanded social welfare programs, and vigorously defended the interests of their working-class supporters. The Labour Party is located to the left of both the American Democrats and the German SPD on this dimension. The British Liberal Democrats are a small centrist party that occupies a midpoint on this dimension. The party was traditionally a representative of liberal, middle-class values. In recent years it has formed and reformed itself, but still holds a centrist position on issues of the government's socioeconomic role.

Margaret Thatcher's Conservative Party government aggressively attempted to roll back the scale of national government during the 1980s. Thatcher's government privatized many government-owned industries, reduced government social and educational programs, sold off public housing, and generally tried to lessen the scope of the government's involvement in society. These policies reinforced the Conservatives' traditional image as a party that favors business interests and that draws disproportionate support from middle-class voters. Reagan and Thatcher became synonymous with the retrenchment of government programs in the 1980s (Pierson 1994). The present Conservative administration of John Major has continued these policies.

The major representative of Old Left in Germany is the Social Democratic Party (SPD). The SPD emerged from the socialist working-class movement and still consistently represents working-class interests. Although German labor unions no longer have institutional ties to the SPD, the relationship nevertheless remains close.[12] Because of these liberal traditions, the SPD favors increased social spending. In 1980 the Greens joined the German party system. Herbert Kitschelt (1989) has described the Greens as a Left-libertarian party because it combines an advocacy for New Left causes with a distinctly liberal position on many traditional issues of the social spending and the welfare state. Thus political experts position the Greens to the left of the SPD on the social spending dimension in figure 7.2.[13]

The Christian Democratic Union/Christian Social Union (CDU/CSU) is the major political force on the right in Germany. The CDU was formed after the war as a conservative-oriented catchall party (*Volkpartei*). In the state of Bavaria the CSU runs as the party of the conservative bloc. As their names imply, both conservative parties represent religious voters on the church-state cleavage. The Union parties also advocate conservative economic policies and a free-market economy. The CDU/CSU now forms a governing coalition with the small Free Democratic Party (FDP). The CDU/CSU and FDP occupy similar conservative positions on the services/taxes dimension. Indeed, during the 1980s the CDU/CSU–FDP government limited benefits for every single social program, decreased the government's budget deficits, and pursued conservative economic reform. The exceptional costs of German unification have forced these parties to turn temporarily away from these policies, but their commitment to smaller government remains strong. The National Democratic Party (NPD) is a small, extreme-Right party known for its nationalistic and reactionary policies, more so than for its economic agenda. Nevertheless, experts locate the NPD at the conservative end of the social services dimension.

France has two major parties that represent traditional Old Left positions: the Communist Party (PC) and the Socialists (PS). The PC strongly believes that the government is responsible for social needs and is the most Leftist party in all four nations. The PC depends very heavily on working-class votes and has formal ties with the communist labor union, the CGT. Furthermore, while other communist parties have lost their Marxist ideology with the collapse of the Soviet Union, the French Communist Party remains committed to these values. The French Socialists, by comparison, have moderated their ideological image during the 1980s to appeal to liberal middle-class voters. Still, political experts see the PS as strongly committed to extensive governmental social programs.

France has two major conservative parties, the Rally for the Republic (RPR) and the Union for French Democracy (UDF). The RPR is the modern successor to the Gaullist forces that created the Fifth Republic and governed the republic for most of its history. The party is a representative of conservative business interests and the middle class; it favors a reduction of government social programs and taxes. The UDF is a moderate conservative party that attracts liberal elements of the middle class. Together the RPR and UDF form a conservative majority in the present parliament, advocating a traditional conservative economic agenda. The president of France, Jacques Chirac, is a leader of the RPR. At the far right of the political spectrum is the National Front (FN). The FN is an example of a New Right party, focusing its attention on cultural and social issues, such as opposition to foreigners, a nationalistic foreign policy, and traditional social values. Its identity is formed more as a backlash to the liberal themes of the

New Politics than by traditional economic issues; but on issues of social spending it is perceived as sharply conservative.

If Old Politics issues, such as government social spending, were the only factors structuring electoral competition, then Lipset and Rokkan would still be correct in describing contemporary party systems in terms of the cleavages of the 1920s. The class-based Left/Right party alignment that historically structured partisan politics remains clearly visible in how political experts position the contemporary parties on the services/taxes dimension.

The content of the political agenda, however, now includes more than the economic and security concerns of the Old Politics. The New Politics introduce new interests into the political debate, and this has led to a different alignment of parties. The partisan alignments along the New Politics cleavage can be seen in the bottom panel of figure 7.2, which positions parties on the environment/economy policy dimension.

In the United States, we find the same Left/Right ordering of the parties. The Democrats are seen as the advocates for environmental protection. The Republicans are perceived as more concerned with protecting the economy even at a cost to the environment. This party cleavage was aptly illustrated in the 1992 presidential election. The Democrats nominated Albert Gore, a political figure who is closely identified with environmental protection and the author of a best-selling book on the environment, as their vice-presidential candidate. Despite earlier claims to be the environmental president, Bush opposed environmental regulations and, in the heat of the campaign, took to slurring Gore as the "Ozone Man" because of Gore's concern about the depletion of ozone in the upper atmosphere. In the United States, the alignment of the two parties is now similar on both Old Politics and New Politics dimensions.

In most other party systems, the environmental issue creates a new pattern of partisan alignment (Dalton 1994, chap. 9). In Britain, for example, the centrist Liberal Democrats have distinguished themselves among the established parties as the most sympathetic to the environmental issue.[14] In Germany, the Green Party is seen as a strong advocate for environmental causes and is located at the far end of this continuum. Over time the SPD has become more sympathetic to the environment, but experts still position the SPD near the center of this policy scale. The Social Democrats are closer to the conservative CDU and FDP on this dimension than they are to the Greens. On the far right of this continuum is the extremist NPD, which illustrates where this party and the New Right Republikaner would be located on the New Politics dimension. As the Greens are advocates for modernization and liberal issues, the NPD (and more recently the Republikaner) are the most vocal critics of social and cultural change. Overall, the major cleavage on the environmental dimension separates the Greens from all the other German parties.

The ability of New Politics to transform party alignments is most clearly illustrated in the French party system. The French Greens are strong supporters of the environment, occupying an extreme New Left position. But the traditional Leftist parties are neutral or critical of environmental protection. The French Socialists are at the center of this scale and have an ambivalent record on environmental matters. The French Communists, who are extremely Leftist on Old Politics issues, are positioned between the conservative UDF and RPR on the environmental dimension. On the environmental dimension, the Communists and the National Front hold similar positions. Overall, as we saw in the German party system, the New Politics cleavage separates the Greens from all the other French parties.

If we combine the evidence in this section, we can begin to map the sociopolitical space that voters use to orient themselves to partisan politics. In each nation there is a clear representation of political positions along the traditional socioeconomic issues that formed the initial structure of party competition in these democracies. In addition, the political controversies of advanced industrial societies are bringing new issues to the fore, and this is prompting the formation of new parties or the realignment of the established parties to represent these positions. Much of the current research on electoral politics can be seen as an attempt to assess the relative position of the political parties on both dimensions and the relative weight of both dimensions in structuring political choice for the electorate. The mix of these forces is what fuels the current processes of electoral change in these nations.

Contemporary Party Systems

This chapter has described broad similarities in the ideological structure of contemporary party systems. Most political parties are still organized around the Old Politics cleavages of class and religion. Even if these cleavages have become less salient, the group ties and institutional structure of the parties have perpetuated these images. Parties are, after all, still turning to the same interest groups and associations for the core of their support. Contemporary publics see Rightist parties as linked to business interests (and sometimes the Catholic church) and Leftist parties as allied with the labor unions.

While major party differences exist on the Old Politics dimension, there are indications of the increasing importance of the New Politics cleavage. Earlier chapters (5 and 6) found that citizens are developing post-material values that lead to new policy interests. These new issue demands initially manifested themselves outside the established parties. The growth of citizen-action groups, for example, often reflected a mix of the new style of citizen participation and New Politics issue concerns. These interests are now gaining representation through partisan politics, which places new demands on the established parties.

Some indications of partisan change along the New Politics dimension are already evident. New parties, such as the German and French Greens, have been formed to represent New Politics concerns. These small parties have drawn their support from the young, the better educated, and post-materialists—key groups defining the New Politics cleavage. A more basic change would occur if the larger established parties adopted clearer positions on New Politics issues. There is some evidence of this change in the recent actions of the German SPD and French Socialists. Both parties are attempting to combine Old Left and New Left issue appeals into a single program; the French PS found this an especially difficult task for a governing party. The Democratic and Republican parties in the United States also have developed closer ties to New Left and New Right groups respectively.

Despite these indications of partisan change, we should not underestimate the difficulty of integrating the New Politics cleavage into party systems based on the Old Politics cleavage. The established parties have been understandably hesitant to formalize close ties to New Left or New Right groups, especially in Western Europe where the Old Politics ties remain strong. Parties are naturally cautious about taking clear stands on a new dimension of conflict until the costs and benefits are clear. The major European Leftist parties are divided on many issues that involve Old Politics/New Politics conflicts. While most industrial labor unions favor economic development projects that will strengthen the economy and produce jobs, Leftist environmentalists often oppose these same projects because of their ecological consequences. Many conservative parties also face divisions between conservative business elites and liberal middle-class voters. Political alliances between Old Politics and New Politics groups so far have been temporary because of the conflicting values of these groups.

Added to these uncertainties are the new questions of partisan identities in the post–Cold War era. The end of communism requires a rethinking of the foreign policy stances of many parties. Many conservative parties used anticommunism as part of their political image, and this must now be replaced by other political themes. Similarly, the collapse of East European socialism has weakened the ability of social democratic parties to advocate programs to expand the role of government. In short, parties of the Left and the Right are rethinking some of the themes that created their electoral identities. It is too soon to know what the implications of these reevaluations will be.

Because of the uncertainties facing the parties and the difficulties in integrating a new political cleavage into the existing party systems, future partisan change is likely to follow a slow and uncertain course. Continuing changes in citizen values and issue interests mean that the potential for further partisan change is real.

Notes

1. There are several good analytic studies of recent American elections (Pomper 1989, 1993; Abramson et al. 1994), British elections (Butler 1995; Heath et al. 1985, 1994), German elections (Dalton 1993b, 1996), and French elections (Boy and Mayer 1993).

2. Vote share was based on most recent national election: United States (1992), Britain (1992), Germany (1994), and France (1993). Years in government is complicated by the separation of powers in the United States and France; we decided to count the number of years a party was part of the legislative majority between 1970 and 1995 as the most comparable cross-national statistic.

3. In 1994 the Republican seats in the House rose to 230, and the Republicans had a majority of Senate seats (54). In addition, the party made broad gains in state and local offices (Wattenberg 1996).

4. Because of the single-member district electoral system, the Liberal Democrats are routinely disadvantaged in winning seats in Parliament. In 1992, for example, the party won 18 percent of the popular vote nationwide but won only 3 percent of the seats in the House of Commons.

5. In 1994 the western Greens allied themselves with the eastern Alliance 90 and ran under the heading Alliance 90/Greens.

6. The German electoral law requires that a party win 5 percent of the national vote on the second ballot, or three district seats, in order to share in the proportional distribution of Bundestag seats. In 1990 this requirement was separately applied to East and West; in 1994 the PDS won four district seats in East Berlin and thus received additional seats in parliament based on its national share of the vote.

7. Bartolini and Mair (1989) forcefully argue that earlier historical periods were also marked by high levels of partisan volatility. But their methodology underestimates the degree of the current levels of partisan change (Dalton 1993c).

8. For instance, the 1984 Democratic primaries featured a confrontation between Old Left and New Left Democrats. Walter Mondale was identified with the traditional New Deal policies of the Democratic Party and won early endorsements from labor unions and the party establishment. Gary Hart, in

contrast, explicitly claimed that he was the New Politics candidate, the representative of new ideas and a new generation. Hart's core voters were the Yuppies—young, urban, upwardly mobile professionals—one of the groups linked to the New Politics cleavage.

9. These are the so-called feeling thermometer questions that measure positive and negative feelings toward each object. Respondents are given a thermometer-like scale to measure their "warmth" or "coldness" toward each group.

10. The group items were factor analyses using a principal components analysis involving the methods described in Barnes, Kaase et al. (1979, 581–83) and extracting only two dimensions. For earlier analyses of similar sociopolitical spaces, see Barnes, Kaase et al. (1979), Inglehart (1984), Dalton (1988, chap. 7). Cees Middendorp (1991) has conducted an extensive longitudinal analysis of the Dutch political space using a different methodology, and he identifies two very similar dimensions.

11. Similar results are obtained from the American portion of the Cross National Election Project. This study found even stronger evidence of a convergence in Old Politics and New Politics cleavages using a question on political representation. Furthermore, a follow-up question asking about the partisan leanings of social groups found that Clinton was perceived as the preferred candidate for the women's movement (73 percent), the civil rights movement (68 percent), labor unions (66 percent), and environmental groups (64 percent). Bush was perceived by a plurality as the favored candidate of business associations (48 percent) and religious fundamentalists (45 percent). See Beck and Curtice (forthcoming).

12. The German portion of the Cross National Election Project also contained a question on the partisan leanings of social groups. About three-quarters of the German public saw labor unions as leaning toward the SPD, and an equal number saw business associations and the Catholic church as leaning toward the CDU/CSU; nearly 80 percent saw environmental groups as favoring the Greens. See Dalton (1993a, 266) and Wessels (1993).

13. A new entrant to the German party system is the Party of Democratic Socialism (PDS), a successor of the communist party of the German Democratic Republic. The PDS would be positioned on the far left of this scale.

14. Even the Liberal Democrats' advocacy of environmental issues was insufficient for some environmentalists. In the 1989 European Parliament election a newly formed British Green Party won 14 percent of the vote. The structure of the British electoral system handicaps minor parties, however, and the Greens have been unable to institutionalize this support.

8. The Social Bases of Party Support

There is a well-worn saying that people act politically as they are socially, and this has been the case for electoral politics. The preceding chapter discussed how party systems were formed to provide political representation for class, religious, and other social groups. Contemporary political parties maintain ties to their clientele groups and project images in group terms: Labour is a working-class party, the Republicans are the party of business, the Christian Democrats represent religious voters, and so forth. Although the issues and personalities of the campaign change from election to election, parties generally maintain their institutional and ideological ties to specific social groups. Most parties depend on the votes of their clientele groups to provide a stable base of electoral support.

Several processes determine the influence of social characteristics on a voter's choice of party. First, a person's social position often indicates his or her values and political beliefs. A French steelworker is more likely than a shopkeeper, for example, to favor an expansion of social services or government regulation of business. Opposition to liberal abortion laws is more likely among devout Catholics than the nonreligious. Thus social characteristics are an indirect measure of attitudinal differences between groups of voters and their perceptions of which party best represents these policy positions.

Second, social characteristics indicate some of the political cues to which an individual is exposed. A British mineworker, for example, hears about politics from his coworkers or other working-class neighbors and friends; the mineworker also receives political persuasion from the union representative at work and union publications at home. This social milieu provides repeated cues on which policies will benefit people like oneself, and which party best represents one's interests—a strong Labour Party bias in these cues is inevitable. Similarly, a Bavarian Catholic hears about political issues at weekly church services, from Catholic social groups, and from predominately conservative Catholic friends. This information generally encourages a favorable opinion of the Christian Social Union and its program.

Third, social groups can be an important reference point in orienting voters to political issues and providing information about politics. Even if an individual is not a member of a labor union or a regular churchgoer, the knowledge that unions favor one party and the Catholic church another can help voters locate themselves in relation to the parties. For many citizens, the cues provided by social networks and group-party cues can help guide their political orientations and voting behavior.

Voter reliance on social-group cues is an example of the model of satisficing decision making presented in chapter 2. Social cues can narrow the voter's choice to parties that are consistent with the voter's social position. Voters enter an election favoring the party (or parties) that historically has supported the class or religious groups to which they belong, while excluding parties with unsupportive records. Political parties nurture such ties. The parties communicate their group loyalties to the voters, most obviously when they call themselves "Labour" or "Christian Democrats."

Voters can decide between competing parties based on the cues provided by social groups—the endorsements of labor unions, business associations, religious groups, and the like—as well as the group appeals of the parties themselves. The stable group ties of the parties mean that many voters develop standing partisan predispositions that endure across elections, simplifying the decision process still more. When British industrial workers cast their votes for Labour because the party represents people like themselves, this is a reasonable electoral decision.

Reliance on social characteristics thus is a shortcut in making voting decisions. A citizen who is knowledgeable about all the issues and all the candidates is well prepared to make an informed voting choice and justify this decision in issue-oriented and ideological terms. Social characteristics provide a simpler, although less certain, method of choosing which party represents the voter's interests. Still, when strong social-group identities are matched by clear party positions on these social cleavages, as they are in most European nations, then social characteristics can provide a very meaningful guide for voting behavior.

From its beginnings, electoral research has stressed social-group attachments as an important influence on voting behavior. One of the first empirical studies of American voting focused on the social bases of partisanship (Lazarsfeld et al. 1948). This study found that an *index of political predispositions* based on social class, religion, and rural/urban residence was a strong determinant of voting choice. Social stratification is even greater in Europe, producing even sharper group differences in voting patterns. There is a well-known cliché that social class is the basis of British politics, and all else is just embellishment and detail. Both class and religion are strong correlates of voting in Germany and France.

This chapter examines the group basis of voting in contemporary democracies. We highlight both the stability and change in group-based voting. On the one hand, the partisan loyalties generated by social characteristics produce stable party coalitions, since the parties routinely attract the same kinds of core voters. This constancy in the bases of party support reinforces the partisan images presented in chapter 7.

On the other hand, there is strong evidence that the social bases of partisanship are changing. The socioeconomic and political trends discussed in earlier chapters have been linked to shifts in the group bases of party support (Franklin et al. 1992; Dalton et al. 1984). In addition, the increasing sophistication of contemporary electorates may lessen voter reliance on social cues, as individuals make their own political decisions. We examine these theories by tracking group voting patterns over time and across nations.

The Class Cleavage

Class politics taps the essence of what we have described as the Old Politics—a conflict between the haves and have-nots. The class cleavage represents the economic and material problems of industrial societies: providing economic security for all and ensuring a just distribution of economic rewards. Issues such as unemployment, inflation, social services, tax policies, and government management of the economy reinforce class divisions.

Social scientists have probably devoted more attention to the class cleavage than to any other social characteristic as a predictor of mass voting behavior. Theoretically, the class cleavage involves some of the most basic questions of power and politics that evolve from Marxian and capitalist views of political development. Empirically, one's position in the class structure has been a strong predictor of voting choice. Seymour Lipset's early cross-national study of electoral politics described the class cleavage as one of the most pervasive bases of party support:

> Even though many parties renounce the principle of class conflict or loyalty, an analysis of their appeals and their support suggests that they do represent the interests of different classes. On a world scale, the principal generalization which can be made is that parties are primarily based on either the lower classes or the middle and upper classes. (1981a, 230)

Similarly, Arend Lijphart's (1981) overview of modern party systems identified social class as a major dimension of ideological cleavage in virtually all democracies. Other early empirical studies generally supported these conclusions.

Research on the class cleavage normally defines social class in terms of occupation. Following Karl Marx's still influential writings, occupations are classified on the basis of their relationship to the means of production. The bourgeoisie are the owners of capital and the self-employed; the proletariat are the workers who produce capital through their labor. This schema is then generalized to define two large social classes: the middle class and the working class. These class differences provided the basis for the creation of Socialist and Communist parties that represent the interests of the working class; conservative parties, in turn, defend the interests of the middle class.

While this Marxian dichotomy once defined the class cleavage, the changing nature of advanced industrial societies has reshaped the class structure. The traditional bourgeoisie/proletariat cleavage has been joined by a "new" middle class, or what others have called a "salatariat." This stratum consists primarily of salaried white-collar employees and civil servants (Kerr 1990; Heath et al. 1991). Daniel Bell (1973) defined a "postindustrial" society as one in which most of the labor force holds new middle-class positions. This new middle class rapidly expanded in most Western societies so that by the 1980s nearly all had passed the postindustrial threshold.

The new middle class is an important addition to the class structure because it lacks a clear position in the traditional class conflicts between the working class and the old middle class. The separation of management from capital ownership, the expansion of the service sector, and the growth of government (or nonprofit) employment created a social stratum that does not conform to Marxian class analysis. The new middle class does not own capital as the old middle class did, but it also differs in lifestyle from the blue-collar workers of the traditional proletariat. Members of the new middle class seem less interested in the economic conflicts of the Old Politics and are more attuned to New Politics issues. Consequently, the identity of the new middle class differs from both the bourgeoisie and the proletariat.

Table 8.1 presents the varying voting preferences of these social classes in the most recent election for which data are available.[1] The persistence of historical class alignments is clearly evident. The working class in each nation gives disproportionate support to Leftist parties, ranging from 51 percent in Britain to 66 percent in France (the combined PC, Socialist, and other Left vote). At the other extreme, the old middle class is the bastion of

TABLE 8.1

SOCIAL CLASS AND PARTY SUPPORT

(IN PERCENTAGES)

	Working class	New middle class	Old middle class
United States, 1992			
Democrat	66	58	47
Republican	34	42	53
Total	100	100	100
Great Britain, 1992			
Labour	51	24	18
Liberal Democrats	14	21	20
Conservatives	36	55	62
Total	100	100	100
Germany, 1994			
PDS	3	5	4
Alliance 90/Greens	3	12	6
SPD	51	38	17
FDP	2	7	16
CDU/CSU	42	38	58
Total	101	100	101
France, 1988			
PC	12	7	10
Socialists	51	47	30
Other Left	3	2	0
Greens	10	6	4
UDF	9	15	20
RPR	12	19	30
National Front	4	3	7
Total	101	99	101

SOURCES: *United States,* 1992 American National Election Study. *Great Britain,* 1992 British Election Study. *Germany,* September 1994 Politbarometer Study. *France,* Eurobarometer 30 (Fall 1988).

NOTE: American data are based on congressional vote; German data are for East and West electorates combined. Social class is based on the occupation of the head of the household where this information is available; otherwise, it is the occupation of the respondent.

support for conservative parties. This traditional proletariat/bourgeoisie cleavage remains strong in each nation—but in each nation less than half of the electorate now belongs to either of these two classes.

The new middle class constitutes the majority of contemporary electorates and, more important, holds ambiguous partisan preferences (Kerr 1990). The new middle class is always located between the working class and the old middle class in its Left/Right voting preferences. In addition, the new middle class gives disproportionate support to parties that represent a New Politics ideology, such as the German Alliance 90/Greens. The new middle class is a key element in the changing political alignments of advanced industrial societies.

Before we continue, one significant feature of class voting in Germany that deserves mention. The data for Germany combine two divergent patterns. In western Germany, as in most other Western democracies, the parties of the Left gather most of their support from the working class, and the parties of the Right draw their support from the middle class. If one simply calculated the difference in the percentage Leftist (SPD, Greens, and PDS) between working-class and middle-class voters in western Germany, the class voting gap in 1994 was fourteen points. Data from eastern Germany, however, display a *reversal* of this partisan alignment in the 1990 and 1994 Bundestag elections (Dalton and Bürklin 1996). Most of the working class in the East voted for the Christian Democrats; most middle-class voters in the East supported parties of the Left. The simple voting gap between working class and middle class in 1994 was a *negative fifteen points*. This reversal is caused by the differences in the class structure of East and West, as well as the different political values that followed from the historical experiences of the German Democratic Republic. To an extent, similar patterns can be found in other new democratic party systems in Eastern Europe. These differences will likely persist as long as the eastern middle class contains the remnants of the former leadership class of the communist regime. Furthermore, these two contrasting class alignments distort and weaken the impact of class in German electoral politics (Dalton and Bürklin 1996; Rohrschneider and Fuchs 1995).

To place class voting in our four nations in comparative perspective, figure 8.1 compares the strength of the class differences in partisan preferences for seventeen advanced industrial democracies.[2] The strongest Cramer's V correlation statistics, and thus the greatest degree of class polarization, are for Scandinavian party systems: Norway (.22), Denmark (.21), Iceland (.19), and Sweden (.16). Not only are these highly fragmented party systems, which encourages the representation of social interests (Dalton 1991), but the Social Democratic parties in these nations have a strong

FIGURE 8.1

THE OVERALL LEVEL

OF CLASS VOTING, 1990

SOURCE: 1990–91 World Values Survey.

NOTE: Values in parentheses are Cramer's V correlations. Respondents without a party preference are excluded from the calculation of correlations.

class identity. In addition, class voting tends to be stronger where unions have large memberships and are politically involved; this also fits the Scandinavian case (Nieuwbeerta 1995).

British class differences also rank in this upper tier, reflecting the continuing importance of class interests in British politics—and class cues in British voting behavior. Germany and France display moderate levels of class voting, close to the cross-national average of (.15). Finally, the United States stands out for the weak class differences in party preferences. As many others have observed, the American party system blurs the value of social class as a basis for voting choice (Huckfeldt and Kohfeld 1989; Abramson et al. 1994, chap. 5).

Although social class remains a significant influence on voting choice in many democracies, electoral research has found that class cues carry much less weight than they did a generation ago. This pattern can be seen in figure 8.2, which presents the Alford index of class voting for the election series in our four core nations. To maximize the comparability of these analyses, we focus on the Left/Right voting patterns of the working class versus the combined middle class (old and new). The Alford index measures class voting as the simple difference between the percentage of the working class voting for the Left and the percentage of the middle class voting Left.[3]

The general trend in figure 8.2 is obvious; class differences are declining. The size of the class voting index in Britain has decreased by almost half across post–World War II elections and in Germany by more than two-thirds.[4] Class voting patterns follow a less regular decline in American

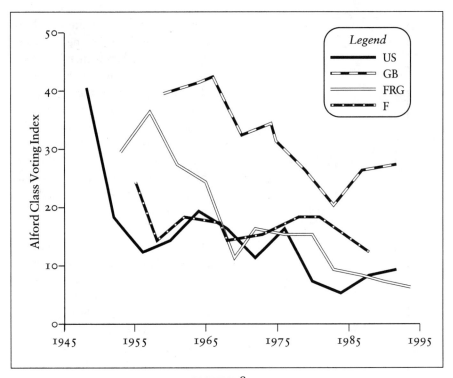

FIGURE 8.2

TRENDS IN CLASS VOTING

SOURCES: *United States,* 1948–92, American National Election Studies. *Great Britain,* 1959, Civic Culture Study; 1964–92, British Election Studies. *Germany,* 1953–94, German Election Studies. *France,* 1955, MacRae (1967, 257); 1958, Converse and Dupeux study; 1962, IFOP survey; 1967, Converse and Pierce study; 1968, Inglehart study; 1973–88, Eurobarometer studies.

NOTE: American data are based on congressional elections, except for 1948. German data for 1990 and 1994 are from unified Germany. The values plotted are the Alford Class Voting Index, that is, the percentage of the working class voting for Leftist parties minus the percentage of the middle class voting for Leftist parties.

congressional elections, but the downward trend is clear. Paul Abramson and his colleagues (1994, chap. 5) show that the erosion of class voting is even more pronounced in presidential elections (also see Stanley and Niemi 1991). Social class had a modest impact on voting behavior during the French Fourth Republic. The turbulent events surrounding the formation of the Fifth Republic—including the creation of a broad-based Gaullist Party—abruptly lowered class voting in 1958. Class voting in the Fifth Republic stabilized at a level significantly below pre-1958 levels (Lewis-Beck and Skalaban 1992). There are indications, such as figure 8.2, that French class voting has begun to decline during the 1980s (also Boy and Mayer 1993; Dogan 1995).

Evidence from many other nations points to the same downward trajectory for the traditional class cleavage. A decline in class voting is evident for Australia (McAllister 1992), Japan (Watanuki 1991), Scandinavia (Borre 1984), and a host of other nations (Inglehart 1990; Lane and Ersson 1991). Paul Nieuwbeerta (1995) has recently completed a detailed study of class voting in twenty advanced industrial democracies. He finds a general erosion in class voting differences for these polities.

Despite broad evidence that class voting differences are narrowing, some researchers have argued that the new class alignments of advanced industrial societies are perpetuating class voting, albeit in new forms. John Goldthorpe (1980), for example, proposed a new categorization of social class incorporating notions of job autonomy and authority relationships into traditional class criteria such as income level and manual labor. Others have created an expanded list of class categories that incorporate new social contexts, such as the middle-class salatariat or affluent blue-collar workers (Hout et al. 1996; Heath et al. 1985, 1991; Pappi 1990). Researchers have explored criteria other than employment as potential new bases of socioeconomic cleavage. Some have suggested that education might form the basis of a political cleavage separating the information rich and technologically sophisticated from the information poor and unskilled voter. Others have argued that conflicts between the public and private sectors are supplanting traditional class conflicts (Dunleavy and Husbands 1985). Some of the most innovative research tries to define social position by lifestyle characteristic, distinguishing between industrial employees and Yuppies, for example (Gluchowski 1987; Hammond 1986; Delli Carpini and Sigelman 1986).

This reconceptualization of social class implies that social cues now function in more complex and differentiated ways than in the past. Yet the empirical reality remains: even these complex new class frameworks have only a modest value in explaining how citizens vote. Rose and McAllister (1986, 50–51) compare several of these alternative models for British voting behavior in the 1983 election and find that they all explain a very modest share of the vote (also Crewe 1986). Nieuwbeerta (1995) shows that alternative statistical measures of class voting proposed by Heath and his colleagues (1985) or Hout et al. (1996) do not change these results. Similarly, the analyses of figure 8.1 are based on a more extensive measure of social class that includes a separate new middle-class category. Yet the average level of class differences in these seventeen nations is quite modest

(Cramer's V = .15). The most persuasive evidence comes from the longitudinal comparative analyses of Mark Franklin and his colleagues (1992, chap. 19). Combining occupation, union membership, income, education, and other class traits, they tracked a general decline in the ability of these social characteristics to explain electoral choice in most Western democracies.

Using a conceptual framework of group-based voting that David Butler and Donald Stokes developed (1969, 85–87), there are two possible explanations for the decline in class voting: either there have been changes in the relationship between voters and class groupings or there have been changes in the relationship between class groupings and the political parties. The former explanation, for example, highlights the changing class structure of contemporary societies. Members of the traditional social strata—industrial workers, farmers, and the self-employed—often remain integrated into class networks and remain distinct in their voting preferences. But there are simply fewer of these voters today. The growth of the new middle class has lessened the percentage of the electorate for whom traditional class ties are directly relevant.

Besides lacking ties to traditional class groups, new middle-class voters have mixed policy positions (and hence unclear partisan leanings). Thus white-collar workers have been a major source of electoral volatility in the United States (Hout et al. 1996; Abramson et al. 1994). Moreover, the new middle class was a prime source of narrowing class differences in Germany (Baker et al. 1981, chap. 8). A more refined analysis of the French data in figure 8.2 finds that the French new middle class has been a major source of electoral change in this party system.[5]

The blurring of the relationship between voters and class groupings also arises from a general narrowing in the life conditions of social classes. Improving incomes and the spread of middle-class lifestyles are leading to the *embourgeoisement* of some sectors of the working class. At the same time, the expanding ranks of low-paid and low-status white-collar employees and the growth of white-collar unions are producing a *proletarianization* of part of the middle class. Few individuals possess exclusively middle-class or working-class social characteristics, and longitudinal studies show that the degree of class overlap is increasing.[6] In sum, a convergence of life conditions contributes to the convergence of class voting patterns.

Increasing social and occupational mobility also may weaken the link between citizens and traditional social classes. All the nations in this study experienced a decline in the agricultural sector and an increase in middle-class employment during the postwar period. Dramatic changes in the size of economic sectors often occurred within a few decades. High levels of social mobility mean that an individual's ultimate social position is often different from that of his or her parents. Many farmers' children of conservative political upbringing moved into unionized, Leftist, working-class environments in the cities; many working-class children from urban, Leftist backgrounds have careers in traditionally conservative, white-collar occupations. Some socially mobile individuals will change their adult class identity and voting behavior to conform to their new social contexts; others will not. This mix of social forces blurs traditional class and partisan alignments.

The other possible source of declining class voting involves a changing relationship between class groups and the political parties. Over the past generation many Western political parties have tried to broaden their electoral appeals, partially to attract new middle-class voters, which led to more moderate party programs on traditional class-based issues. Socialist parties in Europe shed their Marxist programs and adopted more moderate domestic and foreign policy goals. Conservative parties also tempered their views and accepted the basic social programs proposed by the Left. Socialist parties vied for the votes of the new middle class, and conservative parties sought votes from the working class. Historical analyses of party programs document a general convergence of party positions on socioeconomic issues during the last half century (Thomas 1980; Robertson 1976; Budge et al. 1987). With smaller class-related differences in the parties' platforms, it seemed only natural that class cues would become less important in guiding voting behavior.

Initially at least, this seemed to be another plausible explanation for the decline in class voting differences. Recently, however, various studies have shown that party positions on the class cleavage remain clearly differentiated. For example, a survey of political experts documented a clear awareness of the continuing party differences on the socioeconomic issues that underlie the class cleavage (Laver and Hunt 1992). Evidence from Germany shows that the partisan clarity of class cues actually has increased over the same period that class voting has diminished (Dalton 1992, 60). Furthermore, chapter 7 showed that the American public still clearly perceives the partisan leanings of unions and business associations; comparable data are available for Germany (Wessels 1994). In short, it does not appear that ambiguity about the class positions of the parties is the prime reason for decreased class voting—instead, these cues are less relevant to today's voters.

The decline in class voting patterns therefore seems to represent a weakening of the political bonds linking voters to structured and politically organized class groups, rather than a narrowing of political positions by the parties. Reinforcing this interpretation, the revival of economic issues and the class-based appeals of parties in response to economic recession—a pattern found in all four core nations—has not significantly revived class voting in the 1980s and 1990s. Thus the nature of these changes implies that the long-term decline in class voting should continue.

The Religious Cleavage

The other major basis for social division in most Western party systems has been the religious cleavage in its various forms. The relationship between religion and politics arises from a centuries-old interplay of these two forces. The Reformation created divisions between Catholics and Protestants that carried over into politics. Control of the nation-building process often became intermixed with religious differences. In Anglican England, for example, the Protestant Church supported national independence and became identified with the dominant national culture. In Germany, the tensions between Lutherans and Catholics were a continuing source of conflict and even open warfare. Gradually the political systems of Europe accommodated themselves to the changes wrought by the Reformation, and a new status quo developed. Then the French Revolution renewed religious conflicts in the nineteenth century. Religious forces—both Catholic and Protestant—mobilized to defend church interests against the liberal, secular movement spawned by the events in France. Conflicts over church/state control, the legislation of mandatory state education, and disestablishment of state religions occurred across Europe.

As was true with the class cleavage, conflicts over religion defined the structure of elite conflict and the political alliances that existed in the late nineteenth century. The political parties that formed during this period often allied themselves with specific religious interests: Catholic or Protestant, religious or secular. Thus the party alignments developed at the start of the twentieth century institutionalized the religious cleavage, and many features of these party systems have endured to the present (Lipset and Rokkan 1967).

Early empirical research on voting behavior underscored the continuing importance of the religious cleavage. Richard Rose and Derek Urwin (1969) examined the social bases of party support in sixteen Western democracies. Their oft-cited conclusion maintains that "religious divisions, not class, are the main social bases of parties in the Western world today" (p. 12). Arend Lijphart (1979) compared the religious, class, and linguistic cleavages in four democracies where all three cleavages exist. He found that religion was the strongest influence on voting choice. Numerous other cross-national and longitudinal studies have documented the persisting importance of the religious cleavage (Rose 1974; Baker et al. 1981, chap. 7; Wald 1983; Lewis-Beck and Skalaban 1992).

Measuring the impact of religious cues on voting behavior is more complex than the analyses of class voting. The class composition of most industrial democracies is similar, but their religious composition is more varied. Britain is largely Protestant, and nearly two-thirds of the population are nominally Anglicans. In contrast, nearly all French citizens are baptized Catholics, and the Protestant minority is very small. Germany is a mixed denominational system, with Lutheran Protestants slightly outnumbering Catholics. The United States represents yet another pattern of religious pluralism. The United States lacks a dominant national religion; there are a significant number of Catholics, Reformation-era Protestants (Anglicans, Calvinists, Lutherans, etc.), Pietist Protestants (Methodist, etc.), other Protestant and Christian groups (Southern Baptists, Pentacostals, Mormons, etc.), and Jews.

In addition to the diverse religious composition of nations, the partisan tendencies of religious denominations also vary cross-nationally. Catholics customarily support parties of the Right, and Protestants customarily support parties of the Left. This pattern generally holds for Western democracies, but historical events sometimes led to different patterns of religious alignment. This means that the voting cues provided by religious affiliation may differ across national boundaries, in contrast to the consistent working-class/middle-class pattern on the class cleavage.

Table 8.2 presents the relationship between religious denomination and party support in the four core nations. Religious differences in voting behavior are often large; however, each nation displays its unique pattern for the religious cleavage. The historical conflict between the Catholic church and Liberal/Socialist parties still appears in German voting alignments. Most Catholics support the CDU/CSU, which defends traditional values and the church's prerogatives. Among Catholics who are closely tied to the church, those who attend church weekly, the CDU/CSU received 80 percent of the vote in 1994. In contrast, the Leftist parties—SPD, Greens and PDS—garnered greater support from Protestants and nonreligious voters.

Although more than 80 percent of the French population have been baptized in the Catholic faith, sizable differences in voting behavior still separate French Catholics and non-Catholics. In 1988, only 14 percent of non-Catholics voted for conservative parties, compared to 46 percent among Catholics. Because the French public is overwhelmingly Catholic, the political consequences of this imbalance on election outcomes is limited.

TABLE 8.2
RELIGIOUS DENOMINATION AND PARTY SUPPORT
(IN PERCENTAGES)

United States, 1992	No reli-gion	Jewish	Catholic	Pietist Protes-tant	Other Christian	Reforma-tion Prot-estant
Democrat	66	72	62	62	60	45
Republican	34	28	38	38	40	55
Total	100	100	100	100	100	100

Great Britain, 1992	No religion	Catholic	Other Protestant	Church of Scotland	Anglican
Labour	39	52	34	39	28
Liberal Democrats	20	15	20	12	18
Conservatives	41	34	46	49	55
Total	100	101	100	100	101

Germany, 1994	No religion	Protestant	Catholic
PDS	14	1	1
Alliance 90/Greens	10	8	9
SPD	38	47	32
FDP	5	4	8
CDU/CSU	33	41	51
Total	100	101	100

France, 1988	Non-Catholic	Catholic
PC	18	5
Socialists	55	41
Other Left	3	2
Greens	10	6
UDF	5	17
RPR	5	25
National Front	4	4
Total	100	100

SOURCES: *United States,* 1992 American National Election Study. *Great Britain,* 1992 British Election Study. *Germany,* September 1994 Politbarometer Study. *France,* Eurobarometer 30 (Fall 1988).

In Britain the religious cleavage follows another pattern. The Anglican church historically has been identified with the political establishment; thus most Anglicans vote for the Conservative Party. Catholics are aligned with the Labour Party because of their minority status and the question of Irish independence. Nonconformist Protestants have long given disproportionate support to the Liberal Democrats.

Religious and moral conflicts have been a central element in American history (Wald 1993); yet the formal separation of church and state has limited the impact of religion on partisan politics. Table 8.2 shows that the Protestant denominations from the Reformation era predominately support the Republicans; the other major religious blocs support the Democrats. These differences are modest, however, and may reflect other factors more than religion per se. For example, neofundamentalist Protestants are a heavily Democratic group, but this is largely a reflection of regional cleavages in American politics and the concentration of this denomination in the conservative, though Democratic, South. Similarly, the Democratic ties of American Catholics are primarily the result of ethnic and class influences rather than explicitly religious values.

To place these religious voting patterns into a cross-national context, the left side of figure 8.3 displays the levels of denominational-based voting in seventeen nations. The starkest religious differences are found in the Netherlands, which has historically been a religiously divided society. There are also significant denominational differences in Germany, dividing Protestants, Catholics, and the nonreligious. In France, the correlation largely results from differences between religious and nonreligious voters.[7] Both Britain and the United States rank near the bottom in the extent to which religious denomination provides a basis for partisan choice.

Another aspect of the religious cleavage is the division between secular and religious voters. In predominately Catholic nations, such as France, this dimension represents a voter's integration into the Catholic culture. In mixed denominational systems the secularization process has often stimulated an alliance between Protestants and Catholics in a joint defense of religious interests, so denominational differences are replaced by a secular/religious cleavage. In Germany, for example, the Christian Democratic Union bridged the historic religious cleavage by uniting both Catholics and Protestants in a single religious party. Even in the United States, similar phenomena have been observed. Ronald Reagan and George Bush campaigned for the votes of religious conservatives from all denominations. The Republicans hoped to tap a common concern with the preservation of traditional values and opposition to abortion and the supposed moral decline of American society.

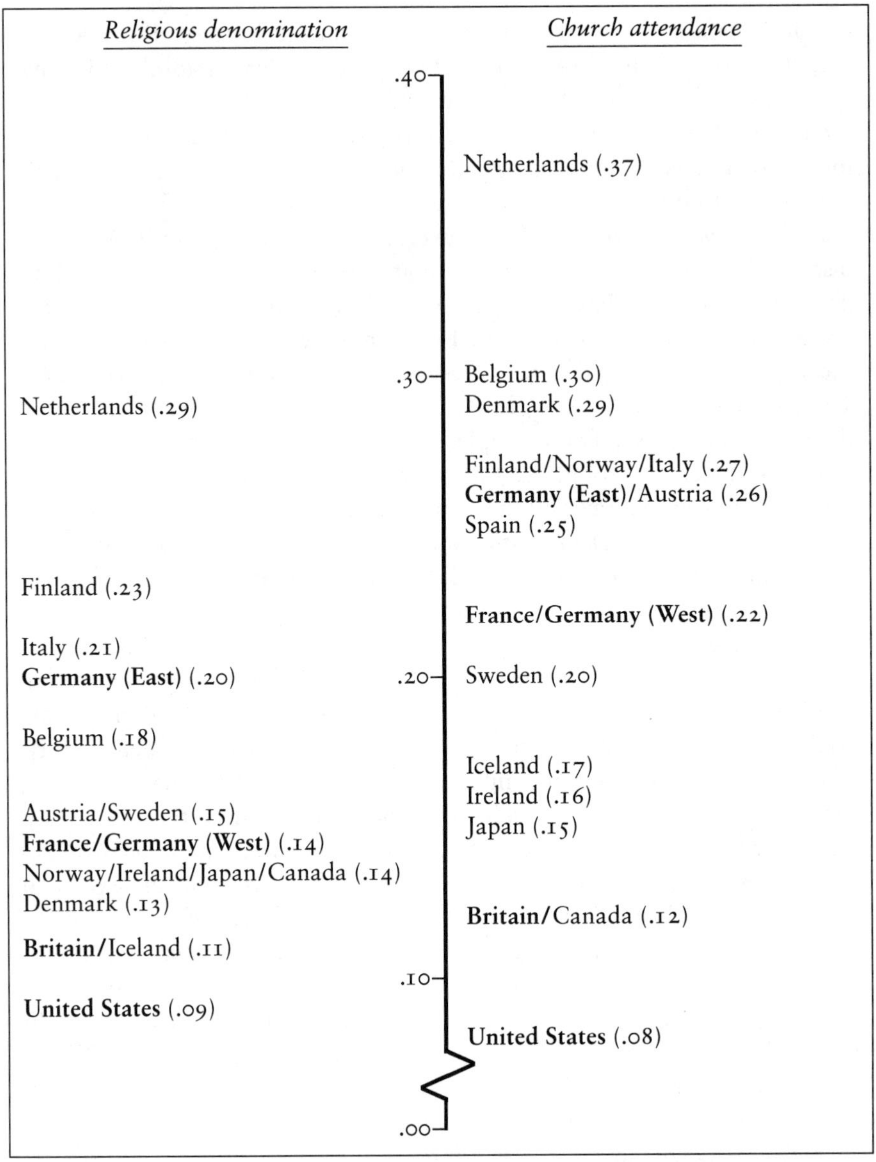

Religious denomination	Church attendance

.40—

Netherlands (.37)

.30— Belgium (.30)
Netherlands (.29) Denmark (.29)

Finland/Norway/Italy (.27)
Germany (East)/Austria (.26)
Spain (.25)

Finland (.23)
France/Germany (West) (.22)
Italy (.21)
Germany (East) (.20)   .20— Sweden (.20)

Belgium (.18)

Iceland (.17)
Austria/Sweden (.15) Ireland (.16)
France/Germany (West) (.14) Japan (.15)
Norway/Ireland/Japan/Canada (.14)
Denmark (.13) **Britain/**Canada (.12)

Britain/Iceland (.11)

.10—
United States (.09)

United States (.08)

.00—

FIGURE 8.3

THE OVERALL LEVEL OF RELIGIOUS VOTING, 1990

SOURCE: 1990–91 World Values Survey.

NOTE: Values in parentheses are Cramer's V correlations. Respondents without a party preference are excluded from the calculation of correlations.

TABLE 8.3

CHURCH ATTENDANCE AND PARTY SUPPORT

(IN PERCENTAGES)

	Never	*Occasionally*	*Weekly*
United States, 1992			
Democrat	66	60	55
Republican	34	40	46
Total	100	100	101
Great Britain, 1992			
Labour	39	29	33
Liberal Democrats	17	18	21
Conservatives	44	53	47
Total	100	100	101
Germany, 1994			
PDS	7	1	1
Alliance 90/Greens	11	6	2
SPD	43	44	19
FDP	6	6	4
CDU/CSU	34	42	74
Total	101	99	100
France, 1988			
PC	15	4	3
Socialists	52	43	25
Other Left	3	2	2
Greens	10	6	1
UDF	7	17	30
RPR	9	25	37
National Front	5	3	1
Total	101	100	99

SOURCES: *United States,* 1992 American National Election Study. *Great Britain,* 1992 British Election Study. *Germany,* September 1994 Politbarometer Study. *France,* Eurobarometer 30 (Fall 1988).

Table 8.3 presents the relationship between religious involvement, measured by the frequency of church attendance, and party preference. The voting gap between religious and nonreligious citizens is considerable in both France and Germany. For instance, only 30 percent of French citizens who attended church weekly preferred a Leftist party in 1988, compared to 70 percent among those who never went to church.

Religious involvement has little impact on voting patterns in Britain.

Because of the Erastian nature of the Anglican church, religious conflicts have not been a major factor in partisan politics since early in this century. Similarly, the partisan influence of religious feelings is limited in America.

The right-hand side of figure 8.3 compares the strength of party differences between secular and religious voters in seventeen nations. The secular/religious divide (average correlation is .22) is a more potent explanation of the vote than either class or religious denomination. Despite the paucity of explicitly religious issues and the lack of religious themes in most campaigns, religious attachments are often a strong predictor of party choice. Religion constitutes a hidden agenda of politics, tapping differences in values and moral beliefs that might not be articulated in a campaign but nevertheless influence voter choices. Indeed, there is a variety of evidence that indicates that moral or religious images continue to divide the parties in many Western democracies.[8]

Figure 8.3 also underscores the diversity of the religious cleavage across the four core nations. Both religious denomination and church attendance are significantly related to partisan preferences in Germany. The religious cleavage in France is based on the voting differences between devout Catholics and the nonreligious. In Britain there are only modest partisan differences by religious denominations or church attendance. The weakest social differences, however, are found in the United States, which ranks last among these democracies in voting differences by denomination or church attendance.

Despite this evidence of a strong relationship between religious values and partisan preferences, we might expect the religious cleavage to follow the same pattern of decline as the class cleavage. Social modernization may disrupt religious alignments in the same manner that social-class lines have blurred. Changing lifestyles, and religious beliefs, have decreased involvement in church activities and diminished the church as a focus of social (and political) activities. Most Western publics display a steady decline in religious involvement over the past fifty years (Ashford and Timms 1992; Franklin et al. 1992, chap. 1). In the Catholic nations of Europe, for instance, frequent church attendance has decreased by nearly half since the 1950s. Predominately Protestant countries, such as the United States and the nations of northern Europe, began with lower levels of church involvement but have followed the same downward trend. By definition, this secularization trend means that fewer voters are integrated into religious networks and exposed to the religious cues that can guide the vote.

Expectation about a decline in religious voting can be tested by observing the pattern of religious voting over time. Similar to the class voting index, figure 8.4 plots a religious voting index based on the difference in

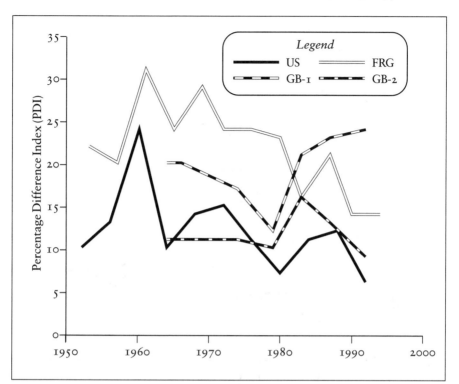

FIGURE 8.4

TRENDS IN DENOMINATIONAL VOTING

SOURCES: *United States, 1952–92,* American National Election Studies. *Great Britain, 1964–92,* British Election Studies. *Germany, 1953–92,* German Election Studies.

NOTE: Comparisons for the United States and Germany are between Protestants and Catholics. "GB-1" is a comparison of the Labour Party vote of Anglicans and Catholics; "GB-2" is a comparison of the Conservative Party vote of Anglicans and nonconformists.

party preferences between religious denominations. For instance, the differences in Conservative Party support between Anglicans, nonconformist Protestants, and Catholics have changed only slightly across British elections since 1959. Similarly, the gap in Leftist voting support between German Catholics and Protestants averaged in the 20- to 25-point range for much of the Federal Republic's existence. This gap has narrowed over the past decade, however, and the merger of a secular eastern electorate has further dampened religious voting differences since unification.

The partisan divisions between American Catholics and Protestants vary across elections; the religious cleavage intensified with John Kennedy's candidacy in 1960, while other elections display weak religious voting.

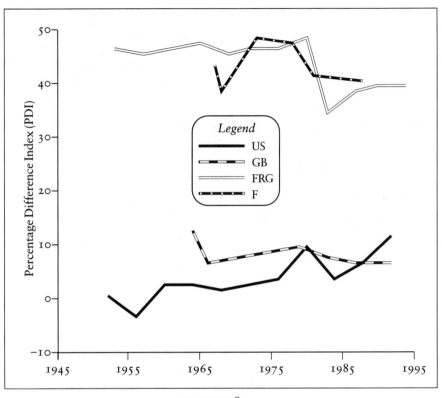

FIGURE 8.5
TRENDS IN RELIGIOUS VOTING

SOURCES: *United States,* 1952–92, American National Election Studies. *Great Britain,* 1964–92, British Election Studies. *Germany,* 1953–92, German Election Studies. *France,* 1967, Converse and Pierce study; 1968, Inglehart study; 1973–88, Eurobarometer studies.

NOTE: The values plotted are the differences between Leftist voting preferences of those who never attend church from those who attend weekly.

Overall, however, there is only a slight convergence in religious voting patterns in American congressional elections (see Abramson 1994, chap. 5, for evidence on presidential elections).

Figure 8.5 describes the long-term trends in voting differences between citizens who attend church weekly and those who seldom or never attend church. Religious involvement in France has a strong and persisting impact on voting preferences, averaging over a 40 percent difference in Leftist party support. The religious cleavage in Germany was relatively strong and stable until the 1980s; it is weaker in more recent elections, even those after unification. British party differences on the religious voting index are initially quite small and display little change over time. The recent attempts of the Republican Party to court religious voters has heightened religious differences over the past three U.S. elections—but the overall magnitude of this gap remains limited.

In summary, the time lines for religious voting (figures 8.4 and 8.5) do not show the marked dropoff found for class voting (figure 8.2, p. 172). Despite the paucity of explicitly religious issues and the lack of religious themes in most campaigns, religious characteristics can still be a strong predictor of party choice. Where religious voting patterns are weak, as in the United States and Britain, this reflects an ongoing characteristic of the party system rather than the recent erosion in religious voting. The stability of religious voting indices is all the more surprising because advanced industrial societies have undergone a secularization process during the past few decades. In addition, many of the societal changes that weakened the class cleavage presumably should have the same effect on religious voting.

Despite these appearances, the importance of religion as a basis of voting behavior is declining, but the pattern of decline is less obvious than for the class cleavage. Comparisons of the voting patterns of religious denominations examine only those voters with religious attachments. Individuals who attend church regularly remain well integrated into a religious network and maintain distinct voting patterns; however, there are fewer of these individuals today. By definition, the growing number of secular voters do not turn to religious cues to make their electoral choices. Thus as the number of individuals relying on religious cues decreases, the partisan significance of religious characteristics and their overall ability to explain voting choices have weakened.

Other Traditional Social Cleavages

The decline of sociologically based voting is most apparent for the class and religious cleavages, but a similar erosion of influence occurred for most other sociological characteristics.

Regional differences have occasionally flared up as a basis of political division. Britain, the United States, and now the unified Germany have seen regional interests polarize over the past generation. In other societies, such as Spain, Canada, and Italy, sharp regional differences from the past have persisted to the present (Rose 1982; Clarke et al. 1980). Yet in most nations region exerts only a minor influence on voting preferences. In most advanced industrial democracies, urban/rural residence displays only modest differences in voting patterns. Furthermore, these differences often have narrowed as the forces of modernization decreased the gap between urban and rural lifestyles.

The media have devoted considerable attention to debates about an emerging gender gap in voting patterns. Nevertheless, the available empirical evidence points to a narrowing of male/female voting differences in most Western party systems (De Vaus and McAllister 1989). In contemporary elections, gender is seldom a major explanation of voting patterns, although there are significant differences if one combines gender and life-status measures (Abramson et al. 1994, chap. 5).

One possible exception to the pattern of declining social cleavages is race and ethnicity. There are sharp racial differences in partisan support within the American electorate, and these differences have widened over time (Tate 1993; Abramson et al. 1994). For instance, 89 percent of African Americans gave their congressional votes to Democrats in 1992, compared to 56 percent of white Americans. The minority immigrant populations in Europe may produce similar differences in these party systems. Ethnicity has the potential to be a highly polarized cleavage because it may involve sharp social differences and strong feelings of group identity. Yet most societies remain ethnically homogeneous or nearly so, and this limits the impact of race or ethnicity as an overall predictor of vote choice. For example, the Cramer's V correlations for race and vote were modest in both the United States (.20) and Britain (.11) in their respective 1992 elections.

When all the evidence is assembled, one of the most widely repeated findings of modern electoral research is the declining value of the sociological model of voting behavior. Mark Franklin and his colleagues have compiled the most comprehensive evidence supporting this conclusion (Franklin et al. 1992). They tracked the ability of a set of social characteristics (including social class, education, income, religiosity, region, and gender) to explain partisan preferences. Across fourteen Western democracies, they found a marked and consistent erosion in the voting impact of social structure. The rate and timing of this decline varied across nations, but the end product is the same. In party systems such as the United States and Canada, where social-group-based voting was initially weak, the decline has occurred slowly. In other electoral systems, such as Germany, the Netherlands, and several Scandinavian nations, where sharp social divisions once structured the vote, the decline has been steady and dramatic. They conclude with the new "conventional wisdom" of comparative electoral research:

One thing that has by now become quite apparent is that almost all of the countries we have studied show a decline during our period in the ability of social cleavages to structure individual voting choice. (Franklin et al. 1992, 385)

The New Politics Cleavage

The weakening of party bonds based on Old Politics cleavages of class and religion creates the potential for new political cleavages to develop. Many citizens are open to new political appeals and might be mobilized by new issues and innovative programs.

The New Politics (or postmaterial) cleavage discussed in chapter 7 may provide the basis for a new partisan alignment. The erosion of Old Politics cleavages is at least partially the result of the increasing salience of New Politics issues (Knutsen 1987). Environmental protection, women's rights, and other social issues are not easily related to traditional class or religious alignments. Furthermore, New Politics issues attract the attention of the same social groups that are weakly integrated into the Old Politics cleavages: the young, the new middle class, the better educated, and the nonreligious.

The development of a new basis of partisan cleavage is a long and difficult process (Dalton et al. 1984, chap. 15). Groups must organize to represent New Politics voters and mobilize their support; the group bases of these issues are still ill-defined. The parties also must develop clear policy images on these issues. So far, many established parties have been hesitant to identify themselves with these issues because the stakes are still unclear and many parties are internally divided on the issues (Rohrschneider 1993b; Dalton 1994, chap. 9).

Despite these limiting factors, the potential partisan impact of the New Politics has increased in recent years. Small Green or New Left parties now compete in many West European democracies (Müller-Rommel 1989). In response, the established parties are being forced to become more receptive to the political demands of New Politics groups. For instance, in response to the inroads of British environmentalists, Margaret Thatcher developed a new appreciation for issues of global environmental change in the late 1980s. In the 1988 U.S. presidential election, George Bush claimed to be the environmental president.

Western publics also seem willing to base their voting choices on New Politics concerns. A cross-national survey in 1982 found that many Americans, Britons, and Germans said that a party's environmental policy would affect their voting decisions (Milbrath 1984). Many Europeans express a willingness to vote for an environmental party—the potential electorate for a green party rivals that of socialist and Christian democratic parties (Inglehart 1990, 266)!

Chapter 7 suggested that the initial structure of this new cleavage may focus on the conflict between New Politics and Old Politics adherents. To measure the present development of this cleavage, we used the material/postmaterial values index presented in chapter 5. Materialists emphasize security, stability, economic well-being, and other Old Politics objectives. Postmaterialists place greater stress on New Politics goals, such as participation, social equality, and environmental protection.

Table 8.4 displays the relationship between value priorities and party preferences using data from the 1990–91 World Values Survey. We find a consistent relationship between postmaterialism and support for Leftist parties. In every nation, postmaterialists favor the Left by a significant margin. The influence of changing values is especially clear for the New Left environmental parties in France and Germany. For example, 21 percent of French postmaterialists supported the Greens, compared to only 3 percent of materialists.

The overall size of these voting differences is considerable, often exceeding the Alford index scores for class or religious voting. There is a 44-percentage-point gap in support for the Labour Party between British materialists and postmaterialists. Sizable PDI scores also appear in Germany (35) and France (33), while value differences are less pronounced in the United States (17).

The extent of values-based voting in advanced industrial democracies is described in figure 8.6 (p. 190). As other studies have noted (Dalton 1994; Rohrschneider 1993), voting based on postmaterial issues is exceptionally strong in Denmark and the Netherlands (and Finland), where established political parties have responded to these new issue concerns. There is also a significant level of values-based voting in Britain, Germany, and France; in all three nations the influence of values exceeds class-voting differences (compare to figure 8.1, p. 171). Repeating a pattern we have seen for other cleavages, this political cleavage is only weakly tied to American electoral behavior.

Previous electoral research found that the extent of values polarization is partially a function of the diversity of choice in a party system; with more parties, it is more likely that one will choose to represent these concerns. In addition, affluence stimulates postmaterial concerns. This is most clearly evident in the East/West German comparisons. Postmaterial values have a significant influence on the voting choices of many Westerners (Cramer's V = .21). Eastern Germans, however, are less likely to possess postmaterial values and are still preoccupied with the economic problems

TABLE 8.4

VALUE PRIORITIES AND PARTY SUPPORT

(IN PERCENTAGES)

	Postmaterial	—	—	*Material*
United States				
Democrat	67	59	52	50
Republican	33	42	48	50
Total	100	101	100	100
Great Britain				
Labour	70	56	47	26
Liberal Democrats	9	8	3	5
Conservatives	22	37	50	70
Total	101	101	100	101
Germany				
Alliance 90/Greens	14	4	1	2
SPD	52	38	33	29
FDP	11	8	10	4
CDU/CSU	21	46	52	61
Other party	2	4	3	5
Total	100	100	99	101
France				
PC	6	6	5	3
Socialists	46	42	35	35
Other Left	3	1	0	2
Greens	21	17	12	3
UDF	15	20	30	29
RPR	6	8	16	19
National Front	3	6	3	10
Total	100	100	101	101

SOURCE: 1990–91 World Values Survey.

NOTE: Value priorities are measured with the twelve-item index (see chapter 5).

that accompanied German union. Thus values play a smaller role in their voting behavior (Cramer's V = .14) even though they are voting on the same party choices. Figure 8.6 also shows that the average weight of value priorities (Cramer's V = .17) now exceeds the weight of social class in party choice (figure 8.1).

Extensive long-term trend data are not available for the twelve-item index, but we can gain some idea of these trends by comparing results

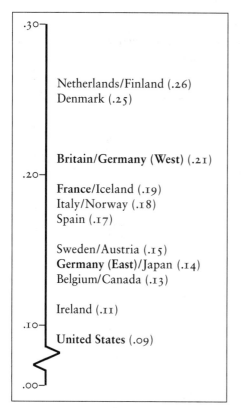

<table>
<tr><td>.30—</td><td></td></tr>
<tr><td></td><td>Netherlands/Finland (.26)
Denmark (.25)</td></tr>
<tr><td></td><td>Britain/Germany (West) (.21)</td></tr>
<tr><td>.20—</td><td></td></tr>
<tr><td></td><td>France/Iceland (.19)
Italy/Norway (.18)
Spain (.17)</td></tr>
<tr><td></td><td>Sweden/Austria (.15)
Germany (East)/Japan (.14)
Belgium/Canada (.13)</td></tr>
<tr><td></td><td>Ireland (.11)</td></tr>
<tr><td>.10—</td><td></td></tr>
<tr><td></td><td>United States (.09)</td></tr>
<tr><td>.00—</td><td></td></tr>
</table>

FIGURE 8.6

THE OVERALL LEVEL

OF VALUES VOTING, 1990

SOURCE: 1990–91 World Values Survey.

NOTE: Values in parentheses are Cramer's V correlations. Respondents without a party preference are excluded from the calculation of correlations.

from a survey in the 1970s to our current findings (figure 8.7). In contrast to class voting, which has been decreasing over time, the impact of the values cleavage has strengthened in most nations.[9] For example, the voting difference between materialists and postmaterialists in Germany was 22 percentage points in 1973; by 1990 this gap had increased to 35 points. Similarly, a more extensive analysis of German voting trends describes the growing impact of postmaterial values since 1970 (Dalton 1992). Thus the sources of partisan cleavage are changing in advanced industrial democracies —the long-standing Old Politics cleavage is being joined by a new values cleavage.

It would be a mistake to assume that the New Politics cleavage means an inexorable increase in support for Leftist parties. We have repeatedly stressed that the Old Politics cleavage will remain the major force structuring party competition for some time. Furthermore, the partisan consequences of the New Politics depends on how parties respond to these issues. For instance, while American environmentalists normally feel closer to the Democratic Party, an early Republican president (Teddy Roosevelt) nurtured the modern environmental movement and another Republican president (Richard Nixon) created the Environmental Protection Agency. Similarly, the conservative Kohl government has taken more forceful action than its SPD predecessors in dealing with acid rain, pollution of the North Sea, and other environmental problems in Germany. Environmentalism is not a Left or Right issue in the traditional Old Politics meaning of these terms; the partisan re-

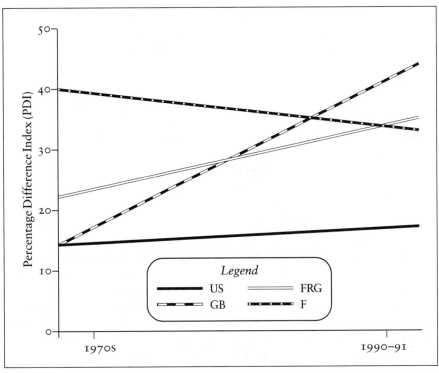

FIGURE 8.7

TRENDS IN NEW POLITICS VOTING

SOURCES: 1990–91 World Values Survey, 1973 European Communities study, and 1975 Political Action Survey.

NOTE: The values plotted are the Percentage Difference Index (PDI) correlating postmaterial value priorities with Leftist party preference.

sults of these issues depend on how parties respond (see Dalton 1994, chap. 9). The real lesson of these data is that public interests and party alignments are changing, and the party systems in advanced industrial democracies are affected by these trends.

The Transformation of Social Cleavages

This chapter has described a general decline in the social cleavages that have traditionally structured democratic party systems. Throughout much of this century, the dominant social cleavage in most democracies distinguished between working-class and middle-class parties. But the socioeconomic transformation of advanced industrial societies is weakening class alignments. Similarly, the number of churchgoers available for mobilization by confessional parties is decreasing, leading to a declining influence of religion on voting behavior. These class and religious trends are often accompanied by declines in the influence of regional, residential, and other social cleavages (Franklin et al. 1992).

Since there is a natural logic (and political rationale) to thinking about party systems as the representation of social-group differences, one response to the erosion of the Old Politics cleavage has been to search for potential new social bases of partisan alignment. Political scientists term this a *partisan realignment*. A realignment is defined as a significant shift in the group bases of party coalitions, usually resulting in a shift in the relative size of the parties' vote shares.

There have been many prior examples of realignment in Western party systems, in which one system of group cleavages was supplanted by another. For example, the 1930s New Deal realignment in the United States is traced to the entry of large numbers of blue-collar workers, Catholics, and blacks into the Democratic Party coalition. Realignments have been a regular feature of American electoral politics for well over a century and probably since the emergence of the first mass party coalitions around 1800 (Clubb et al. 1980). Similar historical realignments have occurred in European party systems, such as the Labour Party's rise in the early 1900s and the Gaullist realignment at the beginning of the French Fifth Republic.

Some analysts have suggested that New Politics issues—environmental protection, nuclear energy, sexual equality, consumer advocacy, and human rights—may provide the basis of a new partisan alignment. These issues are attractive to voters who are weakly integrated into the Old Politics alignments. Eventually, these interests may coalesce into broad social movements that will realign electorates and party systems. The growing partisan polarization along the New Politics value cleavage apparently supports this realignment thesis. Value priorities have become a more important influence on voting choice, and new parties have even formed to represent these perspectives.

I am not convinced that it is accurate to think of contemporary partisan politics in the same terms as past partisan realignments. The process of partisan realignment is normally based on clearly defined and highly cohesive social groups that can develop institutional ties to the parties and provide clear voting cues to their members (Zuckerman 1982). A firm group base provides a framework for parties to develop institutional ties to the groups and for groups to socialize and mobilize their members. There are few social groupings that might establish the basis of a New Politics realignment. Generational differences in support for New Politics parties might indicate an emerging New Politics cleavage, but age groups provide a very transitory basis for party alignment. Other potential group bases of partisan cleavage, such as education or alternative class categorizations, so far remain speculative, without firm evidence of realigning effects.

Postmaterial values are related to partisan preferences, but these values are unlikely to provide a basis for a new group-party alignment. Values are attitudinal states that define clusters of like-minded people. One cannot identify a postmaterialist in the same way that class, religion, or region provides a basis of personal identity and group mobilization. Indeed, postmaterial values are antithetical to such traditionally structured organizations as unions and churches. Instead, a vast array of single-issue groups and causes are developing to represent New Politics concerns: from the women's movement to peace organizations to environmental groups. These groups generally are loosely organized, with ill-defined memberships that wax and wane.

The lack of a group basis for the New Politics cleavage highlights another aspect of the new style of citizen politics. The kinds of cleavages that divide modern electorates and the kinds of groups they define are changing. Electoral politics is moving from cleavages defined by fixed social groups to value and issue cleavages that identify communities of like-minded individuals. The growing heterogeneity, secularization, and *embourgeoisement* of society is weakening social-group ties generally (Putnam 1995). Increasing levels of urbanization, social mobility, and geographic mobility work against the continued existence of exclusive, cohesive social groups. The revolutions in education and cognitive mobilization work against the dominance of disciplined, hierarchic, clientelist associations.

In summary, two kinds of changes are affecting contemporary electoral politics. First, the shift from the Old Politics toward the New Politics marks a transformation from social-group cleavages to issue-group cleavages. Because issue-group cleavages are more difficult to institutionalize or "freeze" via social-group ties to mass organizations, they may not be as stable. Because many of the new issue concerns involve only a narrow sector of the public, the linkage between these cleavages and party support may remain less clear. Some parties may adopt vague issue stands to avoid offending specific interests; other parties may cater to special interest groups and lose their broader programmatic image.

A second change affects all cleavages. Social grouping may still emerge to represent the changing political interests of contemporary electorates. Nevertheless, all forms of political mobilization are subject to the atomizing influences of advanced industrial societies. Interest mobilization along any cleavage dimension necessarily will be characterized by more complex, overlapping, and crosscutting associational networks; more fluid institutional loyalties; and looser, more egalitarian organizational structures. Thus the question is not whether labor union leaders support Leftist parties (they do) but whether the union rank and file will follow their leaders any more. This change affects the breadth, effectiveness, and stability of any future partisan alignment. Not only is the style of the Old Politics cleavage fading, but the prognosis for an eventual revival is not optimistic.

The new style of citizen politics therefore includes a more fluid and volatile pattern of party alignments. Political coalitions and voting patterns will lack the permanence of past class and religious cleavages. Without clear social cues, voting decisions will become a more demanding task for voters, and voting decisions will become more dependent on the individual beliefs and values of each citizen.

Notes

1. Most American voting studies analyze presidential elections. Because of the importance of candidate image, presidential elections reflect a different set of electoral forces than normally found in European parliamentary elections. To assure comparability of American and European results, the American data in this chapter are based on voting patterns in congressional elections.

2. We measured social class by the occupation of the head of the household, coded into the following categories: (1) old middle class, (2) new middle class, (3) working class, (4) farming, and (5) other occupation.

3. In the United States, this is the percentage voting Democratic in congressional elections; in Britain, the percentage voting Labour; in Germany, the percentage voting SPD of the two-party vote (SPD and CDU/CSU) before 1980, and the Leftist percentage in later elections; in France, the percentage voting for Leftist parties (PC, Socialist, and other Left).

4. Generational patterns in class voting also reinforce the argument for the long-term erosion in this cleavage (Dalton 1988, chap. 8; Abramson 1975; Franklin et al. 1992, chap. 19). Research generally finds strong and persisting relationships between class and vote among older generations. Among younger generations, these relationships are weak and decreasing.

5. The following table gives the percentage of the Leftist party vote among members of the new middle class at each election:

1962	1967	1968	1973	1978	1981	1988
42	40	42	54	51	57	56

6. Analyses in Dalton (1988) found that three-quarters of the public in each nation have a mix of middle-class and working-class characteristics across four measures of social status: occupation, income, education, and union membership.

7. Finland, Italy, and Belgium are relatively homogeneous societies in their

religious composition. The strong correlations in these nations arise because of differences between religious and nonreligious electors.

8. Laver and Hunt (1992) show that political elites in most Western democracies still perceive significant party differences on dimensions such as pro- and anticlerical and the permissiveness of social policy. Dalton (1992, 60) presented evidence that Germans can clearly differentiate the parties in their religious leanings, and these perceptions have grown more distinct over time (also Wessels 1994). Finally, chapter 7 found that the American public perceives a developing tie between the Republican Party and conservative religious groups.

9. Value polarization in France decreased between 1973 and 1990. This may be coincidental to these two surveys or may reflect the initial polarization over postmaterial issues that occurred as a result of the May Revolts. The French case deserves additional research.

9. Partisanship and Electoral Behavior

Social cleavages may provide the foundations of modern party systems, as seen in the two previous chapters, but this represents only the beginnings of the process of electoral decision making. Each election presents voters with choices among policy proposals and the qualities of the candidates. While social characteristics may be a basis for making decisions, citizens also hold a variety of political beliefs and values that affect their electoral calculus. Often, these considerations go beyond group ties or the perceptions derived from group cues.

Consequently, contemporary electoral research emphasizes the attitudes and values of voters as key factors in understanding electoral choice. Most elections are presented not as conflicts over historical cleavage alignments but as choices about more contemporary problems (which may reflect long-term conflicts). Citizens make judgments about which party best represents their interests, and these perceptions guide voting behavior. Attitudes toward the issues and candidates of an election are a necessary element in any realistic model of voting. Attitudes are also changeable, and their incorporation into a voting model helps explain variation in party results across elections.

A Sociopsychological Model of Voting

Faced by evidence on the limitations of a purely sociological approach to voting, early electoral researchers developed voting models to include psychological factors, such as attitudes and values, as influences on voting decisions and other political behavior. A team of researchers at the University of Michigan first formalized a model integrating both sociological and psychological influences on voting (Campbell et al. 1960, 1966). This sociopsychological model describes the voting process in terms of a *funnel of causality* (figure 9.1). At the wide mouth of the funnel are the socioeco-

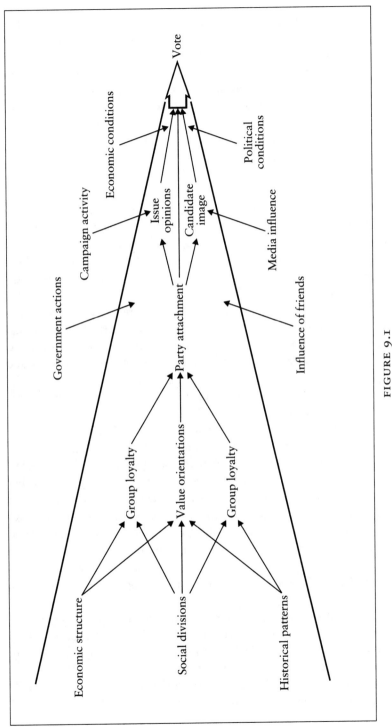

FIGURE 9.1

THE FUNNEL OF CAUSALITY PREDICTING VOTE CHOICE

nomic conditions that generate the broad political divisions of society: the economic structure, social divisions such as race or religion, and historical alignments such as the North-South division in the United States. These factors influence the structure of the party system (see chapter 7) but are far removed from the voting decisions of individual citizens.

As we move through the causal funnel, socioeconomic conditions influence group loyalties and basic value orientations. For instance, economic conditions may bond an individual to a social class, or regional identities may form in reaction to social and political inequalities. Thus social conditions are translated into attitudes that can directly influence the individual's political behavior.

The causal funnel narrows further as group loyalties and value priorities are linked to more explicitly political attitudes. Angus Campbell and his colleagues explained individual voting decisions primarily in terms of three attitudes: partisanship, issue opinions, and candidate images. These beliefs are most proximate to the voting decision and therefore have a direct and very strong impact on the vote.

Although the funnel of causality appears simple by contemporary standards of social science, it represented a major conceptual breakthrough for voting research. This model provides a useful heuristic device for organizing the factors that potentially influence voting behavior. To understand voting decisions, one has to recognize the causal relationship between the many factors involved. The wide end of the funnel represents broad social conditions that structure political conflict but are temporally and psychologically far removed from the actual voting decision. As we move through the funnel, attention shifts to factors that are explicitly political, involve individual beliefs, and are more proximate to voting choice. Social characteristics are therefore seen as an important aspect of the voting process, but their primary influence is in forming political attitudes; most of the direct impact of social characteristics on voting is mediated by attitudinal dispositions. Attitudes, in turn, depend on the group loyalties and value orientations of the individual, as well as external stimuli such as friends, media, government actions, and the activities of the campaign. There is a place in the funnel of causality for each element of the voting process, and we can understand each element in relation to the others.

In addition to the heuristic value of the model, the sociopsychological approach also very successfully predicts voting choices. Attitudes toward the parties, issues, and candidates of an election are psychologically very close to the actual voting decision and therefore are strongly related to voting choices. In fact, the model can predict voting decisions more accurately than individuals can predict their own behavior (Campbell et al. 1960, 74)!

The sociopsychological model has defined a paradigm of voting behavior that has structured how we think about elections and how researchers analyze the voting process. Researchers have tested and applied the basic elements of the model in a variety of nations. This chapter examines partisan attachments as a central concept in the sociopsychological model of voting. Then, chapter 10 examines how specific issue opinions provide another element in this model.

Partisan Attitudes

The sociopsychological model focused on the specific issue opinions and candidate evaluations that determine voting behavior. Yet it soon became clear that many citizens determined their political beliefs through feelings of party loyalty. As one elderly voter once commented to me while waiting to vote, "I vote for the candidate and not the party. It just seems like the Democrats always choose the best candidate." Many voters begin each electoral season with already-formed partisan predispositions. These partisan loyalties are a central element in an individual's belief system, serving as a source of political cues for other attitudes and behaviors.

The Michigan researchers describe these party attachments as a sense of *party identification,* similar to identifications with a social class, religious denomination, or other social group. Party identification is a long-term, affective, psychological identification with one's preferred political party (Campbell et al. 1960, chap. 6; Miller 1991).[1] These party attachments are distinct from voting preferences, which explains why some Americans vote for the presidential candidate of one party while expressing loyalty to another party. Indeed, it is the conceptual independence of voting and party identification that initially gives the latter its theoretical significance.[2] Partisanship is the psychological basis of stable party alignments and influences other attitudes and behaviors. The discovery of party identification is one of the most significant findings of public opinion research. The concept has become a key to understanding citizen political behavior.

The export of the party identification concept to the study of public opinion in other democracies has yielded mixed results (Butler and Stokes 1974; Baker et al. 1981; Budge et al. 1976; Converse and Pierce 1986, chap. 2). Often the problem is finding an equivalent measure of partisanship in multiparty systems or in nations where the term *partisanship* holds different connotations for the voters. The concept of a partisan "independent" is not common in other electoral systems, as it is in the United States. Thus researchers could not simply translate the American party identification question into French or German; they had to find a functional equivalent for partisan attachments.[3] Still most studies agree that voters hold some sort of party allegiances that endure over time and strongly influence other opinions.

The Learning of Partisanship

The importance of party identification for understanding political behavior partially results from the early origins of party attachments. Socialization studies find that children develop basic partisan orientations at a very early age, often during the primary school years (Hess and Torney 1967, 90). Children learn party loyalties before they can understand what the party labels stand for, a process similar to the development of many other group ties. These early party attachments then provide a reference structure for future political learning (which often reinforces early partisan biases).

The early-life formation of party identities means that parents play a central role in the socialization of these values. The transmission of partisanship within the family can be seen by comparing the party identifications of parents and their children. A cross-national socialization study interviewed parents and their children to compare their opinions directly (table 9.1). These researchers found relatively high levels of partisan agreement within American, British, and German families.[4] In the United States, for example, 70 percent of the 16- to 20-year-old children of Democratic parents were themselves Democrats, and 54 percent of Republican parents had Republican children. Less than 10 percent of the children actually favored the party in opposition to their parents. These levels of partisan agreements are similar to those found in a larger and more representative study of American adolescents (Jennings and Niemi 1973). The British and German surveys also showed that the party attachments of these parents are frequently re-created in the values of their offspring. Measures of partisan transfer are not available for French family pairs, but Left/Right ideological orientations display strong generational agreement (Percheron and Jennings 1981). Parents apparently have a strong formative influence on the partisan values of their children, even before most children become active in the political process.

There are many reasons why parents are so successful in transmitting their partisanship to their children. Partisan loyalties are formed when parents are the dominate influence in a child's life, and the exposure to partisan cues from the parent is common. Parties are very visible and important institutions in the political process, and virtually all political discussion includes some partisan content: we identify candidates and judge them by their party affiliation; we evaluate policies by their party sponsor. It does not take long for a child to identify the parents' partisan leanings from

TABLE 9.I

THE TRANSMISSION OF PARENTAL PARTISANSHIP

(IN PERCENTAGES)

	United States		
	Parental party preference		
	Democrat	*Republican*	*Independent*
Child's party preference			
Democrat	70	25	40
Republican	10	54	20
Independent	20	21	40
Total	100	100	100
N	128	77	30

	Great Britain			
	Parental party preference			
	Labour	*Liberal*	*Conservative*	*None*
Child's party preference				
Labour	51	17	6	29
Liberal	8	39	11	6
Conservative	1	11	50	6
None	40	33	33	59
Total	100	100	100	100
N	83	18	54	17

	West Germany			
	Parental party preference			
	SPD	*FDP*	*CDU/CSU*	*None*
Child's party preference				
SPD	53	8	14	19
FDP	4	59	1	3
CDU/CSU	9	—	32	12
None	34	33	53	66
Total	100	100	100	100
N	68	12	78	67

SOURCE: Political Action Survey.

their reactions to television news and statements in family discussions. Furthermore, most parents have strong party attachments that endure across elections; children are thus exposed to consistent and continuous cues on which party their parents prefer. For example, one of my university colleagues was openly proud that he had conditioned his preschool child to groan each time a specific former president appeared on television. Either through explicit reinforcement or subconscious internalization of parental values, many children learn of their parents' partisan preferences and take them as their own.

Once individuals establish party ties, later partisan experiences often follow these early predispositions. Thus electoral experience normally reinforces these partisan tendencies because most citizens cast ballots for their preferred party.[5] The accumulated experience of voting for the same party and the political agreement that leads to such partisan regularity both tend to strengthen partisan ties. Consequently, researchers generally find that partisan loyalties strengthen with age or, more precisely, with continued electoral support of the same party (Converse 1969, 1976).[6]

Figure 9.2 displays this increasing strength of party identification with age.[7] Regardless of which party one supports, party bonds are stronger among older age groups. Most of the public in the United States and Britain develop a strong sense of party identity by middle age, which continues to strengthen through the rest of the life cycle. The strength of French partisanship also increases with age, but the level of partisanship is limited by the general instability of the French party system. French parties frequently change their names or political orientations, and this impedes the development of strong party attachments as occurs in stable party systems such as the United States and Britain.

At one time, the Federal Republic of Germany was an exception to this general pattern (Baker et al. 1981, chap. 9; Norpoth 1983). Prewar generations had spent a significant portion of their lives under nondemocratic regimes, or the turbulent Weimar Republic, that were not conducive to the development of strong party ties. With the maturation of German democracy, however, nearly all western voters today were raised under the present democratic system. Thus we now find the normal increase in partisanship with age among Westerners. The current German anomaly involves eastern Germans. Residents of communist East Germany obviously did not have the same opportunity as their western cousins to develop attachments to the democratic parties of the West. Their experience with the current party system dates only to 1990. Thus residents of eastern Germany display significantly fewer strong partisans compared to the West. Furthermore, partisanship does not appreciably strengthen with age among

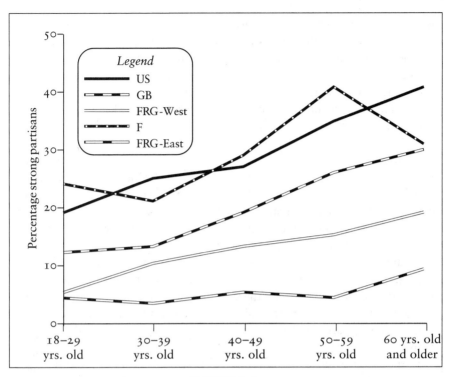

FIGURE 9.2

THE STRENGTH OF PARTISAN ATTACHMENTS BY AGE

SOURCES: *United States,* 1992 American National Election Study. *Britain,* 1992 British Election Study. *Germany,* September 1994 German Election Study. *France,* Eurobarometer 30.

NOTE: Each nation uses a differently worded question on partisanship, so direct comparisons of the level of partisan attachments cross-nationally are not appropriate.

Easterners. As eastern Germans accumulate more experience with democratic electoral politics, the life-cyle pattern of partisan learning should become more apparent in future elections.

Partisan attachments thus are learned early in life, become deeply embedded in a child's belief system, and are normally reinforced by later partisan experiences. Partisanship may change in reaction to later life experiences, but these attachments are not easily altered once they have formed. For example, party identification is one of the most stable political attitudes, far exceeding the stability of opinions on several long-standing national issues: race relations, economic programs, and foreign policy. Only issues that touch strongly held moral values, such as opinions on abortion, rival the stability of partisanship (Converse and Markus 1979). Additional evidence of long-term partisan constancy comes from a panel study of high school seniors and their parents. M. Kent Jennings and Greg Markus (1984) found that 78 percent of the adult sample and 58 percent of the adolescent sample did not change their partisan ties across one of the most turbulent political periods in recent American history (1965–73).

Evidence from other nations mirrors this pattern. Party attachments are significantly more stable than other political beliefs across a two-year British panel survey (Dalton 1988, chap. 9). On the average, between 80 and 90 percent of the British public retain constant party ties from one election to the next. Hilde Himmelweit and her colleagues (1981) interviewed a sample of British middle-class males over a twelve-year period. They found that a clear majority of voters supported the same party in 1959 and 1974; conversions between Labour and Conservative partisans were exceedingly rare. Longitudinal studies in Germany have found that partisanship is a very stable political attitude (Norpoth 1978). The limited evidence for France shows that below the surface of substantial turbulence in the actions of party leaders, there is considerable continuity in the partisan orientations of the French public (Converse and Pierce 1986, chap. 3). The process of partisan change moves slowly in most established party systems.

Important evidence on the relative permanence of partisan attitudes comes from comparing the stability of partisanship and voting preferences (table 9.2). For instance, reinterviews with the same American voters in 1972 and 1976 found that 93 percent had stable party identifications, while only 75 percent had stable congressional voting preferences. Moreover, when there was some variability, more voters maintain a stable party identification while changing their vote (22 percent) than the other way around (4 percent). Party preferences are also more stable than voting preferences in Britain and Germany, but this difference is more modest than in the United States (LeDuc 1981; Norpoth 1978; cf. Heath and Pierce 1992). In Europe there is a greater tendency for partisanship and vote to travel together; when one changes, so does the other (Holmberg 1994; cf. Converse and Pierce 1986, chap. 3). Because of their limited amount of election opportunities, Europeans are less likely to distinguish between long-term partisanship and current voting preferences. Still partisanship generally is a political orientation that continues over time, even in the face of vote defections.

In sum, partisanship is a core element in an individual's belief system. This orientation is formed early in life and thus may condition later life learning. It is easy to see why researchers give it a central role in a sociopsychological model of voting choice.

TABLE 9.2

THE RELATIVE STABILITY OF PARTY ATTACHMENTS
AND VOTE (IN PERCENTAGES)

_____ United States, 1972–76 _____

Party identification	Vote	
	Stable	Variable
Stable	71	22
Variable	4	3
N = 539		

_____ Great Britain, 1970–74 _____

Party identification	Vote	
	Stable	Variable
Stable	75	10
Variable	5	10
N = 795		

_____ West Germany, 1976 _____

Party identification	Vote	
	Stable	Variable
Stable	71	22
Variable	4	3
N = 707		

SOURCES: LeDuc (1981, 261); Berger (504).

NOTE: The tables present percentages of the total N based on those who were voters and identified with a political party at each time point. American and British results are based on changes between two elections; West German data are based on changes during a three-wave 1976 election panel.

The Impact of Partisanship

In sports, loyalty to a specific team helps one know whom to root for and which players to admire, and it motivates individuals to participate in support of their team. People often develop such ties early in life, and they endure through the ups and downs of the franchise. Moreover, one's loyalty to the Dodgers (in my case), strengthens with repeated trips to root on my team, even if they lose.

It is the same with feelings of partisan attachment (Fiorina 1990; Miller 1976; Borre and Katz 1973). The funnel of causality implies that partisanship provides valuable political cues on how citizens can judge the specific candidates and issues of a campaign. A policy advocated by one's party is more likely to meet favor than one advocated by the other team. Moreover, in comparison to social-group cues such as class and religion, party attachments are relevant to a much broader range of political phenomena because parties are so central to the political process. Issues and events frequently are presented to the public in partisan terms, as the parties take positions on the political questions of the day or react to the statements of other political actors. Thus reliance on partisanship may be the ultimate example of the satisficing model of politics.

The *Washington Post* performed an interesting experiment that illustrates the power of partisanship as a political cue (Morris 1995). A question on a fictitious government act was included on one of its opinion surveys. One form of the question included reference to either Clinton's or the Republicans' position on the issue, and another form discussed the act without any partisan cues. The survey found that the number of people expressing an opinion on this act increased when a partisan cue was given. Moreover, there were dramatic partisan effects: Democrats were far more likely to oppose the fictitious act when told Clinton wanted repeal; Republicans disproportionately opposed the act when told the Republicans in Congress wanted repeal.

An example from the 1992 American National Election Study demonstrates the power of partisanship to shape even nonpartisan opinions. Before the 1992 U.S. elections, the survey asked the public to judge whether the national economy would improve or worsen over the next twelve months. With George Bush in the White House, Republicans were more optimistic about the nation's future than Democrats by a 15 percent margin. After the election, with Clinton entering the presidency, Republican optimism waned and Democrats became more positive about the economy by a 29 percent margin.

This reversal of the relationship between preelection and postelection surveys illustrates the power of partisanship to shape citizen perceptions of the political world. Partisanship has an even stronger influence on opinions that are more closely linked to the parties, such as evaluations of governmental performance and candidate images (Abramson et al. 1994, chap. 8; Shanks and Miller 1990; Erikson and Tedin 1995, chap. 3). Partisans root for the players (candidates) on their team and save their catcalls for the opponents.

Party ties also perform a mobilizing function. Just like sports loyalties, attachment to a political party draws an individual into the political process to support is or her side. Voting turnout and participation in campaign activities are generally higher among strong party identifiers (chapter 2). The 1992 American Election Study, for example, found that turnout was 17 percent higher among strong partisans than among independents, although Perot's populist campaign mobilized an unusual number of nonpartisans. In addition, strong partisans were more likely to have tried to influence others, to display campaign paraphernalia, to attend a rally, or to give money to a candidate in the 1992 campaign. Partisanship functions in a similar way in Britain. Strong partisans voted at a slightly higher rate in the 1992 House of Commons election and were more likely to have attended a campaign meeting or read the party brochures on the election. While 92 percent of strong British partisans cared which party (team) won the election, only 62 percent of weak partisans shared their concerns.

The cue-giving function of partisanship is strongest for voting behavior. Partisanship means that voters enter an election with a predisposition to support their preferred party. Philip Converse (1966) described partisanship as the basis for a "normal vote"—the vote expected when other factors in the election are evenly balanced. If other factors come into play, such as issue positions or candidate images, their influence can be measured by their ability to cause defections from standing partisan commitments. For the unsophisticated voter, a long-term partisan loyalty and repeated experience with one's preferred party provides a clear and low-cost cue for voting. Even for the sophisticated citizen, a candidate's party affiliation normally signifies a policy program that serves as the basis for reasonable electoral choice.

Researchers generally find a close relationship between partisanship and voting in parliamentary elections (Holmberg 1994). Even with multiple parties to choose from, only 10 percent of British partisans defected from their preferred party in the 1992 election. Defection is also low in Germany, since one of the votes that citizens cast is directly for a party list. In 1994, 11 percent of partisans in western Germany defected. The limited voting opportunities in most European nations tend to lessen the separation between partisanship and vote.

The American elector, on the other hand, "has to cope simultaneously with a vast collection of partisan candidates seeking a variety of offices at federal, state, and local levels; it is small wonder that he becomes conscious of a generalized belief about his ties to a party" (Butler and Stokes 1969, 43). Thus the separation between attitudes and behavior is most noticeable in American elections, especially when voters are asked to make a series of choices for local, state, and federal offices (Beck et al. 1992). In highly visible and politicized presidential elections, candidate images and issue appeals have the potential to counteract partisan preferences, and thus party defections are common in these elections. The success of Republican presidential candidates in the 1980s occurred because they attracted defectors from the Democratic majority. Even in the two-party contest of 1988, for instance, more than 12 percent of American partisans cast presidential votes contrary to their party identification.

A similar situation exists in France. The two-candidate runoff in French presidential elections is decided by the size of the vote the candidates can attract from parties other than their own (Boy and Mayer 1993). In French parliamentary elections, however, voting choice more closely conforms to standing partisan preferences. In summary, when partisan attachments exist, they are routinely among the strongest predictors of voting behavior in virtually all advanced industrial democracies.

Partisan Dealignment

Partisanship is a central variable in the study of many different aspects of citizen political behavior. For the individual citizen, partisanship is an enduring and very useful source of political guidance. For the political system, widespread party attachments promote continuity in party alignments and reinforce the stability of the political process.

Thus it came as some surprise when party ties began to weaken in many democracies during the 1970s. At first, the signs of partisan decline were difficult to detect against the normal background of partisan change between elections. Gradually, the evidence of real change became more obvious. In many nations, new political parties emerged to challenge the established partisan order. The fluctuations in party fortunes between elections increased in magnitude (Crewe and Denver 1985). Political observers frequently discussed the crisis of confidence facing parties and party systems. In the past decade, these doubts have intensified.

Partisan change is a normal element of the electoral process, and periods of heightened partisan volatility and fragmentation dot the electoral histories of most democracies. In this instance, however, partisan decline apparently reflects a more fundamental change in citizen political behavior. Many advanced industrial democracies are experiencing a process of *partisan dealignment* (Dalton et al. 1984). Voters are not simply defecting from their preferred party in one or two elections. Instead, there is a continuing erosion in partisan loyalties.

The weakening of party ties first became apparent in the United States (figure 9.3). American partisanship was extremely stable from the 1950s to

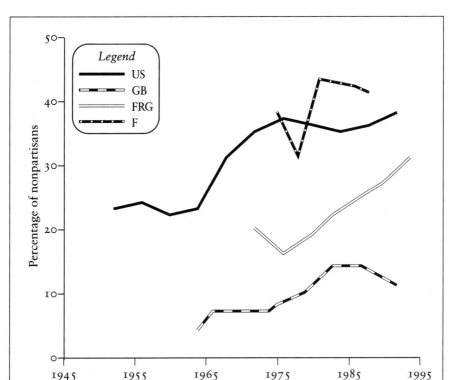

FIGURE 9.3

THE PERCENTAGE OF NONPARTISANS

SOURCES: *United States, 1952–92*, American National Election Studies. *Great Britain, 1964–92*, British Election Studies. *Germany, 1953–94*, German Election Studies. *France,* Eurobarometer studies.

NOTE: German data for 1990 and 1994 are from western Germany.

the early 1960s; the percentage of party identifiers remained within the 70–75 percent range, and less than a quarter of the public claimed to be "independents," without standing partisan ties. Partisan loyalties began to weaken after the 1964 election. By the 1980s, more than a third of the electorate were nonpartisans. Perot's candidacy pushed the percentage of independents up to 39 percent in 1992 (Wattenberg 1996; Abramson et al. 1994, chap. 8).

An almost identical pattern of declining party ties has occurred in Britain. Because of the traditions of the British party system, and the format of the British partisanship questionnaire, fewer Britons claim to be nonpartisans. In the 1964 British election study, only 4 percent claimed to lack a standing partisan preference. By the 1980s, the number of nonpartisans had trebled to roughly 14 percent. Questions asking about the strength of attachments among partisans displays a similar pattern. More than 40 percent of the British public were strong partisans during the late 1960s. Less than 20 percent of Britons claim to be strong partisans in the most recent elections.

Germany initially deviated from the pattern of partisanship found in other advanced industrial democracies. Researchers found a large increase in partisanship between 1961 and 1976, as West Germans developed initial commitments to the postwar party system (Baker et al. 1981, chap. 8; Norpoth 1983). Over the past decade, however, evidence of dealignment has became clear. Nonpartisans numbered only 16 percent of the public in 1976; by 1994 they accounted for more than 30 percent among Westerners. The extent of partisanship is even lower among Easterners, since they lack prior partisan experience and are just beginning to develop party attachments (Kaase and Klingemann 1994). In September 1994, 42 percent of eastern Germans claimed to lack any party ties.

The series of comparable French survey data is much shorter (for a discussion of French long-term trends, see Lewis-Beck 1984). Because of the volatility of the French party system, a relatively large number claim to lack any standing partisan commitment. Since the 1970s, the number of partisans may have increased further, although the evidence is less certain than for the other three nations (e.g., Boy and Mayer 1993, chap. 9). Longitudinal data from national election studies in the Netherlands, Italy, Scandinavia, and Australia display a similar erosion in the strength of party attachments over the past decades (Dalton et al. 1984; McAllister 1992; Holmberg 1994; cf. van Deth and Janssen 1994 for an opposing view).

Some scholars have argued that the decline in party identification in the United States has been vastly exaggerated. For instance, Bruce Keith and his colleagues (1992) maintained that Americans have merely become hesitant to express their partisan loyalties. According to these researchers, the independents who lean toward the Democrats or Republicans are not an uncommitted and unmobilized bloc but are largely "closet" partisans. Carsten Zelle (1995) has also questioned whether German partisanship has truly decreased.[8]

Even if researchers debate the precise trends in the party identification questions, the evidence of partisan dealignment is visible in a range of different aspects of electoral behavior (Wattenberg 1991, chap. 2). For instance, split-ticket voting has risen in recent American elections, as weakened party attachments lead fewer voters to cast straight-party ballots

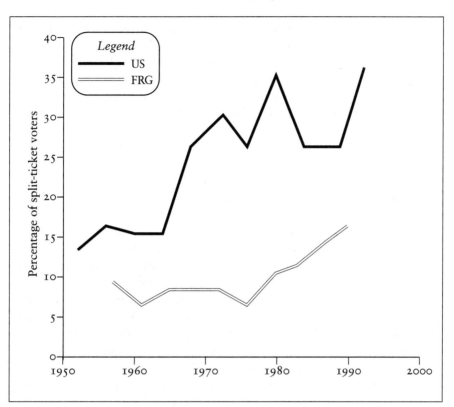

FIGURE 9.4

THE GROWTH OF SPLIT-TICKET VOTING

SOURCES: *United States,* 1952–92, American National Election Studies. *Germany,* Statistisches Bundesamt (various years).

NOTE: For the United States, votes for third-party presidential candidates are counted as split-ticket voting. German data for 1990 are from western Germany.

(figure 9.4). In the 1960s, less than a sixth of Americans split their ballots between a presidential candidate of one party and a congressional candidate of another. By the 1970s and 1980s this had risen to between a quarter and a third of the electorate. With Perot's third-party candidacy in 1992, 36 percent of Americans split their ballots. Split-ticket voting has also increased dramatically between House and Senate votes (Stanley and Niemi 1994, 146). Similarly, Germans can select different parties with their candidate votes (*Erststimme*) and party votes (*Zweitstimme*). Up until the late 1970s, less than 10 percent of all voters split their ballots. This percentage has increased over time. In 1990, 16 percent of western Germans split their two votes between different parties.

The decrease in voting turnout in the United States, Britain, and Germany can at least partially be traced to weakened partisanship. Furthermore, instead of making predetermined voting choices, there is some evidence that more electors are delaying their voting decision until later in the campaign. The erosion of partisanship also has led to an increased volatility of voting patterns. Although most voters continue to support the same party over time, the number of floating voters is increasing in these party systems (Wattenberg 1996; Dalton 1992, 1988, chap. 9). Partisanship was once a stable guidepost for citizen political behavior, and now fewer individuals are following its guidance.

There are several explanations for the spreading pattern of partisan dealignment. At least initially, the decline of partisanship was linked to political events and political crises. In the United States, the dramatic events of the 1970s initially turned many young people away from political parties. The antipartisan sentiments stirred by the Vietnam war, Watergate, and similar crises kept new voters from developing the early-life partisan attachments that could build over time (Beck 1984). The student protests in Europe and a seemingly growing number of party scandals may have had a similar effect in these nations.

The cross-national breadth of dealignment trends suggests that more than a series of coincidental political crises lie behind these trends. The sources of partisan dealignment more likely reflect broader patterns of social and political change in advanced industrial democracies. The declining role of parties as political institutions seems to play a key part of this process. Many of the parties' traditional political functions have been taken over by other institutions. A myriad of special-interest groups and single-issue lobbies have developed in recent years, and political parties have little hope of representing all these groups. Instead, these groups press their interests without relying on partisan channels. Party leaders are even losing some control over the selection of elected party representatives. The most advanced example is the United States, where the expansion of open primaries and nonpartisan elections has undermined the parties' hold on recruitment. The British Labour Party has experienced a similar shift in nomination power away from the party in Parliament to party conventions and local constituency groups. In 1994, the German SPD selected its chancellor candidate through a mail ballot of its members. These and other developments lessen the importance of parties in the political process and therefore weaken the significance of parties as political reference points.

Changes in the mass media also contribute to dealignment trends. The mass media are assuming many of the information functions that political parties once controlled. Instead of learning about an election at a campaign rally or from party canvassers, voters now find their primary sources of campaign information in television and newspapers (see chapter 2). Furthermore, the content of the mass media has changed to downplay the importance of political parties. Martin Wattenberg (1996, chap. 6) has shown that the American media have shifted the campaign focus away from the political parties toward the candidates. A similar personalization of campaign coverage is occurring in Europe.

Partisan dealignment is also encouraged by the failure of parties to deal successfully with contemporary political issues (Lawson and Merkl 1988; Zelle 1995). On the one hand, contemporary parties are struggling with problems of maintaining social services in the face of mounting government deficits. Some of the economic and welfare issues traditionally associated with the class cleavage have not been fully resolved. On the other hand, the new issues of advanced industrial societies often appear unsuited for mass political parties. Many of these issues, such as nuclear energy, minority rights, or local environmental problems, are too narrow to affect mass partisan alignments on their own. The rise of single-issue interests does not translate well into partisan attachments because of the uncertain electoral impact of these issues and the difficulty of accommodating these issues within large political coalitions. In the United States, this has led to a proliferation of citizen interest groups and direct-action politics; in Europe this has spawned similar groups as well as a variety of small parties on the Left and Right (Müller-Rommel and Pridham 1991). Thus political parties have lessened their critical programmatic function of aggregating and articulating political interests.

Finally, changes in the characteristics of contemporary electorates may contribute to the dealignment trend. We examine this possibility in detail in the following section.

Cognitive Mobilization and Apartisans

The early literature on partisanship held a negative view of nonpartisans (Campbell et al. 1960). Nonpartisans were at the margins of the electoral process; they were uninvolved in elections and unsophisticated about politics. If the growth of independents merely expanded the numbers of these nonpartisans, it would be a negative development for the contemporary electoral process.

Part of the dealignment thesis, however, holds that advanced industrial societies are producing a new type of independent. The process of cognitive mobilization has increased voters' political sophistication and their ability to deal with the complexities of politics (chapter 2). At the same time, the growing availability of political information through the media reduces the costs of making informed decisions. Thus the functional need for partisan cues to guide voting behavior, evaluate political issues, and mobilize political involvement is decreasing for a growing sector of society.

This argument builds on W. Phillips Shively's (1979) research, which suggests that the development of party ties partially depends on the functional value of partisanship. Shiveley maintains that voters develop party identifications as a shortcut to help them handle difficult and often confusing political decisions. Relying on cues coming from a party identification often lessens the costs of political involvement.

Russell Dalton (1984) used this theory to suggest that the process of cognitive mobilization in advanced industrial societies is decreasing the proportion of the public who need to rely on partisanship to guide their political behavior. Some voters remain oriented to politics based on their partisan attachments. In addition, cognitive mobilization produces another group of politically interested and well-educated voters who orient themselves to politics on their own. The combination of both traits defines a typology of four types of citizens (figure 9.5). *Apoliticals* are neither attached to a political party nor cognitively mobilized; this group conforms to the independents originally described by Campbell and his colleagues (1960, 143–45). *Ritual partisans* are mobilized into politics primarily by their strong party attachments, and are not cognitively mobilized. *Cognitive partisans* are highly ranked on both mobilization dimensions. They have strong party attachments, and they are psychologically involved in politics even when party cues are lacking.

Apartisans are the "new independents." It is vitally important to distinguish apartisans from traditional independents (apoliticals). Apartisans are cognitively mobilized, which implies high levels of political involvement and sophistication, though these citizens remain unattached to any political party.

Dalton (1984) found that apartisans are concentrated among the young, the better educated, and postmaterialists. Other research shows that the continuing development of advanced industrial societies has both increased the proportion of apartisans within contemporary publics and shifted the ratio of ritual and cognitive partisans. Data from the American National Election Studies find that the number of apartisans has more than doubled over the past forty years—to a quarter of the electorate.[9] In addition, the number of cognitive partisans has grown slightly, while the proportion of ritual partisans has decreased by more than half. Ronald

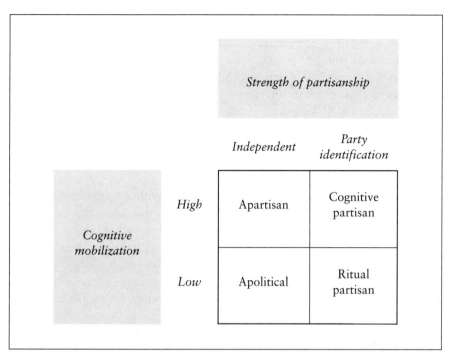

FIGURE 9.5
PATTERNS OF POLITICAL MOBILIZATION

Inglehart found that the percentage of apartisans in Europe increased significantly over a single decade (1976–87) (Inglehart 1990, 366). Furthermore, Inglehart found sharp differences in the percentage of apartisans across European generations, which suggests that the number of apartisans will continue to grow. Sören Holmberg's (1994) longitudinal analyses of Swedish partisanship yields similar findings.

The recognition of apartisans has several implications for contemporary political behavior. Apartisans have the political resources to follow the complexities of politics, and they are free of affective party ties. Thus these new independents are less consistent in their voting patterns because voting behavior is not dependent on long-standing party predispositions. This group also should inject more issue voting into elections and demand that candidates are more responsive to public opinion.

Apartisans should press for an expansion of citizen input beyond the narrow channel of elections and other party-related activities. The political skills of apartisans enable them to organize effective citizen-action groups, citizen lobbies, protest demonstrations, and other unconventional political activities. The nonpartisan and issue-oriented characteristics of these activities make them ideal participation modes for apartisans.

Finally, ongoing processes of socioeconomic change gradually should increase the number of apartisans. The actions of parties in specific elections may hasten or retard this process in the short term. Nevertheless, the evidence suggests a long-term trend toward partisan dealignment in advanced industrial societies.

The Consequences of Dealignment

What is stunning about partisan dealignment, as with the weakening of the sociological model, is the relative simultaneity of political trends in various nations. Long-term sources of partisan preferences—social characteristics and partisanship—are weakening in most advanced industrial societies. In a single nation such developments might be linked to the specific trials and tribulations of the parties. When a pattern appears across a wide variety of nations, however, it suggests that the causes are common to advanced industrial societies. Indeed, the linkage between the process of cognitive mobilization and partisan dealignment seems to represent yet another feature of the new style of citizen politics.

Weakening party bonds have real consequences for the operation of the political process. For instance, erosion of the long-term bonds between voters and parties creates the potential for greater volatility in results from election to election. David Butler illustrated this pattern for Britain: the average fluctuation in Gallup polls measuring Conservative Party support was 7.5 percent for the 1955–64 period and 20.6 percent for the 1985–92 period (Butler 1995, 71). This volatility increases the unpredictability of elections. The political parties may lament the loss of their stable and predictable voting bases. But the increasing uncertainty of electoral outcomes may also encourage parties and candidates to be more responsive to voter interests.

Weakened party-line voting also may have contributed to the unprecedented level of split-party control of both the federal and state governments in the United States (Brody et al. 1994). In 1988 only 40 percent of the states had one party in control of both legislative houses and the governor's office (see Fiorina 1992). Not since the formation of the Republican Party in the 1850s can one find any comparable split in the history of state party politics. Similarly, between 1981 and 1986 different parties controlled the House and Senate for the first time since 1916. Most visible, of course, is the division in partisan control of the presidency and the Congress since 1952. From 1952 to 1996 the same party controlled the presidency and the House for just sixteen out of forty-four years. The culmination of these trends was the dramatic shift in partisan control of the U.S. Congress following the 1994 elections. After more than forty years of Democratic domination, the House fell to the Republicans without a corresponding realignment in partisan attachments.

The Federal Republic of Germany also has a federal system, and the same pattern is found there. For the first twenty years of the FRG's history, the same party coalition controlled the Bundestag (the directly elected lower house of parliament) and the Bundesrat (which represents the majority of state governments). From 1976 until 1996, federal and state control has been divided for about one-third of the period. In Britain, one sees a growing regionalization of voting patterns, as local electoral results are less closely tied to national patterns.

Of course, one of the best signs of dealigned politics is Perot's candidacy in the 1992 election. A candidate without prior political experience and without the support of a party apparatus garnered 19 percent of the U.S. presidential vote. The rise of "flash parties," such as the British Greens in the 1989 European Parliament elections, or the success of the Berlusconi's Forza Italia in the 1994 Italian parliamentary elections are additional indicators of the volatility now present in contemporary party systems. Similarly, the collapse of the Japanese party system in the early 1990s was another sign of how partisan change had reached even the most entrenched party systems.

Finally, the erosion of the influence of long-term sources of partisanship would suggest that factors further along the funnel of causality can play a larger role in voter choice. Citizens are still voting, even if they are not relying on party cues or early-learned partisanship to the degree they once did. On the one hand, this might encourage the public to judge candidates and parties on their policies and governmental performance—producing a deliberative public that more closely proximates the classic democratic ideal. On the other hand, the lack of long-standing partisan loyalties may also make electorates more vulnerable to manipulation and demogogic appeals (Holmberg 1994, 113–14). Dealignment has the potential to yield both positive and negative consequences for electoral politics, depending on how party systems and voters react in this new context. The following chapters consider how the changing role of issues and candidate images is affecting the calculus of elections.

Notes

1. The standard party identification question is one of the most frequently asked questions in U.S. public opinion surveys. It measures both the direction of partisanship and the strength of party attachments: "Generally speaking, do you think of yourself as a Republican, a Democrat, an Independent, or what? (For those expressing a party preference:) Would you call yourself a strong Republican/Democrat or a not very strong Republican/Democrat? (For Independents:) Do you think of yourself as closer to the Republican or Democratic Party?" The question yields a seven-point measure of partisanship ranging from strong Democratic identifiers to strong Republican identifiers.

2. One of the current debates in the American voting literature is the question of how closely aggregate levels of partisanship track current voting preferences. For the contrasting sides of this debate, see MacKuen et al. (1989), Abramson and Ostrom (1991, 1994).

3. For instance, the German version of the party identification question specifically cues the respondent that it is asking about long-term partisan leanings: "Many people in the Federal Republic lean toward a particular party for a long time, although they may occasionally vote for a different party. How about you?"

4. These data are drawn from the Political Action study. The study supplemented its national sample of adults with additional parent-child interviews in families where a 16–20 year old was still living in the parent's home. For additional analyses, see Barnes, Kaase et al. 1979, chap. 15).

5. Morris Fiorina (1981) describes partisanship as a "running tally" of an individual's accumulated electoral experience. If early partisan leanings are reinforced by later voting experience, party ties strengthen over time. If voting experiences counteract partisanship, then these party loyalties may gradually erode. Also see Niemi and Jennings (1991).

6. Researchers have debated whether age differences in American partisanship represent generational or life-cycle effects (Converse 1976; Abramson 1979). We emphasize the life-cycle (partisan learning) model because the cross-national pattern of age differences seems more consistent with this explanation.

7. Part of these relationships is due to patterns of accumulated partisanship over the life cycle. In addition, the lower levels of partisanship among the young can be traced partially to decreasing attachments among younger generations.

8. Zelle (1995) claims to present German data that directly contradict the dealignment statistics displayed in this chapter. His analyses are partially limited by the time range in some of his analyses, beginning in the 1970s and ending before 1994. Also, he excludes the Greens from his analyses of vote switching or codes them in ways to minimize their impact. Excluding new parties while measuring partisan volatility seems a logical contradiction.

9. We define cognitively mobilized citizens as having a combination of interests and skills; that is, "very interested" in the election and/or having at least some college education. The following table presents the distribution of types

using data from the American National Election Studies (also see Dalton 1984, 282).

	1952	1980	1992
Apartisans	10%	18%	24%
Cognitive partisans	32	35	41
Ritual partisans	42	28	20
Apoliticals	16	19	16

10. Attitudes and Electoral Behavior

Party conflict may begin as a competition between social groups or party camps, but elections inevitably revolve around the issues and candidates of the campaign.[1] These two factors are important because they give political meaning to the partisan attachments and social divisions we have discussed in earlier chapters. The political meaning of partisanship (or class attachments) is expressed in the cluster of issue positions and candidate preferences that evolve from long-term partisan ties. Labour supporters, for example, support the party not just out of blind loyalty but because they share a belief in policies that the party normally advocates.

Issue beliefs and candidate images are also important because they represent the dynamic aspect of electoral politics. The distribution of partisanship may define the broad parameters of electoral competition. Nevertheless, specific campaigns are fought over the policies the contenders advocate, the images of the candidates, or the government's policy performance. The mix of these factors almost always varies across elections, and thus issue beliefs and candidate images explain the ebbs and flows of voting outcomes. This is why the funnel of causality locates issue beliefs and candidate images as proximate to voting choice. Although partisanship may partially determine these attitudes, the content of a campaign also shapes these attitudes and thus the ultimate voting decision.

Finally, as the electoral impact of long-term partisan attachments and social cues has eroded in recent decades, many political scientists have found a corresponding increase in the influence of issue opinions on voting choice (Franklin 1985; van der Eijk and Niemoller 1983; Franklin et al. 1992). Martin Wattenberg (1991) has written provocatively about the rise of candidate-centered choices by American voters, and the role of candidate images is now more widely debated in European party systems (Kaase 1994; Crewe and King 1994; McAllister 1996).

This chapter examines the role of issues and candidate images in electoral choice. We consider both the conditions that determine the potential influence of these attitudes on the vote, as well as their actual impact in contemporary party systems. This evidence enables us to complete our model of voter choice and discuss the implications of our findings for the democratic process.

Principles of Issue Voting

The study of issue voting has been closely intertwined with the scholarly debate on the political sophistication of contemporary publics. In theoretical terms, issue voting was presented as the defining feature of a sophisticated, rational electorate; voters evaluate the government and opposition and then thoughtfully cast a ballot for their preferred party. To the skeptics of mass democracy, this theoretical ideal seldom existed in reality. Instead, they saw voters as lacking knowledge about the party's or their own positions, and often voting on the basis of ill-formed or even incorrect beliefs (see chapter 2).

The early empirical voting studies were often critical of the electorate. The authors of *The American Voter* maintained that meaningful issue voting must meet three requirements: citizens should be interested in the issue, they should hold an opinion on the issue, and they should know the party or candidate positions on the issue (Campbell et al. 1960, chap. 8). *The American Voter* argued that on most policy issues, most voters fail to meet these criteria. These researchers classified a third of the public, or less, as possible issue voters on each of a long list of policy topics. Moreover, the Michigan researchers believed that these small percentages reflected the conceptual and motivational limits of the electorate; the lack of issue voting was presumably an intrinsic aspect of mass politics (Converse 1990). These political scientists therefore rejected the notion that elections rationally assessed the policy choices of the public.

Even from the beginning of empirical voting research, there were critics of this negative image of issue voting. A leading scholar, V.O. Key, was one of the first to present survey evidence showing that citizens were "moved by concern about the central and relevant questions of public policy, of government performance, and of executive personality" (Key 1966, 7–8). In short, Key's unorthodox argument stated that "voters are not fools." Key's position gradually has become less unorthodox as our understanding of citizen voting behavior has grown.

Because only a minority of the public may fulfill the criteria of rational issue voting for each specific issue, this does not mean that only a third of the total public are capable of issue voting. Contemporary electorates are composed of overlapping *issue publics,* groups of people interested in a specific issue (see chapter 2). These issue publics vary in size and composition. A large and heterogeneous group of citizens may be interested in political issues such as taxes, inflation rates, budget deficits, and the threat of war. On more specific issues—agricultural policy, nuclear energy, transportation policy, foreign aid—the issue publics normally are smaller and politically distinct. Most voters are politically attentive on at least one issue, and many voters may belong to several issue publics. When citizens define their own issue interests, they can fulfill the issue-voting criteria for their issues of interest. For example, David RePass (1971) found that only 5 percent of Americans were interested in medical programs for the elderly, but over 80 percent of this group could be classified as potential issue voters. Adopting a more diversified view of the electorate—not all citizens must be interested in all issues—greatly strengthens the evidence of issue voting.

The conflicting claims about the nature of issue voting also may arise because researchers think of issue voting in different terms or use contrasting empirical examples to support their claims. Indeed, the literature is full of descriptions of the various types of issues, and why we must differentiate between issues.[2] Issue voting may be more likely for some sorts of issues than for others, and the implications of issue voting also may vary depending on the type of issue.

Table 10.1 introduces a framework for thinking about issue voting. One important characteristic is the content of the issue. *Position issues* involve conflicts over policy goals (Berelson et al. 1954, 182–99; Stokes 1963). A typical position issue might concern debates on whether the U.S. Congress should pass the NAFTA agreement or whether Britain should privatize government-owned industries. Discussions of issue voting often focus on the position issues that define the current political debate.

In contrast to position issues, *performance issues* involve judgments on how effectively the candidates or parties pursue widely accepted goals.[3] For instance, most voters favor a strong economy, but they may differ about how they evaluate a government's job in achieving this goal. Conflicting claims about performance judgments often lie at the heart of electoral campaigns. Finally, voters may judge the *attributes* of the parties or candidates: do they possess desired traits or characteristics? For example, a party must be considered trustworthy if its campaign promises are to be believed. These different issue characteristics reflect on the types of decisions being made and the implications of these decisions for judging voters and electoral outcomes.

Types of issue voting also can be characterized by the time frame of

TABLE 10.1

A CLASSIFICATION OF ISSUES

| Time frame | Content of issue | | |
	Position	*Performance*	*Attribute*
Retrospective	Policy appraisal	Performance evaluation	
			Attribute voting
Prospective	Policy mandate	Anticipatory judgment	

the voters' judgments (Fiorina 1981; Miller and Wattenberg 1985; Miller and Borrelli 1992; Lewis-Beck 1988; Abramson et al. 1994, chap. 7). *Retrospective* judgments occur when citizens rate political actors primarily by their past performance. *Prospective* judgments are based on expectations of future performance. Retrospective and prospective judgments hold different implications for the nature of citizen decision making. Retrospective judgments should have a firmer empirical base because they arise from past experience. Retrospective political evaluations can be a relatively simple decision-making strategy: praise the incumbents if times have been good, criticize them if times have been bad. A pure reliance on retrospective judgments would limit the scope of citizen evaluations, however. Elections enable voters to select a government for the future, and these decisions should include evaluations of a party's promises and its prospects for success. Therefore, voting decisions should consider prospective judgments about a government's likely behavior in the future. Prospective judgments are based on a speculative and complex decision-making process. Individuals have to make their own forecasts and link these projections to the expected performance of political actors—a task that imposes a considerable information burden on the voter. How citizens balance retrospective and prospective judgments thus reflects directly on the nature of electoral decision making.

The combination of both sets of characteristics provides a typology of the different types of issue calculations that voters may use in elections. Some issue voting involves a *policy appraisal* that assesses a party's (or candidate's) past position on a policy controversy. For instance, when some voters opposed George Bush in 1992 because of his support for a tax increase in 1989, they were making a judgment about Bush's past policies.

Alternatively, voters may consider what a party or candidate promises in policy terms as the basis of their voting decision. When Ronald Reagan wanted voters in 1980 to support him in order to reduce the scale of government, he was asking for a *policy mandate* from the electorate.

Policy appraisal and policy mandates represent a sophisticated form of issue voting: citizens are making choices between alternative policy goals for their government. This places high requirements on the voters: they must be informed, have a preferred policy, and see meaningful choices between the contenders. Sometimes this information is acquired directly by the voter, sometimes by using surrogate information sources (Popkin 1991; Lupia 1994).

In comparison, *performance evaluations* involve more general judgments about how a political actor (party or candidate) has been doing its job in the past. If the government has been successful, then voters support its return to office; if the government has struggled, then voters cast their ballots for an acceptable challenger. For example, in 1980 Ronald Reagan asked Americans to make a performance evaluation of Carter's presidency when he asked: "Are you better off than you were four years ago?" In other instances, voters might make *anticipatory judgments* about the future performance of government. For instance, some analysts claim that the Labour Party lost in 1992 because some Britons doubted the party's ability to function effectively as a governing party, although they favored many of Labour's policy proposals.

Finally, some aspects of "issue voting" may involve candidate or party attributes as a basis of choice. This type of voting is less often conditioned by a time frame. Voters judge candidates on their personal characteristics, which although not immediately political in their content are legitimate factors to consider in selecting a candidate (Kinder et al. 1980). As Carter's moral integrity helped him in 1976, Clinton's "Slick Willie" image hurt him in 1992—and both images were politically relevant, although they did not involve explicit policy or performance calculations. Similar stylistic considerations can influence voter choices for a political party. For instance, the German SPD suffered from voter doubts about its trustworthiness and patriotism, until the party dissolved these doubts during the Grand Coalition (Baker et al. 1981, chap. 9).

Electoral researchers consider attribute voting as a low level of political sophistication because this does not involve explicit policy criteria. As we discuss below, however, many attributes involve traits that are directly relevant to the task of governing or to providing national leadership. Thus we should consider attribute voting as a potentially meaningful basis of electoral choice.

The typology of table 10.1 provides a framework for thinking about different aspects of issue voting. For example, Martin Wattenberg's (1991, chap. 6) analysis of support for Ronald Reagan provides an especially insightful example of how policy positions and performance evaluations are theoretically and empirically distinct aspects of issue voting. Some candidates can win because of their policy promises; some win despite their program. We do not explicitly examine each type of issue voting in this chapter. Still we highlight how various types of issues can influence contemporary electoral outcomes, and the implications of each type for the nature of democratic politics.

Position Issues and the Vote

Nearly a generation ago, some social scientists speculated about the imminent end of political conflict. They thought that advanced industrial societies would resolve the political controversies that had historically divided their populations (the controversies of the Old Politics), leading to the end of meaningful policy disagreements. We have witnessed just the opposite.

Contemporary electoral research has documented increased levels of policy-based voting in modern party systems. Real changes in the nature of electorates (and politics itself) have facilitated issue voting. The process of cognitive mobilization has increased the number of voters who have the conceptual ability and political skills necessary to fulfill the issue-voting criteria. The growth of citizen-action groups, new issue-oriented parties, and the general renaissance of ideological debate at election time are obvious signs of the public's greater issue awareness. Political elites have become more conscious of the public's preferences and more sensitive to the results of public opinion polls.

Advanced industrialism obviously has not meant the end of policy differences within these societies. Contemporary issue voting still involves many long-standing policy debates. Economic cycles inevitably stimulate shifting concerns about the economic role of government and the nature of the modern welfare system. Indeed, the past decade has seen a revival of economic controversy, spawned initially by economic recession and then by the "free market" programs of Reagan, Thatcher, Kohl, and other neoconservatives. Similarly, political events can often revive latent conflicts, such as the current debate over affirmative action in the United States or renewed regional tensions in many democratic societies.

Issue controversies also are born from the changing nature of politics. This is most clear for foreign policy. In the 1960s and 1970s, the U.S. elections faced the Vietnam war, Britain and France confronted the consequences of decolonialization, and Germany debated *Ostpolitik*. Now the United States is grappling with a new world order, Germany is preoccupied with the problems of unification, and all the West is struggling with new international conflicts, such as Bosnia and the Middle East.

Another recent set of political controversies involve New Politics issues, such as nuclear energy, women's rights, environmental protection, and related issues. These issues entered the political agenda of most advanced industrial democracies over the past two decades, introducing new political controversies and a heightened degree of policy polarization. Furthermore, these issues have played a special role in providing a political base for many new parties and reorienting the voting patterns of the young.

Faced with a diversity of issues across elections and electoral systems, it is difficult to provide a summary assessment of the impact of issues across time or nations. Indeed, by definition the impact of issues should ebb and flow since they represent a dynamic part of elections. Nevertheless, we can provide a general measure of the impact of policy preferences on voting behavior by examining the relationship between Left/Right attitudes and vote. Chapter 6 described Left/Right attitudes as a sort of "super issue," a statement of positions on the issues that are currently most important to each voter. The salient issues may vary across individuals or across nations, but Left/Right attitudes can provide a single measure of each citizen's overall policy views.[4]

Most citizens can position themselves along a Left/Right scale, and these attitudes are linked to specific policy views, fulfilling the first two criteria of policy voting (Fuchs and Klingemann 1989; Inglehart 1990). Figure 10.1 shows that the publics in each nation can position the major political parties on this Left/Right scale. The figure presents the electorate's average self-placement and the average scores assigned to political parties within each nation. American voters perceive fairly modest political differences between the Democrats and Republicans, a reflection of the large policy overlap between the parties. The perceived party differences are greater in the three European party systems. The French Communist Party is at the far left of the political spectrum, counterbalancing the National Front on the far right. The German partisan landscape ranges from the Greens on the far Left to the neo-Right Republikaner on the far Right.[5] In Britain the Labour and Conservative parties assume distinct positions on the Left/Right scale, opening a void in the center that the Liberal Democrats occupy. Most political observers would agree that these party placements are accurate portrayals of actual party positions (e.g., Laver and Hunt 1992). Therefore, in overall terms citizens fulfill the third issue voting criterion: knowing party positions.

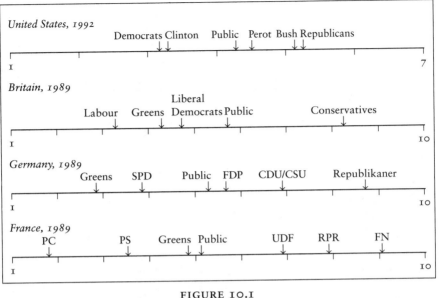

FIGURE 10.1

LEFT/RIGHT PLACEMENT OF THE PARTIES
AND VOTER SELF-PLACEMENT

SOURCES: 1992 American National Election Study; Eurobarometer 31A (June 1989).

NOTES: The values represented in the figure are mean scores. Note that a 7-point Liberal/Conservative scale was used in the American survey and a 10-point Left/Right scale was used in the Eurobarometer survey.

Table 10.2 presents the relationship between Left/Right attitudes and party choice using the 1990–91 World Values Survey. Left/Right attitudes are strongly related to voting choice in every nation. The impact of these attitudes is greatest in France, where the large number of parties offers the clearest policy options. A full 88 percent of self-identified French Leftists favored a Leftist party in 1990, compared to only 4 percent among self-identified Rightists. Even in the United States, there is a 29 percentage point gap in Left/Right voting preferences. These voting gaps are much larger than the effects of social characteristics noted in chapter 8. The substantial influence of Left/Right attitudes is due to the fact that policy evaluations are located closer to the end of the funnel of causality.

The patterns of Left/Right voting also show the relative positions of the parties along this continuum. For instance, the most extreme Leftist party in France, the PC, attracts the greatest share of its vote among the most extreme Leftists; the Socialists do best among more moderate Left-

TABLE 10.2

LEFT/RIGHT ATTITUDES AND PARTY SUPPORT

(IN PERCENTAGES)

	Left	—	Center	—	Right
United States					
Democrat	76	76	59	41	47
Republican	24	24	41	59	53
Total	100	100	100	100	100
Great Britain					
Labour	94	88	49	16	22
Liberal Democrats	1	6	12	4	3
Conservatives	4	6	40	81	75
Total	99	100	101	101	100
Germany					
Greens	19	15	4	1	0
SPD	71	74	37	12	6
FDP	6	4	13	9	4
CDU/CSU	4	7	47	78	91
Total	100	100	101	100	101
France					
PCF	25	4	3	1	4
Socialists	53	79	27	6	0
Other Left	10	2	3	0	0
Greens	10	13	25	5	0
UDF	3	2	28	50	22
RPR	0	0	10	32	22
National Front	0	1	3	7	52
Total	101	101	99	101	100

SOURCE: 1990–91 World Values Survey.

NOTE: The German results are based on western Germany only.

ists. This pattern is mirrored in support for the UDF and RPR on the Right. Another significant contrast is between the Greens in Germany and the Ecologists in France. The German Greens garner disproportionate support from Leftists, while the French Ecologists are more likely to draw support from the center; this reflects both parties' relative positions in figure 10.1.

We can add more detail to how issue positions affect vote by studying the relationship between specific policy attitudes and party preferences.

The 1990–91 World Values Survey includes a set of issue positions across a variety of policy domains (see chapter 6 for additional discussion of these items). Table 10.3 describes the relationship between these issue positions and party choices in our four nations.[6] We should be cautious about overinterpreting these data. The strength of each relationship reflects both the varying size of the relevant issue public and the clarity of party positions. The dynamic, short-term nature of issue beliefs means that either of these factors, and thus the impact of an issue, may greatly change between elections. These data therefore are only a snapshot description of the relationship between issue opinions and party preferences and not an explanation. Still snapshots provide a valuable picture of reality.

TABLE 10.3

THE CORRELATION BETWEEN ISSUE OPINIONS
AND PARTY PREFERENCES

Issue	United States	Britain	Germany	France
Left/Right attitudes	.23	.34	.35	.50
Socioeconomic issues				
Worker management	.11	.17	.17	.28
Income equality	.17	.20	.14	.18
Government ownership	.19	.21	.17	.19
Unemployment benefits	.15	.21	.19	.15
Governmental responsibility	.18	.24	.14	.16
Environmental issues				
Income vs. environment	.02	.11	.11	.19
Taxes vs. environment	.05	.06	.08	.21
Pollution vs. jobs	.04	.05	.13	.18
Environmental movement	.20	.06	.13	.18
Gender issues				
Male job preference	.01	.08	.15	.17
Abortion justified	.11	.12	.19	.13
Women's movement	.16	.10	.16	.17
Foreign policy issues				
Confidence in NATO	.01	.09	.17	.22
Confidence in EU	.13	.05	.08	.23
Disarmament movement	.16	.19	.18	.27
Human rights movement	.11	.06	.11	.23

SOURCE: 1990–91 World Values Survey.

NOTE: Table entries are Cramer's V coefficients.

The traditional economic issues of the Old Politics—such as worker co-management of industry, measures to lessen income inequality, and government ownership of industry—display strong relationships with party preferences in all four nations. The impact of these issues is greatest in France, where the Communist Party and the Right vie over distinctly different economic programs. In each nation, the strongest correlation involves an economic issue. This pattern probably holds for most elections because economic topics have large issue publics and most political parties have clear policies on issues of the government's role in the economic and related economic policies (see figure 7.2, p. 157). The weaker correlations for the American electorate may reflect the general consensus on many structural questions of the economy as well as the lack of differentiation in a two-party system.

New Politics issues dealing with the environment and women's rights have only a modest impact on party choice. In Britain, for instance, the average correlation for Old Politics economic issues is .21; for New Politics issues the average is .08. Although many people are interested in issues such as environmental protection, the translation of policy attitudes into party preferences has been limited by the hesitancy of most parties to adopt clear policies on these issues. For instance, while the German Greens have a distinct profile on environmental issues, the positions of the CDU/CSU, SPD, and FDP are less clear-cut (figure 7.2). This same pattern applies to many gender-related issues. This reflects the tendency of New Politics issues to cut across traditional party lines. New Politics issues are significant more for their potential impact than for their present influence on electoral outcomes.

Foreign policy issues are weakly related to party preferences in most cases. France is the one nation where foreign policy issues are consistently related to partisanship; this reflects continuing conflicts over France's role in the international system, ranging from its relation to NATO to the policies of European unification. Foreign policy can sometimes influence partisan choice (Aldrich et al. 1989), but its impact is normally secondary to domestic issues. Foreign policy issues attract the primary attention of only a small share of the public, except at times of international crisis. Party differences on most foreign issues are also modest in comparison to party polarization on many other topics.

A much richer compendium of information on issue voting exists for each nation separately (Abramson et al. 1994; Heath et al. 1994; Boy and Mayer 1993). This literature indicates that many position issues potentially influence the partisan preferences of contemporary electorates. Although the impact of any one issue for the entire public is often modest, this is because not all issues are salient to all voters. A more refined analysis of specific issue publics would find that individual voting decisions are heavily influenced by each voter's specific issue interests. When these findings are combined with evidence of increasing issue voting overall, V.O. Key's positive assessments of the public's voting decisions no longer appear so unorthodox.

Performance Issues and the Vote

Another element of issue voting involves performance as a basis for electoral choice. Many voters may turn to performance criteria, judging the success of the incumbents or their prospects for the future, as part of their voting decision. Morris Fiorina (1981, 5) put it best when he stated that citizens "typically have one comparatively hard bit of data: they know what life has been like during the incumbent's administration. They do not need to know the precise economic or foreign policies of the incumbent administration in order to judge the results of those policies." In other words, performance-based voting offers people a reasonable shortcut for ensuring that unsuccessful policies are dropped and successful policies continued.

This literature argues that it is only important that voters dispense electoral rewards and punishments—regardless of whether the policies and the outcomes are connected. Benjamin Page (1978, 222), for example, writes that "even if the Great Depression and lack of recovery were not at all Hoover's fault ... it could make sense to punish him in order to sharpen the incentives to maintain prosperity in the future." He acknowledges that blame may be placed unfairly, yet "to err on the side of forgiveness would leave voters vulnerable to tricky explanations and rationalizations; but to err on the draconian side would only spur politicians on to greater energy and imagination in problem solving." Therefore, performance voting requires that voters have a target for their blame when the government falters in some respect. Typically, this is due to poor economic performance, though voters can consider foreign policy performance or other policy areas.

The literature on performance-based economic voting has burgeoned in recent years. Considerable evidence documents the importance of macroeconomics on micropolitics, both in the United States (Tufte 1978; Kiewiet 1983; Rosenstone 1983; Markus 1988) and Europe (Lewis-Beck 1988; Anderson 1995; Norpoth 1992). Even a simple measure of performance evaluations—overall judgments about the performance of the national economy over the past twelve months—displays a significant relationship with party preferences in the United States (.22), Great Britain

(.15), Germany (.13), and France (.17).[7] In simple percentage terms, Bush won 86 percent of the vote from those who thought the nation's economy had improved in the year prior to the election; he received only 21 percent from those who felt the economy had worsened. Obviously, a rising economic tide benefits the incumbents.

The importance of economically based evaluations of parties and candidates is generally acknowledged, but the evidence on the exact scope and nature of this influence remains problematic. One point of debate concerns whether voters base their political evaluations on their own personal economic situation (pocketbook voting) or on the performance of the broader national economy (sociotropic voting). Most of the evidence suggests that voters follow the sociotropic model, which implies that policy outcome rather than narrow self-interest is the driving force behind performance voting (Kinder and Kiewiet 1981; Kiewiet 1983; Lewis-Beck 1988). Researchers also disagree on whether voters evaluate performance retrospectively or base their judgments on prospective expectations (see Fiorina 1981; Miller and Wattenberg 1985; MacKuen, Erickson, and Stimson 1992).

So important is the state of the economy that it can often override other policy considerations. Many election analysts claim that incumbent parties are virtually unbeatable during strong economic upturns and extremely vulnerable during recessionary periods. For example, researchers argue that Americans and Britons elected conservative governments in 1979 and 1980 not for ideological reasons but merely because they were the only instruments available for defeating incumbents who had failed to deliver the economic goods (Crewe and Searing 1988; Wattenberg 1991). Four years after coming to power, both Margaret Thatcher and Ronald Reagan won reelection on the basis of improved economic performance (and the Falklands War in the case of Thatcher)—in spite of continuing policy differences with most of their country's voters (Norpoth 1992). Others have documented the role of economic performance in German elections (Anderson 1995).

While narrow performance voting does not conform to democratic theory's emphasis on policy evaluation, researchers defend performance voting as entirely rational. Does it make sense, they would ask, to pay much attention to the positions of an ineffective administration that seemingly cannot make good on its promises and program? Retrospective voting theorists emphasize that the only really effective weapon of popular control in a democratic regime is the electorate's capacity to throw a party from power.

Candidate Images and the Vote

Democratic theorists describe issue voting in positive terms, but they view candidate evaluations less positively. Voting researchers have described voting on the basis of personality characteristics as "irrational" (cf. Converse 1964; Page 1978). They view candidates images as commodities packaged by image makers who manipulate the public by emphasizing traits with special appeal to the voters. People's judgments about alternative candidates are, in this view, based on superficial criteria such as the candidate's style or looks (e.g., Sullivan and Masters 1988). Indeed, Shawn Rosenberg and Patrick McCafferty (1987) showed that in an experimental setting it is possible to manipulate a candidate's personal appearance to affect voters' choices.

Recently, a different approach to candidate assessments has appeared in the literature. This emerging view holds that candidate evaluations are not necessarily superficial, emotional, or purely short-term. Voters may focus on the personal qualities of a candidate to gain important information about characteristics relevant to assessing how the individual will perform in office (Kinder et al. 1980; Kinder 1986; Miller et al. 1986; Rahn et al. 1990). This new approach presumes that individuals organize their thoughts about other people into broad preexisting categories. These category "prototypes" are used in making judgments when limited factual information is available. Donald Kinder et al. (1980), for example, explored the features that citizens use to define an ideal president. They showed that people can choose attributes they believe would make for an ideal president, but these prototypic concepts are only related to ratings of the incumbent president.

Arthur Miller et al. (1986) have presented data to support a rational voter interpretation of candidate evaluations. They argued that "candidate assessments actually concentrate on instrumental concerns about how a candidate would conduct governmental affairs" (p. 536). Analyzing candidate image data from the American National Election Studies, they found that the three most important dimensions of candidate image for Americans are integrity, reliability, and competence. Such criteria are hardly irrational, for if a candidate is incompetent to carry out policy promises or too dishonest for those promises to be trusted, it makes perfect sense for a voter to pay attention to personality as well as policies. Interestingly, both David Glass (1985) and Arthur Miller et al. (1986) found that college-educated voters are the most likely to judge the candidates by their personal attributes.

Early electoral research on parliamentary systems suggested that popular images of party leaders had a minor impact on voting choice because these electorates did not directly vote for the chief executive. But recent research has found significant effects. Clive Bean and Anthony Mughan (1989) showed that the perceived effectiveness of party leaders was moderately important in the British election of 1983 and possibly decisive in the Australian election of 1987 (also Crewe and King 1994; McAllister 1996). Analyses of the most recent German parliamentary election similarly emphasized the growing role of candidate images (Anderson and Zelle 1995; Norpoth and Roth 1996).

Although there is growing attention to the role of candidate images in electoral choices, even in parliamentary systems, researchers realize it is very difficult to come to a precise assessment of the influence of candidate images. Candidate images come at the end of the funnel of causality, and thus they reflect the cumulation of prior influences. As we noted in chapter 9, for instance, partisanship can have a potent effect in cuing voters on which politicians to like and which to dislike. Furthermore, by coming at the end of the causal funnel, candidate images are very close to the final voting decision. It is often difficult to use responses to a public opinion survey to separate candidate preferences from party preferences in a parliamentary system. In the 1994 German election, for instance, among those who voted for the CDU/CSU, 92 percent preferred Helmut Kohl as chancellor; among SPD voters, 84 percent favored Rudolf Scharping.[8]

The United States is certainly in the lead in developing a pattern of candidate-centered electoral politics (Wattenberg 1991). Yet in virtually all Western democracies, the abilities and characteristics of party leaders inevitably must play an important role in making electoral choices.

Citizen Politics and Voting Behavior

The last several chapters have described the changing patterns of voting behavior in advanced industrial democracies. One major change is a general decline in the long-term determinants of voting choice. The influence of social class on voting preferences has decreased in virtually all Western democracies, as has the impact of religion, residence, and other social characteristics (chapter 8). Similarly, dealignment trends signal a decrease in the impact of enduring party attachments on voting decisions (chapter 9). Fewer voters now approach elections with standing party predispositions based either on social characteristics or early-learned partisan ties.

As the long-term determinants of party choice have decreased in influence, there has been a counterbalancing growth in the importance of short-term attitudes such as issue opinions (and possibly candidate image) (see

Nie et al. 1979; Miller and Borrelli 1992; Klingemann 1983; Franklin 1985; Rose and McAllister 1986). The most persuasive cross-national evidence comes from a recent study of voting behavior in seventeen Western democracies. In reviewing their findings, Mark Franklin and his colleagues (1992, 400) conclude: "if all the issues of importance to voters had been measured and given their due weight, then the rise of issue voting would have compensated more or less precisely for the decline in cleavage politics."

This trend toward greater issue voting (and possibly candidate voting) in most Western nations is a self-reinforcing process. Issue voting contributes to, and benefits from, the concomitant decline in party voting patterns. The weakening of party ties increases the potential for issue opinions to influence voting choice. In addition, the increasing importance to the voter of policy preferences encourages some party defection and erodes the voter's party attachments.[9] Thus the rise of issue voting and the decline of partisanship are interrelated trends.

The shifting balance of long-term and short-term voting influences represents another aspect of the new style of citizen politics. As modern electorates have become more sophisticated and politically interested, and as the availability of political information has expanded, many citizens can now reach their own voting decisions without relying on broad external cues such as social class or family partisanship. In short, more citizens now have the political resources to follow the complexities of politics; they have the potential to act as the independent issue voters described in classic democratic theory but seldom seen in practice.

Additional evidence in support of this interpretation comes from the work on cognitive sophistication by Paul Sniderman and his colleagues (1991). These researchers find that the better educated and the politically sophisticated place more weight on issues as a basis of their electoral decision making; less sophisticated voters rely more on partisanship and social cues. These findings conform to evidence from chapter 9 that locates sophisticated apartisans among the better educated, especially youth. Taking these two developments together, social change is shifting the basis of electoral choice by transforming the skills and resources of contemporary electorates.

We can illustrate the changing styles of citizen voting behavior by the changing impact of economics on the vote. Traditionally, economic conflicts have been structured by social divisions: the working class versus the middle class, industrial versus agrarian interests. In this situation, one's social position was often a meaningful guide to voting decisions. As social divisions have narrowed and the group bases of political interests have blurred, social class has decreased as a source of voting cues. This does not mean that economic issues are unimportant. Quite the opposite. As recession weakened the economies of the industrial nations in the 1980s, economic issues again rose to the top of the political agenda for many citizens. Contemporary evidence of economic voting is widespread, but now issue positions are individually based rather than group derived. The political cues of a union leader or business association must compete with the voter's own opinions on economic policy and party programs. That a partial return to the old issues of economic growth and security has not revived traditional class divisions provides compelling evidence that a new style of citizen politics now affects voting patterns.

This new style of individually based voting decisions may signify a boon or a curse for contemporary democracies. On the positive side, sophisticated voters should inject more issue voting into elections, increasing the policy implications of electoral results. In the long term, greater issue voting may make candidates and parties more responsive to public opinion. Thus the democratic process may move closer to the democratic ideal.

On the negative side, many political scientists have expressed concerns that the growth of issue voting and single-issue groups may place excessive demands on contemporary democracies (see chapter 12). Without the issue-aggregating functions performed by party leaders and electoral coalitions, democratic governments may face conflicting issue demands from their voters. Governments may find it increasingly difficult to satisfy unrestrained popular demands.

Another concern involves the citizens who lack the political skills to meet the requirements of sophisticated issue voting. These people may become atomized voters if traditional political cues (party and social groups) decline in usefulness. Lacking firm political predispositions and a clear understanding of politics, these individuals may be easily mobilized by charismatic elites or fraudulent party programs. Many political analysts see the rise of New Right parties in Europe, especially those headed by dynamic party leaders, as a negative consequence of a dealigned electorate. Indeed, the development of television facilitates unmediated one-on-one contacts between political elites and voters. Despite its potential for encouraging more sophisticated citizen involvement, television also offers the possibility of trivialized electoral politics in which video style outweighs substance in campaigning.

In summary, the trends discussed here do not lend themselves to a single prediction of the future of democratic party systems. But the future is within our control, depending on how political systems respond to these new challenges. The new style of citizen politics will be characterized by a greater diversity of voting patterns than before. A system of frozen social cleavages and stable party alignments is less likely in advanced industrial societies where voters are sophisticated, power is decentralized, and individual choice is given greater latitude. The diversity and individualism of the new style of citizen politics are major departures from the structured partisan politics of the past.

Notes

1. I want to acknowledge my collaboration with Martin Wattenberg (Dalton and Wattenberg 1993), which helped to develop my thinking on many of these points.

2. For example, Ted Carmines and James Stimson (1980) make a distinction between "hard" issues, which are complex and difficult to evaluate, and "easy" issues, which present clear and simple choices. Donald Kinder and Rod Kieweit (1981) stress the distinction between personal issues of self-interest, such as voting on the basis of narrow economic well-being, and issues that reflect national policy choices, such as voting on the basis of what will benefit most Americans.

3. Berelson et al. (1954) described these as style issues; Stokes (1963) used the term valence issue. Later research made the further distinction between performance and attributes that we present here (Miller and Wattenberg 1985; Shanks and Miller 1990).

4. Anthony Downs conceived of Left/Right labels as a way to reduce information costs, rather than as fully informed ideological orientations. As Downs explained (1957, 98), "with this shortcut a voter can save himself the cost of being informed upon a wide range of issues."

5. This survey was conducted prior to German unification. More recent surveys would find the PDS to the Left of the Greens.

6. The relationship is described by a Cramer's V correlation statistic. A value of .00 means that issue opinions are unrelated to party preference. A Cramer's V or .20 is normally interpreted as a moderately strong relationship; .30 is considered a strong relationship.

7. These Cramer's V correlations are drawn from the 1992 American National Election Study and Eurobarometer 30.

8. Understandably, the relationship between candidate preference and vote is even higher in American presidential elections. Abramson et al. (1994, 168) find that in the three-candidate race of 1992, about 95 percent of those who rated Bush or Clinton as the most favorable candidate followed by voting for their preferred candidate.

9. The conventional wisdom holds that partisanship is often a strong influence on issue opinions, while the reverse causal flow is minimal (figure 9.1,

p. 197). As issue voting has increased, researchers have found that issues can remold basic party attachments. Recent studies show that the causal influence of issues in changing partisanship can be quite large (Niemi and Jennings 1991; Fiorina 1981).

11. Political Representation

Contemporary democracies owe their existence to a relatively modern invention: representative government. From the ancient Greeks up through the time of Rousseau, democracy was equated with the direct participation of the citizenry in the affairs of government. Political theorists believed that democracies must limit the definition of citizenship or the size of the polity so that the entire public could assemble in a single body and make political decisions. The Greek city-state, the self-governing Swiss canton, and the New England town meeting exemplify this democratic ideal.

The invention of representative government freed democracies from these constraints. Instead of directly participating in political decision making, groups of citizens selected legislators to represent them in government deliberations. The functioning of the democratic process depended on the relationship between the representative and the represented.

The case for representative government is largely one of necessity. Democracy requires citizen control over the political process, but in a large nation-state the town meeting model is no longer feasible.[1] Proponents of representative government also stress the limited political skills of the average citizen and the need for professional politicians. Citizen control over government is routinized through periodic, competitive elections to select these elites. Elections should ensure that elites remain responsive and accountable to the public. By accepting this electoral process, the public gives its consent to be governed by the elites selected.

Many early political theorists criticized the concept of representative government and felt that it undermined the very tenets of democracy. Representative government transferred political power from the people to a small group of designated elites. Voters had political power only on the day their ballots were cast and then waited in political servitude until the next election—four or five years hence. Under representative government the citizens may control, but elites rule. Jean-Jacques Rousseau warned that "the instant a people allows itself to be represented it loses its freedom."

Recent proponents of direct democracy are equally critical of representative government. European Green parties, for example, criticize the structure of representative government while calling for increased citizen influence through referendums, citizen-action groups, and other forms of "basic" democracy. Populist groups in the United States display a similar skepticism of electoral politics in favor of direct action. Benjamin Barber has articulated these concerns:

> The representative government principle steals from individuals the ulti-
> mate responsibility for their values, beliefs, and actions. . . . Representation
> is incompatible with freedom because it delegates and thus alienates politi-
> cal will at the cost of genuine self-government and autonomy. (1984, 145)

The democratic principle of popular control of the government is re-placed by a commitment to routinized electoral procedures; democracy is defined by its means, not its ends. Critics claim that other opportunities for increasing popular control are not developed because elections provide the accepted standard of citizen influence. These critics are not intrinsically op-posed to representative government, but they oppose a political system that stops at representation and limits or excludes other (and perhaps more in-fluential) methods of citizen influence.

The linkage between the public and political decision makers is one of the essential questions for the study of democratic political systems. The commitment to popular rule is what sets democracies apart from other po-litical systems. While one cannot resolve the debate on the merits of repre-sentative government, this chapter asks how well the representation pro-cess functions in advanced industrial democracies today.

Collective Correspondence

In the broadest sense of the term, the representativeness of elite attitudes is measured by their similarity to the overall attitudes of the public. Robert Weissberg (1978) referred to this comparison as *collective correspondence*. When the distribution of public preferences is matched by the distribution of elite views, the citizenry as a collective is well represented by elites as a collective.

The representation process obviously goes beyond a definition based simply on citizen-elite agreement. Some political elites may stress their role in educating the public instead of merely reflecting current public prefer-ences. In other instances, the opinions of voters may be contradictory, and the policymaking role of elites may lead them to adopt more consistent, but less representative, opinions. Policy preferences also are not necessarily equivalent to policy outcomes. We could add other qualifiers to this list. Still, citizen-elite agreement is the normal standard for judging the representativeness of a democratic system. This is a meaningful test of representation because it determines whether political decision makers enter the policy process with the same policy preferences as the public. This is a basic goal of representative democracy.

Data comparing the beliefs of top-level political elites and the public for our set of nations are extremely rare. More common are studies that focus on public-elite comparisons in a single nation (Miller and Jennings 1986; Miller 1988; Hoffmann-Lange 1992; Herzog and Wessels 1990; Converse and Pierce 1986; Holmberg 1989; McAllister 1991). Therefore, our comparative analyses must rely on a study of European voters and candidates in the 1979 elections to the European Parliament (EP) (Dalton 1985). Where possible, we update these results with findings from more recent national studies.

Table 11.1 presents the distribution of citizen and elite opinions in Britain, Germany, and France. The broadest measure of political orientations is the Left/Right self-placement scale discussed in chapter 6. The first row in the table shows that EP elites in each nation are significantly more likely than the public to identify themselves as Leftists. This liberal tendency among political elites is a common finding (Thomassen 1994, 255). Political elites apparently consider themselves to be more progressive than their constituencies.

Collective correspondence on specific issues varies across these three nations. British elites are more liberal than the public on most issues. This elite bias is strongest for foreign aid and security issues. Abortion policy is the only area where the British public is much more liberal than elites. Data presented by Richard Rose (1980, 273) also found that members of the British Parliament were more liberal than their voters on issues such as the death penalty, immigrants, and the Common Market.

The German public tends to be slightly more liberal than political elites on the Old Politics issue conflicts of economics and abortion. Conversely, elites are significantly more liberal on foreign aid, dealing with terrorists, and the free-speech issue. Recent German citizen-elite studies find similar patterns of agreement. Ursula Hoffmann-Lange (1992) found that the German public was more liberal than political elites on economic issues such as price controls, government regulation of banks, and codetermination; elites were more liberal on foreign aid and legislation aimed at controlling political radicals. More recently, Bernhard Wessels (1993) compared the issue opinions of Bundestag deputies and the German public. He found close agreement on Old Politics issues such as economic growth and

TABLE 11.1

THE DISTRIBUTION OF OPINIONS FOR THE EUROPEAN
PUBLIC AND ELITES (IN PERCENTAGES)

| | Great Britain | | West Germany | | France | |
	Public	Elites	Public	Elites	Public	Elites
Leftist self-placement	42	46	42	57	47	68
Old Politics						
Public ownership of industry	30	35	34	27	41	48
Government manages economy	44	38	45	32	56	44
Codetermination	52	54	69	60	73	52
Control multinationals	50	66	66	75	72	86
Reduce income inequality	65	64	76	88	93	93
Liberalize abortion	77	58	75	65	77	74
Foreign aid						
Aid EC regions	45	90	47	98	71	90
Aid Third World	35	85	40	93	52	82
Security						
Strengthen defense	18	25	30	22	34	32
Action against terrorists	5	29	12	30	8	15
New Politics						
Nuclear energy	21	23	34	19	34	15
Protest environment	94	92	88	97	94	92
Free expression	72	78	76	79	74	86
Average liberal issue response	46	57	53	60	60	62

SOURCES: 1979 Eurocandidate Survey, Eurobarometer 11; both studies have been weighted to produce representative national samples.

NOTE: Table entries are the percentages of respondents expressing a liberal opinion on each item.

public order and somewhat lower levels of agreement on New Politics goals (also see Herzog and Wessels, 1990, chap. 3).

The closest overall match between citizen and EP elite opinions occurs in France. French citizens and elites generally favor liberal policies on Old Politics issues, and there are no consistent differences between political strata on these issues. The pattern on New Politics and security issues is equally mixed. Only on foreign aid issues are EP elites clearly more liberal than the French public (also see Converse and Pierce 1986, 597).

Comparable data describing the views of American voters and political elites are equally rare. Table 11.2 compares the national electorate to members of Congress in 1978. While the public and elites differed somewhat in their policy views, there was not a systematic bias in the direction of these differences. The public was fiscally more prudent than elites; most voters favored legislation requiring a balanced federal budget while opposing large tax cuts. When Congress followed the opposite course in the early 1980s, enacting tax cuts without budget limits, record federal deficits resulted. The electorate was also significantly more liberal than elites on the social issues of government-funded abortions and national health insurance. Citizen and elite views were most similar on foreign policy issues.[2]

In summary, if we judge collective correspondence by substantive criteria—for example, a 10 percent difference or less in issue opinions—then citizen-elite agreement is fairly common.[3] Most economic, security, and New Politics issues fall within the 10 percent range for the British, German, and French comparisons to European Parliament elites. Only foreign policy issues display sizable opinion differences between citizens and Europarliament candidates. The samples of German and French elites appear most representative of their respective publics. Overall, an average of 53 percent of the German public give liberal responses on the thirteen issue questions, compared to 60 percent of elites. The match of citizen and elite opinions is even closer in France (60 percent versus 62 percent). The voter-elite gap in the United States appears somewhat larger, but this may be caused by the slight differences in question wording between the two sets

TABLE 11.2

THE DISTRIBUTION OF OPINIONS FOR THE AMERICAN
PUBLIC AND ELITES (IN PERCENTAGES)

	Voters	*Elites*
A law requiring a balanced budget	84	65
Large federal income tax cut	43	58
Tax break for tuition costs	67	54
National health insurance	51	38
Government-paid abortions for poor	42	31
Arms limit agreement with the USSR	70	66
Increase defense spending	36	34
A stronger commitment to Israel	33	19

SOURCE: CBS News/*New York Times* Congressional Poll and Voters Survey (Fall 1978).

NOTE: Table entries are the percentages agreeing with each policy.

of interviews (Bishop and Frankovic 1981). Still the general contours of opinion are similar between groups.

Dyadic Correspondence

Collective correspondence between the issue opinions of the public and the political elites does not occur as a collective process. Some degree of popular control is necessary to ensure the responsiveness of elites. Citizen-elite agreement without popular control is representation by chance, not democracy. The normal method of popular control makes political elites electorally dependent on a specific constituency. Weissberg (1978) defined the pairing of constituency opinion and elites as *dyadic correspondence*. In simple terms, liberal constituencies presumably select liberal representatives and conservative constituencies select conservative representatives.

In studying the connection between citizens and elites, researchers initially treated the individual legislator as the primary means of dyadic linkage. One explanation for this approach lies in the historical development of political theory on representation. Edmund Burke's classic "Speech to the Electors of Bristol" in 1774 defined a paradigm of representation that still influences modern political science. Traditionally, a *delegate* model stated the legislator's role in a deterministic fashion. Representative government required that delegates be sent to Parliament and that voters instruct the delegate on constituency preferences. The legislator was obliged to follow the constituency's mandate. Burke proposed a more independent *trustee* role for legislators. He argued that, once elected, legislators should be allowed to follow their own beliefs about what they thought was best for their constituency and the nation.

This theoretical emphasis on the individual legislator was reinforced by the development of modern empirical research on political representation. Representation research, especially from the American perspective, treated the legislator as the basis of political linkage (Miller and Stokes 1963). In part, this reflected the weakness of American parties and the open structure of the American political process. Many American legislators can, and do, act as individual entrepreneurs. Research focused on whether individual legislators followed the delegate or trustee model in representing their constituencies (Kuklinski 1978; Wahlke et al. 1962).

Warren Miller and Donald Stokes' (1963) seminal study of political representation in America incorporated these theoretical models of representation. They designed a complex study of the relationship between public opinion and elite actions. They interviewed a small sample of the public in each of 116 congressional districts across the nation after the 1958 congressional elections, as well as members of the House of Representatives from these same districts. Finally, they assembled the voting records of the members of Congress for the next legislative session.

Miller and Stokes used this information to build a model of the representation process (figure 11.1). Broadly speaking, these researchers envisioned two pathways by which a constituency could influence the voting behavior of its representative (Miller and Stokes 1963). One pathway defined the trustee model of representation; the constituency could select a legislator who shares its views (path *a*), so that in following his or her own convictions (path *b*) the legislator represents the constituency's will. In this case the constituency's opinion and the legislator's actions are connected through the legislator's own policy attitudes. A second pathway follows on the delegate model. A legislator turns to his or her district for cues on constituents' policy preferences (path *c*) and then follows these cues in making voting choices (path *d*). In this case the legislator's perception of constituency attitudes provides the linkage between actual constituency opinion and the legislator's voting behavior.

They applied the model to three policy areas: civil rights, social welfare, and foreign policy. Miller and Stokes found a strong relationship between constituency opinion and the legislator's voting record for civil rights and social welfare issues and a weaker connection for foreign policy.

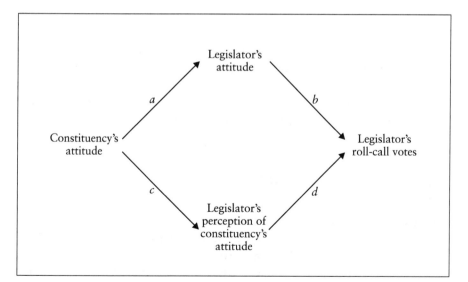

FIGURE 11.1

CONSTITUENCY INFLUENCE IN CONGRESS

In addition, the path of constituency influence varied between policy domains. Civil rights issues primarily functioned by a delegate model; the delegate path was at least twice as important as the trustee path. For social welfare issues, the trustee path through the legislator's own attitude was the most important means of constituency influence.

This study provided hard empirical evidence of the representation process at work. Moreover, the process seemed to work fairly well. Most liberal constituencies were represented by liberal legislators, and vice versa. Although there have been many critics of the methodology of this study, its essential conclusions are still supported by most political scientists (for further discussion, see Erikson and Tedin 1995, chap. 10; Thomassen 1994). In his most recent research, Warren Miller has continued to work within this paradigm, exploring the relationship between party activists and the public and how representational roles affect these relationships (Miller and Jennings 1986; Miller 1988).

The Miller-Stokes model was extended to representation studies in nearly a dozen other Western democracies (Holmberg 1974; Barnes 1977; Farah 1980; Thomassen 1976; Converse and Pierce 1986; Higley et al. 1979). But these studies often found little evidence of policy agreement between constituencies and their legislators. For instance, Samuel Barnes (1977) compared the issue opinions of Italian deputies to public opinion in their respective districts. He found virtually no correspondence between citizen and elite views (average correlation across eight issues was .04). Barbara Farah (1980) documented a similar lack of correspondence between district opinions and the policy views of district-elected deputies in the German Bundestag. The average correlation between district and deputy opinions was actually negative (average correlation across six issues was -.03). The French representation study also found a weak linkage between district and legislator opinions on specific policy issues (Converse and Pierce 1986, chap. 22).[4] It appeared that political representation did not occur in most democracies or that it worked through other means.

The Party Government Model

Research on political representation in non-American political systems gradually turned away from a theoretical model based on individual legislators to one based on the actions of political parties as collectives. This model of representation through parties—responsible party government —is built on several principles (Rose 1984). Elections should provide competition between two or more parties contending for political power. Parties must offer distinct policy options so that voters have meaningful electoral choices. Moreover, voters should recognize these policy differences among the parties. At the least, voters should be sufficiently informed to award or punish the incumbent parties based on their performance. Elections therefore serve as evaluations of the political parties and their activities.

Most descriptions of responsible party government also presume that members of a party's parliamentary delegation act in unison. Parties should vote as a bloc in parliament, although there may be internal debate before the party position is decided. Parties exercise control over the government and the policymaking process through party control of the national legislature. In sum, the choice of parties provides the electorate with a method of control over the actions of individual legislators and the affairs of government.

While the representation process may be based on individual legislators in the United States, political representation in Western Europe largely follows the party government model. In comparison to the United States, the party systems of most European democracies offer the voters greater diversity in party programs, which gives more meaning to party labels (Harmel and Janda 1982, 29). Most democracies are parliamentary systems, where unified legislative parties play a crucial role in determining control of the executive branch. The available evidence shows that party cohesion in European legislatures is considerably higher than in the American Congress (Thomassen 1994, 246; Harmel and Janda 1982, 84). When a party votes as a united bloc, it makes little sense to discuss the voting patterns of individual legislators. Furthermore, public recognition of which party controls the government is more widespread in Western Europe than in the United States, probably as a result of the European parliamentary form of government. Giovanni Sartori maintains that "citizens in Western democracies are represented *through* and *by* parties. This is inevitable" (1968, 471; italics in original).

The party government model thus directs the voters' attention to parties as political representatives, rather than to individual deputies. Indeed, many Europeans (including Germans) vote directly for party lists. Dyadic correspondence is based more on a voter-party model than a district-legislator model. The voter half of the dyad is composed of all party supporters in a nation (even if there are geographic electoral districts); the elite half is composed of party officials as a collective.

If the party government model holds, we should expect a close match between the policy views of voters and party elites taken as collectives. Nevertheless, chapter 9 discussed the general weakening of party organizations and popular attachments to parties. The erosion of party strength is most obvious for activities outside the electoral arena, such as providing political information, social services, and government employment. Parties remain the prime vehicle for electoral politics, but evidence of partisan dealignment is evident here also. Candidate images are playing a more prominent role in elections on both sides of the Atlantic; with the expanding influence of the media and reliance on candidate debates and similar activities, the personalities of the candidates are an important part of elections. Especially in the United States, party campaign organizations are being replaced by the personal staffs of the candidates. Similarly, citizen-action groups and political action committees (PACs) are important actors in the electoral process. In short, the functioning of the party linkage process deserves close study to see if the general weakening of parties has extended to electoral politics as well.

We should stress one other point in comparing dyadic correspondence. We occasionally speak in causal terms—voter opinions presumably influence party positions—but the causal flow works in both directions. Voters influence parties, as parties try to persuade voters. This is why researchers have adopted the causally neutral term *correspondence*. The essence of the democratic marketplace is that like-minded voters and parties search out each other and ally forces. Even if one cannot determine the direction of causal flow, the similarity of opinions between voters and party elites is a meaningful measure of the representativeness of parties.

We examine the party linkage model in Western Europe by comparing the opinions of voters and elites from the 1979 European Parliament study, in which both samples are aggregated by party. This procedure yields comparisons for fourteen parties in Britain, Germany, and France (Dalton 1985). The following figures depict voter-party agreement on several issues. The horizontal axis in each figure plots the average issue position of party supporters; the vertical axis plots the average opinion of the party's elites. These two coordinates define a party's location in the figure. The 45-degree line represents perfect intraparty agreement: when the opinions of party elites exactly match those of their supporters.

Figures 11.2 and 11.3 display party patterns on the economic issue of expanding government ownership of industry and the religious/moral issue of abortion. Party positions on these issues follow traditional Left/Right alignments. The Socialist and Communist parties tended toward the lower-left quadrant; their voters and party elites both held liberal opinions on these issues. For example, in 1979 supporters of the French Communist Party (PCF) were very liberal on the nationalization issues (average score = 1.78), as were PCF elites (score = 1.08). Conversely, the voters and elites of the traditional Rightist parties generally shared conservative opinions on

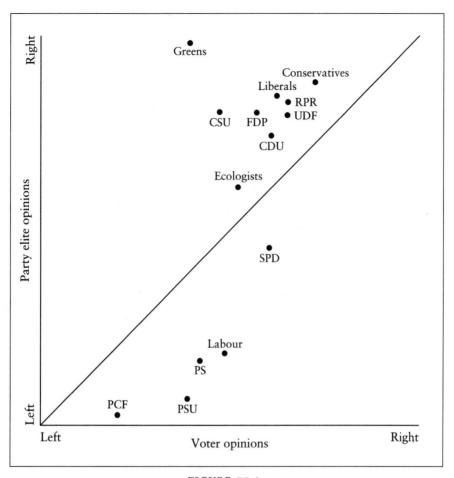

FIGURE 11.2
VOTER AND PARTY ELITE OPINIONS ON FURTHER
NATIONALIZATION OF INDUSTRY

SOURCE: 1979 Europarliament Study.

these issues. Averaged across all parties, the opinions of party elites are less than one scale point (.85 on a five-point scale) from the voter opinions on the nationalization issue, and less than half a point (.45) on the abortion issue. Because economic and religious issues are so important in structuring political conflict, a variety of more recent studies suggest that congruence on these issues remains high (Laver and Hunt 1992; Wessels 1993).

Attitudes toward nuclear power exemplify a salient New Politics issue. Figure 11.4 shows a basic correspondence between party voters and party

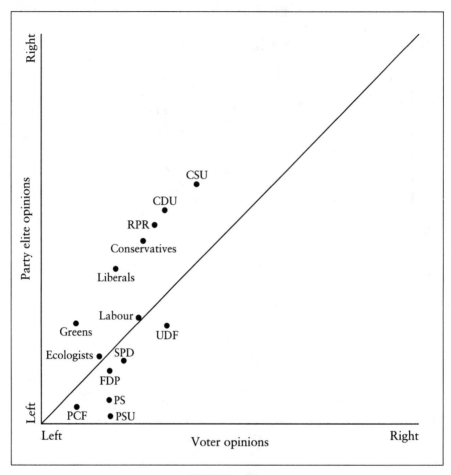

FIGURE 11.3
VOTER AND PARTY ELITE OPINIONS ON ABORTION

SOURCE: 1979 Europarliament Study.

elites on this issue. A voter bloc that favored (or opposed) nuclear energy is represented by party elites who generally shared these opinions. The average difference (.74) between voter and elite opinions is modest.

The pattern of party alignment on the nuclear power issue is also significant. The major established Left and Right parties did not have clear positions on this issue in 1979. The major Left parties—the German SPD, British Labour, and the French PS—all held centrist positions on this issue that were not much different from their conservative party rivals. In fact, the voters and party elites of the French Communist Party favored nuclear

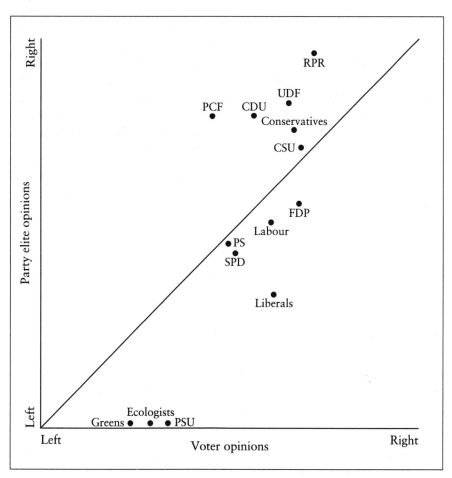

FIGURE 11.4
VOTER AND PARTY ELITE OPINIONS ON
NUCLEAR ENERGY

SOURCE: 1979 Europarliament Study.

power more than many conservative party groups. Opposition to nuclear power was represented by a set of new parties: the German Greens, the French Ecologists, and French PSU. Although these data are aging, more recent studies of the public's environmental attitudes and their party images suggest the pattern described here has not changed fundamentally (Dalton 1994; Rohrschneider 1993b). Party alignments on nuclear power (and New Politics issues) cut across the traditional Left/Right party lines defined by Old Politics issues.

The issue of aid for Third World nations presents an example of the lack of voter-party agreement (figure 11.5). Party elites are consistently more liberal than their voters. Only a single party is within one scale point of its supporters, and the average voter-party difference is great (1.33). In this area West European party elites display considerable independence from the policy opinions of their voters. This result is reminiscent of Miller and Stokes's (1963) finding that foreign policy exhibits the least evidence of dyadic correspondence for their sample of American legislators.

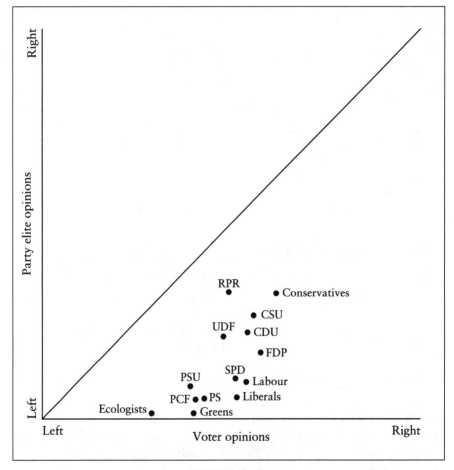

FIGURE 11.5

VOTER AND PARTY ELITE OPINIONS ON AID
TO THIRD WORLD NATIONS

SOURCE: 1979 Europarliament Study.

Except for foreign policy, party elites appear fairly responsive to the views of their voters. Yet there is also a systematic tendency for party elites to exaggerate the issue differences that exist among their supporters. The intensity and ideological commitment of political elites normally generates greater issue differences among elites than among party supporters (Miller and Jennings 1986; Dalton 1985; McClosky 1964). On the nationalization of industry issue, for example, EP elites of the German SPD were significantly to the left of their voters, while CDU elites were to the right of their constituency. The 45-degree line in the figures represents perfect intraparty agreement, and party elites were more polarized than their supporters on the issues of nationalization, abortion, and nuclear energy.

A pattern of accentuated elite polarization also occurs in voter-elite comparisons in the United States (table 11.3). Democratic and Republican voters in 1978 displayed only minor differences in their issue opinions (average difference is 8 percent); but party elites accentuated these differences (average is 36 percent). In other words, party elites tended to *overrepresent* the opinions of their constituencies by maintaining more extreme issue positions. Warren Miller (1988, chap. 3; Jennings 1992) has replicated these analyses by comparing the American public to delegates to national party conventions in 1980 and 1984. He finds that party elites are more polarized than the public on all the items he compared. This general pattern explains the greater clarity of party positions at the elite level and the greater intensity of party conflict among elites.

TABLE 11.3

THE DISTRIBUTION OF VOTER AND ELITE OPINIONS
BY PARTY (IN PERCENTAGES)

	Democrats		Republicans	
	Elites	Voters	Voters	Elites
Balanced budget	48	82	87	85
Income tax cut	23	42	43	97
Tuition costs	36	69	64	26
National health insurance	63	63	37	9
Abortions for poor	45	46	37	16
Arms agreement with USSR	90	73	66	40
Increased defense spending	19	32	41	50
Commitment to Israel	18	35	31	21

SOURCE: CBS News/*New York Times* Congressional Poll and Voters Survey (Fall 1978).

NOTE: Table entries are the percentages agreeing with each policy statement; see table 11.2 for a more complete list of questions.

Just as important as the overall level of dyadic correspondence are the factors affecting voter-party agreement. Some parties consistently achieve a close match between the opinions of voters and party elites, while other parties display less correspondence. These variations in party representation determine the efficiency of the party linkage process.

A study of voter-party agreement for forty party groups across nine nations found that the clarity of party positions is an important influence on the representation process (Dalton 1985). Characteristics that clarify party positions make it easier for voters to select a party compatible with their issue beliefs. Most policy areas display a strong and consistent tendency for centrally organized parties to be more representative of their supporters. Centralized parties may be less open to innovation and allow less internal democracy, as critics suggest, but centralized parties display greater dyadic correspondence. In addition, voter-party agreement is higher among ideological parties (of either the Left or Right). Apparently these characteristics clarify party positions and make it easier for voters to select a party consistent with their issue beliefs. A centralized party is more likely to project clear party cues, and an ideological image helps voters identify a party's general political orientation. At the system level, voter-party correspondence is greater in fractionalized party systems and nations with proportional representation. Diversity in party choices clarifies party options and makes it more likely that voters can find a party that supports their mix of policy preferences.

Patterns of Political Representation

It is regrettable that more recent data on the representation process are not available. After all, we have claimed that the representation process is an important measure of the success of modern democracy. Furthermore, the new style of citizen politics we have described in previous chapters might affect the representation process, though the nature of these effects are uncertain (see Thomassen 1994). On the one hand, a more sophisticated, issue-oriented public might encourage candidates and parties to be more attentive to public interests. On the other hand, partisan dealignment and candidate-centered politics may weaken representation built on a system of responsible party government. Still, broad conclusions about the nature of representation flow from our findings.

This chapter describes two distinct patterns of representative government among Western democracies. Political representation in the United States is more dependent on the relationship between individual legislators and their constituencies. Citizens in most other democracies are primarily represented through their choice of political parties at election time. Some research suggests that this American-European contrast may be lessening. For instance, Warren Miller (1988, chap. 4) discusses how parties play an important role in American representation (also Erikson and Tedin 1995, chap. 10). Other analyses suggest that the strength of the party government model is weakening in Europe (e.g., chapter 9). Still it is probably the case that the contrasts between the American and European patterns of representation continue to hold.

Both models can provide an effective means of citizen-elite linkage, but they emphasize different aspects of representation. The American system of representative government based on individual legislators allows for greater responsiveness to the interests of each legislative district. The political process is more open to new political interests and the representation of minority groups because electoral control at the constituency level is more easily accomplished than control of an entire party. The flexibility of the American style of representation also involves some costs. An entrepreneurial style of representation makes it more difficult for the public to monitor and control the actions of their representative between elections. This representation pattern also encourages campaigns to focus on personalities and district service, rather than policy and ideological orientations. Indeed, studies of congressional elections suggest that personality and constituency service are important influences on voting patterns.

There is a growing body of empirical research showing that policy outcomes in America generally reflect the preferences of the public—although obviously this is, and probably should be, an imperfect linkage. For example, Alan Monroe (1979) found a broad agreement between American policy preferences and policy outcomes for the several hundred specific cases he examined. Benjamin Page and Robert Shapiro (1983) similarly documented a significant correspondence between public preferences for policy change and actual changes in public policy.[5] Sophisticated empirical analyses by James Stimson and his colleagues (1995) are providing new insights into the total impact of public opinion on the policy process and how this influence interacts with the institutional structure of American politics.

A party-government model yields a different pattern of political representation. The choice of parties provides the electorate with indirect institutional control over the actions of individual legislators through party discipline. When a party votes as a united bloc, political responsibility is more clearly established. If the public is satisfied (or dissatisfied) with the party's performance, the next election offers the opportunity to act on these evaluations. While the party model strengthens the policy linkage between citizens and elites, this may produce rigidity and resistance to change. The highly cohesive European parliamentary parties place a necessary premium on party unity and disciplined voting. This hardly provides a fertile ground for experimentation and political change. Parties may be very responsive to their established clientele, but new social groups and internal party minorities may have difficulty gaining representation in the party-government framework.

Research projects working within the party government framework also find that party choices have meaningful policy consequences. For example, Hans Dieter Klingemann and his colleagues (1994) analyzed whether the programs that parties offer to the voters are translated into policy after the election. They find that parties are a meaningful vehicle for policy control in most democracies.

Many roadblocks and pitfalls stand in the way of representation through parties. In these times of change and political turmoil the evidence of party failures is often obvious. Yet parties remain the dominant institution in the area of political representation. Citizen preferences on Old Politics issues are well-represented among the top stratum of political elites. Ironically, some of the strongest evidence for the importance of partisan representation comes from the alternative movement. When the established parties avoided taking clear policy stances on New Politics issues, Green and New Left parties formed to represent these views. In general terms, therefore, parties continue to perform their role as representatives of voter interests.

In summary, even close citizen-elite-policy agreement is not proof that public opinion is efficiently and effectively represented in modern democracies. A large part of the correspondence that does exist must be attributed to an interactive process. Voters migrate to the party (candidate) that best represents their views, and the party convinces supporters to adopt its policies. Congruence does not prove that the public can control government. Beyond the general patterns described here are a host of specific policies on which the impact of public preferences was uncertain. Yet congruence indicates an agreement between public preferences and public policy that is expected under a democratic system. Moreover, it underscores our belief that there is a rationality of public action that elitist theories of democracy doubt exists.

Notes

1. The development of two-way cable television, teleconferencing, and other communication advances may lead us to reconsider the physical limits on

direct citizen participation in large collectives. Indeed, the technology exists for instantaneous national referendums and national town meetings (Pool 1983).

2. Another comparison of public opinion and opinions of members of Congress in 1982 found that the two groups differed by only a few percentage points (Erikson and Tedin 1995, 285). In addition, a comparison of issue positions between the national public and a survey of state legislatures uncovered close correspondence (Uslaner and Weber 1983).

3. In purely statistical terms, almost half of the citizen-elite issue comparisons in these tables yield statistically significant differences (.01 level). This, in part, is because of the large size of the public opinion samples.

4. The power of Converse and Pierce's (1986, chap. 23) analysis was to specify the conditions that strengthen or retard the representation process. They found that citizen-elite congruence varied by policy domain, competitiveness of the district, and the legislator's role conceptions.

5. State-level comparisons provide another opportunity to study the congruence between public opinion and public policy. A recent study by Robert Erikson and his colleagues shows a strong policy correspondence (Erikson et al. 1994).

PART FOUR

Democracy and The Future

12. The Democratic Process

In the decade since I wrote the first edition of this book, one of the most dramatic changes in this research field involves popular concepts of the democratic process. A very short time ago, political experts worried about the fragility of democracy. Governments were struggling with new issue demands, and political institutions were having a difficult time adjusting to calls for a more participatory democracy. Many renowned scholars described this situation as a crisis of Western democracy (Crozier et al. 1975; Huntington 1981; Lipset and Schneider 1983).

There were two contrasting views on the origins of this crisis (Fuchs and Klingemann 1996). From a New Politics perspective, the problem arose because political institutions were not growing to meet the citizenry's new needs and demands. The public's expanding issue interests involved governments in new political controversies. In addition to ensuring the economic and physical well-being of their citizens, governments now were expected to protect the quality of the environment, guarantee consumer rights, arbitrate moral issues, assure equality for minorities and women, and deal with many other new political concerns.

The challenge to democracy arose because established institutions did not respond effectively or efficiently to these demands. Especially in Western Europe, democratic institutions were designed to limit and channel citizen participation, not to maximize popular control of elites.[1] The bureaucratic and institutionalized style of democratic politics thus did not accommodate these new demands. The political parties were hesitant to represent the expanding interests of the public. The citizenry consequently organized on its own and challenged the political establishment through citizen-action groups and other direct-action techniques. This development stimulated public criticism of political elites and the governing process. Adherents of this view called for reforms to open the political process and make democratic institutions more democratic, responsive, and representative. The German chancellor Willy Brandt challenged his fellow Germans: "We must risk more democracy."

Analysts who accepted an elitist theory of democracy offered a different interpretation. These analysts agreed that contemporary governments were being overloaded, but they felt that excessive public demands were the cause and a strengthening of traditional political institutions was the solution (Berger 1979; Crozier et al. 1975; Huntington 1981). Advanced industrialism had weakened the ability of social groups to guide and moderate the demands of individual citizens. Traditional social institutions —such as the church and universities—were losing influence or becoming advocates for change. In addition, the mass media became critics of government and stripped away the cloak of anonymity that once shielded government actions from popular scrutiny. Governments were being "overloaded" by the demands of citizen-action groups and issue-based politics. As Samuel Huntington succinctly stated, the crisis of democracy arose from an excess of democracy on the part of the citizenry (1975, 1981). Thus a strengthening of democracy required a reinvigoration of traditional institutions and a moderation of the new style of citizen politics.

As this debate developed, the signs of democracy's malaise were obvious. In the United States, trust in government began to erode during the 1960s. In 1979 President Jimmy Carter described the crisis in confidence as "a fundamental threat to American democracy." Carter believed that this situation reflected a malaise of the American spirit that struck at the very heart of society and politics. Signs of a similar crisis of confidence spread across the map of Europe. It was claimed that Willy Brandt stated that "Western Europe has only 20 or 30 more years of democracy left in it; after that it will slide, engineless and rudderless, under the surrounding sea of dictatorship" (quoted in Crozier et al. 1975, 2).

These doubts about democracy seemingly disappeared with the end of the Cold War and the collapse of the Soviet Union. Democracy had not perished and was now described as the inevitable end point in political evolution (Fukuyama 1992). Even those who had written most vigorously on the crisis of democracy and democracy's limits were trumpeting the global wave of democratization that was apparently transforming the world.[2]

Have the challenges to democracy evaporated so quickly? There are signs that the malaise continues: the large protest vote for Perot in 1992, the collapse of the dominant party system in Japan and Italy in the early 1990s, and continuing calls for institutional reform in most advanced industrial democracies. There are also claims that we have entered a new age of democratization and international harmony. This chapter determines how citizens judge the democratic process today. In addition, we consider whether the new style of citizen politics marks an evolutionary step in the democratic process or a threat to democracy itself.

The Meaning of Political Support

Political support is a term with many possible meanings. Several political scientists have tried to identify the essential aspects of this concept and link these political attitudes to their consequences.

Gabriel Almond and Sidney Verba (1963) referred to attitudes toward politics and the political system as the *political culture* of a nation. Political culture encompasses everything from beliefs about the legitimacy of the system itself to beliefs about the adequacy and appropriateness of political input structures, government policies, and the role provided for the individual in the political process. The most important of these attitudes is a generalized feeling toward the political system, or *system affect*. Feelings of system affect were presumably socialized early in life (Easton and Dennis 1969), representing a positive attitude toward the political system that was relatively independent of the actions of the current government. Almond and Verba felt that affective feelings toward the political system assured the legitimacy of democratic governments and limited expressions of discontent with the political system.

David Easton (1965, 1975) extended these ideas into a theoretical framework describing the various elements of political support. Easton distinguished between support for three levels of political objects: political authorities, the regime, and the political community. Political authorities are the incumbents of political office, or in a broader sense the pool of political elites from which government leaders are drawn. Support for political authorities focuses on specific individuals or groups of individuals. Regime support refers to public attitudes toward the institutions and offices of government rather than the present officeholders, such as attitudes toward the office of president of the United States, rather than the current chief executive. This level of support also involves public attitudes toward the procedures of government and political institutions, such as the principles of pluralist democracy and support for parliamentary government. Finally, support for the political community implies a basic attachment to the nation and political system beyond the present institutions of government. A sense of being "English" (or "Scottish") exemplifies these attachments.

The distinction between levels of support is essential. Discontent with political authorities normally has limited political implications. Citizens often become dissatisfied with political officeholders and act on these feelings to select new leaders at the next election. Dissatisfaction with authorities, within a democratic system, is not usually a signal for basic political change. Negative attitudes toward a political official often exist with little loss in support for the office itself or the institutional structure encompassing the office. As the object of dissatisfaction becomes more general—the regime or political community—the political implications increase. A decline in regime support might provoke a basic challenge to constitutional structures or calls for reform in the procedures of government. Weakening ties to the political community in a democratic system might foretell eventual revolution, civil war, or the loss of democracy. Therefore, "not all expressions of unfavorable orientations have the same degree of gravity for a political system. Some may be consistent with its maintenance; others may lead to fundamental change" (Easton 1975, 437).

In addition to the objects of political support, Easton distinguished between two kinds of support: diffuse and specific (also see Muller and Jukam 1977). According to Easton, diffuse support is a state of mind—a deep-seated set of attitudes toward politics and the operation of the political system that is relatively impervious to change. For example, the sentiment "America, right or wrong" reflects diffuse support, a commitment to the political system that transcends the actual behavior of the government. In contrast, specific support is closely related to the actions and performance of the government or political elites. This kind of support is object specific in two senses. First, specific support normally applies to evaluations of political authorities; it is less relevant to support for the regime and political community. Second, specific support is based on the actual policies and general style of political authorities.

The distinction between diffuse and specific support is important in understanding the significance of public attitudes toward the political process. Democratic political systems must keep the support of their citizens if they are to remain viable. Yet, since all governments occasionally fail to meet public expectations, short-term failures to satisfy public demands must not directly erode support for the regime or political community. In other words, a democratic political system requires a reservoir of diffuse support independent of immediate policy outputs (specific support) if it is to weather periods of public disaffection and dissatisfaction.

The history of German democracy illustrates the significance of diffuse support. The Weimar Republic was built on an unstable foundation. Many Germans felt that the creation of the republic at the end of World War I, by lessening support for war, contributed to Germany's wartime defeat; from the outset, the regime was stigmatized as a traitor to the nation. Important sectors of the political establishment—the military, the civil service, and the judiciary—and many citizens questioned the legitimacy of the new regime and retained attachments to the political system of the former German Empire. The fledgling democratic state then faced a series of major crises: postwar economic hardships, attempted right-wing and left-wing coups, French occupation of the Ruhr, and explosive inflation in the early

1920s. The political system was never able to build up a pool of diffuse support for the republic. Consequently, the dissatisfaction created by the Great Depression in the 1930s easily eroded popular support for political authorities and the democratic regime. Communists and Nazis argued that the democratic political system was at fault, and the Weimar Republic succumbed to these attacks.[3]

The democratic transition in the German Democratic Republic also illustrates the importance of cultural and institutional congruence. Surveys of East German youth found a marked decrease in support for the communist principles of the GDR during the 1980s (Friedrich and Griese 1990). These youths led the populist revolution in the East that weakened the regime in the fall of 1989. Moreover, revelations in early 1990 about the communists' abuses of power eroded the regime's popular base still further and created a race toward unification with the West.

Early cross-national opinion studies provided empirical support for the proposition that popular support was a requisite of stable democracy. Gabriel Almond and Sidney Verba (1963) found that system affect in the late 1950s was most widespread in the long-established democracies of the United States and Great Britain. For example, 85 percent of Americans and 46 percent of Britons spontaneously mentioned their political system as a source of national pride. This system affect indicated the diffuse support that had developed in these nations over their long democratic histories. Satisfaction with the policy outputs of government was also common in both nations. In contrast, system support was more limited in the newly formed democracies of West Germany and Italy; only 7 percent of West Germans and 3 percent of Italians mentioned their political system as a source of national pride. These findings suggested that diffuse political support was underdeveloped in these systems, raising fears that democracy was still fragile in these two formerly fascist states. The early years of the Federal Republic were closely watched by those who worried that the Bonn Republic would follow the same course as Weimar.

Another cross-national study, by Hadley Cantril (1965), found a similar pattern in public opinions. Cantril showed that positive national self-images were more common among the stable, well-run democracies. More recent research by Ronald Inglehart (1990, chap. 1) found that a democratic political culture was strongly correlated with the stability of democratic institutions. Although one can never be certain whether stable government produces popular support or whether popular support produces stable government, these two phenomena are interrelated.

Authoritarian states may endure without the support of their publics, but popular support is essential for democracies to survive. Therefore, we need to assess the breadth and depth of popular support for democracy as a crucial element in diagnosing democracy's future.

Declining Confidence in Authorities

Public concerns about the democratic process normally begin with questions about the holders of power. Americans do not doubt the institutions of governance, but they may criticize Richard Nixon's actions during Watergate, George Bush's involvement in the Iran-*contra* negotiations, or Bill Clinton's multiple indiscretions. Indeed, a variety of evidence points to Americans' growing skepticism of their leaders. For example, the American National Election Study has measured feelings toward political officials and the government over time (figure 12.1). The early readings described a largely supportive public. Most Americans believed that one can trust the government to do what is right (71 percent), that there are few dishonest people in government (68 percent), and that most officials know what they are doing (56 percent). These positive feelings remained relatively unchanged until the mid-1960s and then declined precipitously. Conflict over civil rights and Vietnam divided Americans and eroded public confidence in their leaders; Watergate and a seemingly endless stream of political scandals pushed support even lower over the next decade.

Distrust of government officials reached a low point in 1980, when the upbeat presidency of Ronald Reagan temporarily reversed these trends. Reagan stressed the positive aspects of American society and politics—and opinions rebounded in 1984. Nevertheless, further declines continued in later elections (Miller 1991). By 1994 these indicators had hit historic lows. Only 22 percent of the American public felt one could trust the government to do the right thing most of the time, only 20 percent believed the government is run for the benefit of all, and only 48 percent thought most government officials are honest.

Questions that focus on specific politicians reaffirm the public's doubts. The American National Election Study found that support for both the Republican and Democratic candidates in 1992 had decreased to nearly historic lowpoints (Weisberg and Kimball 1995, 100). This may be a problem with the candidates themselves; however, there are also signs that the public has become more demanding in judging politics and politicians. For example, during a modest recession in 1992 Bush's popularity hit a low point that nearly matched Nixon's worst approval rating during the Watergate crisis or Harry Truman's in the midst of the Korean War (*Public Perspective,* April/May 1995, 42). The growth of candidate-centered politics

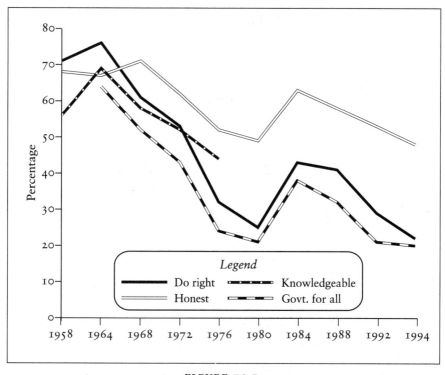

FIGURE 12.1

AMERICAN TRUST IN GOVERNMENT

SOURCES: American National Election Studies, 1958–94.

obviously does not mean that voters will be pleased with the candidates they must choose between.

When one looks back on this span of history, it is easy to see the reasons for the public's doubts about their leaders. Over any four-year electoral cycle one can repeatedly identify actions that have diminished the reputations of Congress and the executive branch: Watergate, Iran-*contra*, the savings and loan scandal, ad infinitum. Candidates promise one thing at election time but regularly fail to deliver on these promises, or even treat them as serious promises after they are elected (for example, Bush's "Read my lips, no new taxes"). And as some of the most distinguished members of Congress have resigned their office, they have left with stinging indictments of the institution. One former representative said on leaving office, "May your mother never find out where you work."

Other survey evidence shows that dissatisfaction with national leadership has spread beyond politics. A series of questions tap public confidence

TABLE 12.1
CONFIDENCE IN AMERICAN INSTITUTIONS (IN PERCENTAGES)

	1966	1971	1973	1976	1980	1984	1988	1993
Medicine	72	61	54	54	52	52	51	39
Higher education	61	37	37	38	30	29	30	22
Military	62	27	32	39	28	37	34	42
Organized religion	41	27	35	31	35	32	20	23
Supreme Court	50	23	32	35	25	35	35	30
Major corporations	55	27	29	22	27	32	25	21
Press	29	18	23	28	22	17	18	11
Executive branch	41	23	29	14	12	19	16	12
Congress	42	19	24	14	9	13	15	7
Organized labor	22	14	16	12	15	9	10	8
Average	48	28	31	29	26	28	25	22

SOURCES: 1966 and 1971, Harris Poll; 1973–93, NORC General Social Surveys.

NOTE: Table entries are the percentage expressing a great deal of confidence in the people running each institution.

in the people running major social, economic, and political organizations (table 12.1). Confidence in the leadership of virtually all institutions has tumbled downward over the past two decades. For instance, in 1966 many Americans expressed a great deal of confidence in the executive branch (41 percent) and in Congress (42 percent); these positive evaluations dropped substantially over the next two decades. Confidence in business, labor, higher education, organized religion, the military, and the medical profession underwent a similar decline. Overall confidence in American institutions reached a new low in 1993.

Greater skepticism and doubts about elites seems to be a common development in other advanced industrial democracies. In Britain, for instance, the low points of prime ministerial popularity have sunk steadily lower over the past five decades. At his nadir, John Major received lower approval ratings than any British PM in the postwar era (*Economist*, 25 September 1993). German politics during the past decade has been rocked by a series of scandals and resignations of leading political figures.[4] The deeply engrained cynicism of the French political culture has been reinforced by scandals ranging from the government's bombing of a Greenpeace ship in the mid-1980s to reports in the 1990s on Mitterrand's sexual affairs. Political scandals are not confined to the banks of the Potomac.

The 1990–91 World Values Survey compared confidence in institutions across our four nations (table 12.2).[5] The question wording and set of institutions differs from table 12.1, so the results are not directly comparable to the previous table. Still the data present a familiar pattern. The public displays its greatest confidence in nonpolitical institutions of government: the police, the legal system, and the armed services. Less than half the public in each nation express confidence in the national legislature, rating it eighth in the list of ten institutions. European confidence in these institutions averages even lower than that in the United States, despite the long-term downward American trend noted above.

Support for the national legislature dropped slightly in three of our four nations since an earlier survey in 1980, but the average rating of societal institutions has remained fairly constant over this decade.[6] Institutional images have not worsened, but they also have not improved. A sense of malaise touches many of the leaders and key institutions of Western society.

The Broadening of Discontent

Increasing public skepticism of political elites appears to be a common development in many advanced industrial democracies, but political scientists

TABLE 12.2

CROSS-NATIONAL CONFIDENCE IN SOCIETAL INSTITUTIONS
(IN PERCENTAGES)

	United States	Great Britain	West Germany	France
Police	75	77	70	65
Legal system	57	52	65	56
Armed services	48	80	39	54
Educational system	55	46	53	64
Churches	67	45	39	48
Major companies	50	46	38	60
Civil service	59	45	38	46
Legislature	42	44	50	43
Trade unions	32	27	36	30
Press	56	15	34	37
Average	54	48	42	50

SOURCE: 1990–91 World Values Survey.

NOTE: Table entries are the percentage expressing "a great deal" or "quite a lot" of confidence in each institution. Missing data are included in the calculation of percentages.

disagree on whether these opinions reflect doubts about political authorities or more fundamental questions about the regime and democratic process.

The debate was first taken up by Arthur Miller (1974a, 1974b) and Jack Citrin (1974). Miller argued that popular dissatisfaction with the repeated policy failures and political scandals of government officials was being generalized into broader criticism of the political process as a whole. Miller spelled out the potentially grave consequences the loss of regime support could have for the American political process.

Citrin felt that Miller overstated the problem. He interpreted the trends in political support as a sign of popular disenchantment with the incumbents of government or political authorities in general, not distrust in the system of American government. Citrin claimed that (1974, 987) "political systems, like baseball teams, have slumps and winning seasons. Having recently endured a succession of losing seasons, Americans boo the home team when it takes the field." Citrin maintained that these boos show opposition not to the process of democratic government but to the players in the lineup and their recent performance on the field. Hence, a few new

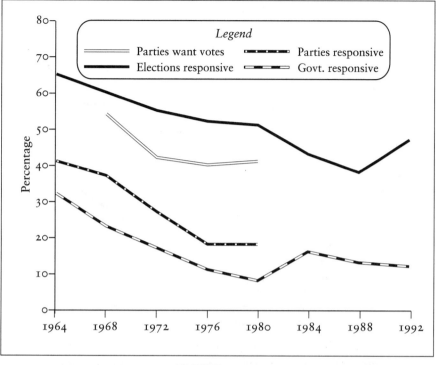

FIGURE 12.2

RESPONSIVENESS OF AMERICAN POLITICAL INSTITUTIONS

SOURCES: American National Election Studies, 1958–92.

stars or a few winning streaks, and the decline in public confidence might be reversed; the trends of distrust had limited significance for Citrin.

Citrin's caution was warranted in 1974, but as two more decades have passed, public disenchantment continues. Accumulating evidence suggests that the decline in public confidence is broader than just dissatisfaction with present political elites. For example, several questions from the American National Election Study examine the perceived responsiveness of government and political institutions (figure 12.2). These questions show a trend of decreasing confidence in parties, elections, and the government in general. One observer of these trends suggested that the political creed for contemporary American politics should read "In God we trust: everyone else pays cash."

This erosion of public confidence in politics is not unique to the United States. British citizens are well known for their deference to political elites and support of democratic institutions. Yet these aspects of the

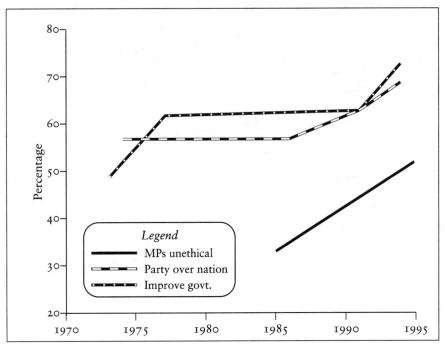

FIGURE 12.3

THE GROWTH OF BRITISH DISTRUST IN GOVERNMENT

SOURCES: Curtice and Jowell (1995); Gallup (1995).

British political culture also have eroded (Curtice and Jowell 1995). The data in figure 12.3 illustrate how British distrust of government has increased over time. In 1974, about half of the public (57 percent) felt the government put partisan interests ahead of the national interest; by 1994, a full 73 percent shared these negative views. Similarly, the percentage who felt the government could be improved "quite a lot" or "a great deal" increased over this time period. Furthermore, these trends began in the mid-1970s, and by this time a substantial growth in political dissatisfaction had already occurred (Kavanaugh 1980; Topf 1989). Feelings of deference are clearly in the past. In 1987, for example, less than half of Britons believed that either civil servants, the national government, or local councils could be trusted to serve the public interest (Jowell and Topf 1988).

Distrust between the citizen and the state is a basic aspect of the French political culture. Many French feel alienated from their overly centralized and bureaucratized political system. Throughout the past decade, most French citizens expressed dissatisfaction with the functioning of their political system (Fuchs et al. 1996). Promised political reforms never materialize under conservative or socialist governments.

Germany was initially an exception to this general trend of declining public confidence in the democratic process. From an undemocratic beginning, popular support for the institutions of democratic government steadily grew during the postwar years (Baker et al. 1981; Conradt 1980). This remaking of the political culture eventually produced nearly universal agreement that democracy is the best form of government, as well as growing commitment to democratic institutions and procedures.

Despite this long-term growth in system support and democratic norms, signs of a new skepticism have begun to appear. In recent years a series of political scandals and exposés on the excesses of the political parties has raised new concerns about the functioning of the democratic system (Kaase 1996). Germans now speak of the crisis of party government, and the German term *Politikverdrossenheit* (political vexation) has become a common part of the public's political vocabulary.

German unification has expanded democracy to the East, but it has also raised new strains within the political system and created some new doubts about the workings of representative democracy. Early public opinion surveys found that East Germans began their modern experience with democracy with positive orientations toward the new political order, broadly supporting the democratic process. As they learn about the realities of democratic politics, however, their ideals are being tested (and probably lowered). For instance, a recent survey found that Westerners are equally supportive of democracy as an ideal form of government and as practiced in the Federal Republic. By comparison, a majority of Easterners are supportive of the democratic ideal but *uncertain about democracy as it is practiced in the FRG*. Residents in eastern Germany are now learning that even in democracies there is a gap between democratic theory and political reality; often this is a rude shock.

Table 12.3 illustrates how widespread criticisms of government have become in our four core nations. Barely half of the public in any of the three Western European states is satisfied with the way democracy works in their nation. Except in the United States, high proportions of these publics feel that they could do nothing if the government passed an unjust law. It is not surprising that 94 percent of East Germans in 1990 believed that government should be made more open to the public—the communist state of East Germany was being dismantled as these interviews were conducted. It is more surprising to see that overwhelming majorities in the established Western democracies share these opinions. Despite the downward trends in political trust we have previously described for the

TABLE 12.3

MEASURES OF POLITICAL SUPPORT

(IN PERCENTAGES)

	United States	Great Britain	West Germany	France	East Germany
Satisfied with functioning of democracy	—	49	57	47	35
Could do nothing to change unjust law	29	48	62	67	55
Government should be more open	83	86	89	85	94
Government should allow more freedom	45	48	39	49	85
Elected officials lose touch with people	78	84	86	85	87
Officials don't care what people like me think	44	35	31	27	29

SOURCES: Satisfaction item is from Eurobarometer 41 (June 1994); the last two items are from the Pulse of Europe study (Times/Mirror 1991); the other data are from the 1990–91 World Values Survey.

NOTE: Missing data were included in the calculation of percentages.

American public, Americans are still relatively supportive compared to these other nations. Political doubts are most common among the French.

Other items in the lower half of the table reflect a general skepticism of political elites. Many individuals believe that officials quickly lose touch with the people, and a significant minority even feel that elected officials do not care what the public thinks.

When the signs of growing popular skepticism first appeared in American public opinion surveys during the late 1960s and early 1970s, there were reasons to link these findings to the immediate problems of American politics. These were exceptionally turbulent years for the United States. A decade of social protest, a divisive and costly war, economic recession, and unprecedented corruption by government officials strained the fiber of American politics far beyond its regular bounds. As politics returned to more "normal" times and the memory of these earlier events faded, trust in government improved during the Reagan years. The players in the game had changed, and the new manager of the home team was a master communicator. And yet the continuation of these American trends into the 1990s and parallel evidence from other advanced industrial democracies suggest that we are witnessing more than a temporary slump in politicians' performance. Contemporary publics have raised their expectations of government: they are more demanding of politicians and their governments. Furthermore, an increasingly critical media and more open public discussion of government reinforces public doubts about the political process. From the Nixon tapes to the Packwood diaries, the public sees reasons for skepticism. Thus, rather than a transient phenomenon, a skeptical public seems to be another feature of the new style of citizen politics.

Feelings of System Support

Many of the survey questions analyzed so far have measured support for the incumbents of government or could be interpreted in these terms. Trust in "politicians" or the "government in Washington" (or Westminster) focuses attitudes on the government or elites in general. Even questions assessing confidence in social and political institutions might be interpreted as evaluations of the present leadership of these institutions. Therefore, we sought out questions that more clearly tap basic feelings of system support to determine whether the malaise reaches to the political system and society.

One aspect of system support involves the "system affect" described by Almond and Verba (1963). A strong emotional attachment to the nation presumably provides a reservoir of diffuse support that can maintain a political system through temporary periods of political stress. One measure of such feelings involves pride in one's nation. Figure 12.4 displays the percentage who feel very proud of their nation in a set of advanced industrial democracies.[7] On the whole, feelings of national pride are relatively stable across this decade. There are, however, marked national differences in these feelings.

National pride is exceptionally high in the United States; 75 percent of the public was very proud to be American in 1991. The chants of *USA! USA! USA!* are not limited to Olympic competition; they signify a persisting feeling among Americans. Most Europeans express their national pride in more moderate tones. Britons express relatively high degrees of national pride; the bifurcated division of the French political culture yields more modest rates of national pride.

Germans are especially hesitant in their statements of national pride. The trauma of the Third Reich burned a deep scar in the German psyche in both west and east. Especially among the young, there is a strong feeling that the nationalist excesses of the past should never be repeated. The Federal Republic therefore avoided many of the emotional national symbols

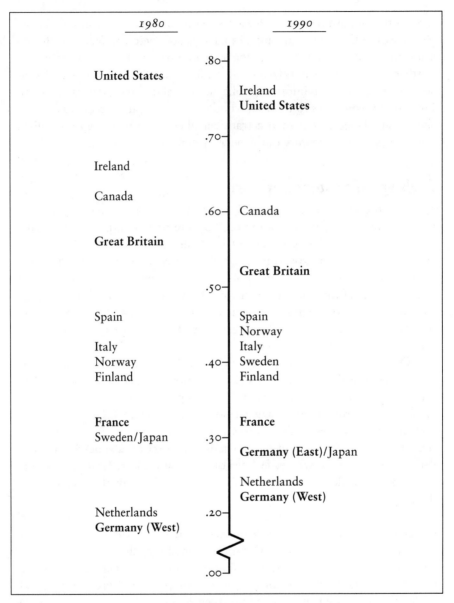

FIGURE 12.4
FEELINGS OF NATIONAL PRIDE
(IN PERCENTAGES)

SOURCES: 1980–81 World Values Survey and 1990–91 World Values Survey.

that are common in other industrial nations. There are few political holidays or memorials, the national anthem is seldom played, and even the anniversary of the founding of the Federal Republic attracts little public attention. Although most citizens are proud to be German, they avoid the unquestioning emotional attachment to state and nation (Dalton 1992, chap. 4; Topf et al. 1989).[8]

Another element of system support involves attitudes toward society and the political system. A standard question in several recent surveys measures public support for social change through revolutionary action. Table 12.4 shows that support for revolutionary social change represents a mere trace element in each nation. Indeed, support for improving society through gradual reforms is consistently the preferred response in each nation.

In summary, these global measures of identification with the nation or support for the basic structure of society do not display the same downward spiral that we have found for other measures of political support. Dieter Fuchs and his colleagues (1996) found that support for the democratic ideal is nearly universal among European publics. Doubts about the incumbents in office or the operation of the political process have not generalized to the democratic system itself.

The Future of Democratic Politics

Western publics have grown more critical of political elites and less positive toward government. The analyses of this chapter have determined the present boundaries of these sentiments. The decline in political trust is most dramatic for evaluations of politicians and political elites in general. The deference to authority that once was common in many Western democracies has partially been replaced by public skepticism of elites. Closer scrutiny of government actions by the public and media uncovers political scandals and policy failures that further erode political trust. The public's distrust of politicians has substantial supporting evidence.

Ironically, there are indications that the collapse of communism in Europe and the end of the Cold War may accentuate these trends (Fuchs et al. 1996). Since 1990, the Eurobarometer surveys have found a broad decrease in satisfaction with the functioning of democracy among European publics. Without the international threat from the Soviet Union—and without the negative example of communist political life—Western publics may feel more open in expressing their doubts about democratic politics. Without the contrast to communism, citizens may judge contemporary democracies against the democratic ideal.

TABLE 12.4
SUPPORT FOR SOCIAL CHANGE
(IN PERCENTAGES)

	United States		Great Britain			West Germany			France		
	1981	1990	1976	1983	1990	1970	1983	1990	1970	1983	1990
Change society by revolutionary action	5	6	7	4	5	2	3	2	5	7	4
Improve society through reforms	66	67	60	59	75	70	48	59	78	64	70
Defend society against subversives	20	16	35	30	13	20	40	28	12	23	20
No opinion	9	11	8	7	8	8	9	11	5	6	7
Total	100	100	100	100	100	100	100	100	100	100	100

SOURCES: 1981 World Values Survey; 1990–91 World Values Survey; Eurobarometers.

In addition, lower levels of political support may reflect changes in how the public evaluates politics and politicians. In place of the diffuse support of the past, when politics was a distant and relatively obscure process, citizens are now more likely to follow politics and to base their evaluations on instrumental criteria (Streek 1987). The old refrain "What have you done for me lately?" is now used more than ever. In addition, the public now expects more of government officials. Personal, financial, or sexual indiscretions were often ignored by the press and treated as irrelevant to politics; higher standards of public behavior are now being applied.

Feelings of mistrust have gradually broadened to include evaluations of the political regime and other institutions in society. The lack of confidence in politics and political institutions is widespread. But public skepticism has not significantly affected support for the political system and national community. As citizens are criticizing the incumbents in government, they are simultaneously expressing support for the democratic creed.

The consequences of declining political trust have become a visible part of contemporary politics. A more skeptical public is more likely to question government policies, and this probably has contributed to the trend toward increased issue voting and growing electoral volatility. Political distrust also is related to the use of protest and other forms of unconventional political action (chapter 4). These changes have often strained the democratic process, as demonstrators challenge established political elites and present government structures. The rise of new social movements and citizen interest groups has further institutionalized the changing nature of citizen politics.

A decade ago it was common to cite these new citizen demands as evidence of a crisis of democracy (Crozier et al. 1975; Huntington 1981). Supposedly excessive public demands were overloading the ability of governments to perform. Some conservatives used the elitist theory of democracy (chapter 2) to offer a solution to this crisis. In a crude exaggeration of the theory, they maintained that if a supportive and quiescent public ensures a smoothly functioning political system, then we must redevelop these traits in contemporary publics. The centrifugal tendencies of democratic politics (and the demands of the public) must be controlled, and political authority must be reestablished. Samuel Huntington assumed the ermine robes as spokesperson for this position:

> The problem of governance in the United States today stems from an "excess of democracy" ... the effective operation of a democratic political system usually requires some measure of apathy and non-involvement on the part of some individuals and groups. The vulnerability of democratic

government in the United States comes ... from the internal dynamics of democracy itself in a highly educated, mobilized, and participatory society. (1975, 37–38)

In short, these analysts argued that the crisis of democracy had developed because too many people wanted to apply the creed of democracy and egalitarian values to themselves, whereas such values were intended only for a small core of political activists. These analysts contended that democracy was overloaded because minorities are no longer apathetic, women are demanding equality, students are no longer docile, and the working class is no longer deferential. If these groups would only leave politics to the politicians, and their expert advisers, "democracy" would again be secure.[9]

The cure offered by the elitist theorists was worse than the problem it addressed; democracy's very goals were ignored in its defense. The critics of citizen politics forgot that democracy means popular control of elites, not elite control over the populace.

The New Politics diagnosis of the problem was fundamentally different from the crisis-of-democracy literature. This view held that if the government was overloaded, it was because government had not modernized and reformed itself to match the new needs and demands of its citizens (Dahl 1989; Dalton and Kuechler 1990; Barber 1984). The decline in political support had not eroded support for democratic principles; the public was criticizing how these principles were functioning in a system of representative democracy. The solution was to improve democracy, not to accept nondemocratic alternatives.

This diagnosis called for the government to address the growing needs of modern societies more effectively. Governments demand a large share of the national wealth and possess tremendous potential. Yet this potential is not always evident when important decisions must be made (see, for example, Feldman and Milch 1982). According to the polls, Americans have favored cost-cutting steps to address the nation's budget deficit, but Washington remains ineffective. The malevolent influence of special interests are used to rationalize inaction, but Congress takes little action to redress the political balance in favor of the national interest. European governments struggle with their own seemingly intractable problems. Governments (and especially incumbent politicians) seem too concerned with preservation of the status quo and too little interested in present and future social needs.

Equally important, democratic governments need to accommodate the expanding political interests of contemporary publics. The potential for citizen participation was limited by the traditional definitions of democratic politics, especially in Western Europe. The opportunities for electoral input are scandalously low for most Europeans. An opportunity to cast a few votes during a multiyear electoral cycle is not a record of citizen input that should be admired. The fundamental structure of contemporary democratic institutions was developed in the nineteenth century; society has changed a good deal since then.

An emphasis on increased citizen action is not simply participation for participation's sake. Expanding citizen participation opens up political systems that have become sclerosed by corporatist policymaking and bureaucratized administration. The triumvirate of business-labor-government in many advanced industrial democracies often restricts the political interests of other groups. A system that distorts access to the political process is necessarily inefficient in meeting all of society's needs. Expanding citizen access to politics is one method to ensure that governments become more responsive to a broader spectrum of political demands. This does not increase the quantity of political needs—the needs of the environment, women, consumers, and other groups exist—instead, it ensures that these needs receive fair attention from the government and thereby improve the government's ability to address all societal needs.

Increased political involvement also educates citizens in the democratic process. James Wright (1976, 260) noted a basic irony in the elitists' criticisms of citizen participation. The critics believe that governments can generate more support by convincing citizens of a lie (a sense of political efficacy that is fictitious) than by encouraging citizens to participate and learn of the necessary limits to their influence. The "big lie" may work for a while, but as soon as someone points out the gap between myth and reality the political credibility of the system falters. It happened to the East German government in 1989, and it happened to George Bush in 1992. Call it co-optation, pragmatism, or Jeffersonian idealism, involving citizens in the democratic process is one method to increase their identification with the process.

Finally, increasing citizen input improves the quality of government decision making. Citizen participation is not a panacea for all of societies' modern ills. Even educated, informed, and politically involved citizens will still make errors in judgment. As Benjamin Barber notes:

> Democracy does not place endless faith in the capacity of individuals to govern themselves, but it affirms with Machiavelli that the multitude will on the whole be as wise or wiser than princes, and with Theodore Roosevelt that "the majority of plain people will day in and day out make fewer mistakes in governing themselves than another smaller body of men will make in trying to govern them." (1984, 151)

Since I presented this evaluation of contemporary democratic politics in the first edition of *Citizen Politics*, there have been encouraging signs that politicians and governments are beginning to respond to these calls for reform. Calls for political reform have become the new catchphrases of politics, ranging from outsiders such as Perot to insiders such as Bill Bradley or Warren Rudman. From Clinton's call for a New Covenant to the Republicans' Contract with America, politicians now claim they want to change the status quo.

Even more significant, there have been institutional reforms that actually change the political process. A recent review of the social movement literature paints a positive picture of the ability of citizen interest groups to increase direct citizen participation in policymaking (Dalton 1993c). In Germany, for example, local citizen-action groups have won changes in administrative law to allow for citizen participation in local administrative processes. Italian environmental legislation now grants individuals legal standing in the courts when they seek to protect the environment from the actions of municipalities or government administrative agencies. There have been similar reforms in the United States that provide individual citizens and citizen groups greater access to the political process (Ingram and Smith 1993). The term-limit movement is another expression of these reformist sentiments. A majority of states have now enacted some form of term-limit legislation, normally through citizen initiatives.

Other forms of direct democracy are also increasing. Citizen groups in the United States and Europe are making greater use of referendums to involve the public directly in policymaking. There have also been reforms within the structured system of party government. The formation of new parties is one sign of adaptation. In addition, even the established parties are changing. The British Labour Party has increased the role of party members in the selection of parliamentary candidates, and the German SPD used a mail ballot of its members to select its chancellor candidate in 1994. These institutional changes are difficult to accomplish and therefore are likely to precede at a slow pace; but once implemented, they restructure the whole process of making policy that extends beyond a single issue or a single policy agenda.

Indeed, these adaptations reflect the very strength of democracy to grow and evolve—the lack of such adaptivity is what brought about the downfall of communism. As the German sociologist Ralf Dahrendorf noted during the high point of the crisis-of-democracy debate:

> What we have to do above all is to maintain that flexibility of democratic institutions which is in some ways their greatest virtue: the ability of dem-

ocratic institutions to implement and effect change without revolution —the ability to react to new problems in new ways—the ability to develop institutions rather than change them all the time—the ability to keep the lines of communication open between leaders and led—and the ability to make individuals count above all. (1975, 194)

These changes in the style of representative democracy are accompanied by some risks. There may be some growing pains as the political process adjusts to increasing citizen participation, especially in the more tightly structured European political systems. One potential problem is the possibility of a growing participation gap between sophisticated and unsophisticated citizens (see chapter 3). Democracies must also face the challenge of balancing greater responsiveness to specific interests against the broader interests of the nation.

Participatory democracy can generate political excesses, but it also contains within it an equilibrium mechanism to encourage political balance. In America this process has generally succeeded in retaining the benefits of new ideas while avoiding the dire predictions about the excesses of democracy. We should remember that democratic politics is not designed to maximize government efficiency and increase the autonomy of political elites. Just the opposite. Efficiency is partially sacrificed to ensure a more important goal: popular control of elites. Expanding participation is not a problem but an opportunity for the advanced industrial democracies to come closer to matching their democratic ideals.

In summary, the crisis of democracy is really a challenge. Democracies need to adapt to present-day politics and the new style of citizen politics. Change may be threatening to some, and it does present a risk—but change is necessary. The challenge to democracies is to continue to evolve, to guarantee political right, and to increase the ability of citizens to control their lives.

Notes

1. Tocqueville made an interesting observation about American and European democracy that still applies. He noted that European democracy was based on the premise that political institutions are a control mechanism, to limit the influence of traditional elites with counterbalancing popular pressure. Democracy in the United States was based on popular sovereignty and was viewed as a method to allow citizens to control their own affairs.

2. In the mid-1980s Samuel Huntington (1984) was explaining why there would be no more democracies in the world, a theme consistent with his elitist

view of democracy. By the end of the decade he was describing democratization as a wave that was transforming the international order (Huntington 1991).

3. The argument is also made that diffuse regime support existed in most other Western democracies. Consequently, dissatisfaction focused on the performance of political elites in these systems. These feelings were channeled within the political process, and the basic structure of democratic government persisted in the United States, Britain, and France.

4. For instance, in the early 1980s a number of leading politicians were implicated in an illegal party financing scandal (Flick affair); another party finance scandal occurred in the mid-1980s; this was followed by a "dirty tricks" election campaign scandal in which the implicated candidate committed suicide; then a few years later the opposing candidate in the "dirty tricks" scandal was forced to resign from his position as SPD leader for his role in the coverup.

5. These data are based on the Gallup question wording that measures confidence in the institutions per se. For a comparison of the different measures of confidence in institutions, see Lipset and Schneider (1983, chap. 3).

6. In 1980 the national legislature received the following ratings: United States (53 percent), Britain (40), West Germany (53), and France (48). For additional discussion of these longitudinal trends see Inglehart (forthcoming).

7. The question asked: How proud are you to be (nationality)? The responses were (1) very proud, (2) quite proud, (3) not very proud, and (4) not at all proud. The figure presents the "very proud" responses.

8. Heavy stress has been placed on Almond and Verba's (1963) finding that few Germans took pride in their political system (7 percent), while many more (33 percent) were proud of their economic system. Surveys in 1978 and 1988 found that almost a third of the West German public was openly proud of the political system and its democratic institutions, and another large group was proud of the policy accomplishments of the political system besides economics (Conradt 1980; Topf et al. 1989).

9. Huntington's advice on limiting political demands overlooks the possibility of constraining the input of Harvard professors, corporate executives, and the upper class. His focus solely on the participation of average citizens suggests that he has confused the definitions of plutocracy and democracy.

Appendix A.
Major Data Sources

The establishment of scientific election surveys began in the United States with local surveys during the 1940 election. In 1948 researchers at the University of Michigan conducted one of the first national election surveys based on scientific sampling methods. The four scholars who directed the early surveys—Angus Campbell, Philip Converse, Warren Miller, and Donald Stokes—wrote the landmark study of American public opinion, *The American Voter.* Since then, the Center for Political Studies (formerly part of the Survey Research Center) has continued this election study series at each biennial national election. The University of Michigan series has become a national resource in the social sciences and is used by researchers in hundreds of universities worldwide.

A comparable series of British election studies was begun by David Butler and Donald Stokes with the 1964 election. These scholars continued the series through the 1966 and 1970 elections; a team of researchers at the University of Essex, led by Ivor Crewe, continued the series in 1974 and 1979. Since 1983, the British election study has been conducted by Anthony Heath, Roger Jowell, and John Curtice of Social and Community Planning, Research (SCPR) in London.

Academic studies of German elections trace their roots back to the 1961 study conducted by Gerhard Baumert, Erwin Scheuch, and Rudolf Wildenmann from the University of Cologne. The Cologne researchers and their students have continued this series to the present through the work of Max Kaase, Hans-Dieter Klingemann, Franz Pappi, and the Forschungsgruppe Wahlen (Manfred Berger, Wolfgang Gibowski, Dieter Roth, and Mattias Jung) in Mannheim.

France lacks a project of continuous monitoring and public dissemination of data on citizen electoral behavior. A number of individual scholars have conducted surveys of specific French elections: Roland Cayrol and his associates, as well as Philip Converse and Roy Pierce. These independent studies provide a limited opportunity to track the evolution of French political behavior during the Fifth Republic.

Most of the data analyzed in this volume were drawn from these data sources; specific listing follows. Most of these data were acquired from the Inter-university Consortium for Political and Social Research (ICPSR) at the University of Michigan in Ann Arbor. Additional data were made available by the ESRC Archive at the University of Essex, England; the Zentralarchiv für empirische Sozialforschung (ZA), University of Cologne, Germany; and the Banque de Données Socio-Politiques, University of Grenoble, France. Neither the archives nor the original collectors of the data bear responsibility for the analyses presented here.

American National Elections Studies (ANES)

1948 American National Election Study ($N = 622$). Angus Campbell and Robert Kahn.

1952 American National Election Study ($N = 1,899$). Angus Campbell, Gerald Gurin, et al.

1956 American National Election Study ($N = 1,762$). Angus Campbell, Philip Converse, et al.

1960 American National Election Study ($N = 1,181$). Angus Campbell, Philip Converse, et al.

1964 American National Election Study ($N = 1,571$). Political Behavior Program.

1968 American National Election Study ($N = 1,557$). Political Behavior Program.

1972 American National Election Study ($N = 2,705$). Warren Miller, Arthur Miller, et al.

1976 American National Election Study ($N = 2,248$). Warren Miller, Arthur Miller, et al.

1980 American National Election Study ($N = 1,614$). Warren Miller et al.

1984 American National Election Study ($N = 2,257$). Warren Miller et al.

1988 American National Election Study ($N = 2,040$). Warren Miller et al.

1992 American National Election Study ($N = 2,485$). Warren Miller et al.

British Election Studies

1964 British Election Study ($N = 1,769$). David Butler and Donald Stokes.

1966 British Election Study (N = 1,874). David Butler and Donald Stokes.

1970 British Election Study (N = 1,885). David Butler and Donald Stokes.

1974 British Election Study, February (N = 2,462). Ivor Crewe, Bo Saarlvik, and James Alt.

1974 British Election Study, October (N = 2,365). Ivor Crewe, Bo Saarlvik, and James Alt.

1979 British Election Study (N = 1,893). Ivor Crewe, Bo Saarlik, and David Robertson.

1983 British Election Study (N = 3,955). Anthony Heath, Roger Jowell, and John Curtice.

1987 British Election Study (N = 3,826). Anthony Heath, Roger Jowell, John Curtice, and Sharon Witherspoon.

1992 British Election Study (N = 3,534). Anthony Heath, Roger Jowell, and John Curtice.

German Election Studies

1953 The Social Bases of West German Politics (N = 3,246). UNESCO Institute.

1961 West German Election Study (N = 1,679, 1,633, 1,715). Gerhart Baumert, Erwin Scheuch, and Rudolf Wildenmann.

1965 West German Election Study, October (N = 1,305). DIVO Institut.

1965 West German Election Study, September (N = 1,411). Rudolf Wildenmann and Max Kaase.

1969 West German Election Study (N = 1,158). Hans Klingemann and Franz Pappi.

1972 West German Election Study (N = 2,052). Manfred Berger, Wolfgang Gibowski, Max Kaase, Dieter Roth, Uwe Schleth, and Rudolf Wildenmann.

1976 West German Election Study (N = 2,076). Forschungsgruppe Wahlen.

1980 West German Election Study (N = 1,620). Forschungsgruppe Wahlen.

1983 West German Election Study (N = 1,622). Forschungsgruppe Wahlen.

1987 West German Election Study (N = 1,954). Forschungsgruppe Wahlen.

1990 German Election Study, November (West = 984; East = 1,095). Forschungsgruppe Wahlen.

1994   German Election Study, September (West = 1,013; East = 1,068). Forschungsgruppe Wahlen.

French Election Studies

1958   French Election Study (N = 1,650). Georges Dupeux. Available ICPSR.
1967   French Election Study (N = 2,046). Philip Converse and Roy Pierce.
1968   French Election Study (N = 1,905). Ronald Inglehart.
1978   French Election Study (N = 4,507). Jacques Capdevielle, Elisabeth Dupoirier, Gerard Frunberg, Etienne Schweisguth, and Colette Ysmal.

Major Crossnational Studies

1959   The Civic Culture Study (U.S. = 970, Great Britain = 963, West Germany = 955). Gabriel Almond and Sidney Verba.
1974   Political Action Study (U.S. = 1,719, Great Britain = 1,483, West Germany = 2,307). Samuel Barnes, Max Kaase, et al.
1981   World Values Survey (U.S. = 1,729, Great Britain = 1,231, West Germany = 1,305, France = 1,200). Gallup Research.
1990   World Values Survey (U.S. = 1,839, Great Britain = 1,484, West Germany = 2,101, France = 1,002, East Germany = 1,336). Ronald Inglehart and the European Values Systems Study Group.
1970–   European Community Surveys/Eurobarometers (ongoing series of opinion surveys conducted by the Commission of the European Union).

Appendix B.
1990–91 World Values Survey

One of the key sources of public opinion data in this book is the 1990–91 World Values Survey. To assist students and instructors in understanding the causes and correlates of public opinion, Chatham House is providing a subset of data from the World Values Survey to instructors using *Citizen Politics* in their courses. Students can use these data for research projects that explore themes discussed in this volume or other elements of public opinion included in this study.

This appendix provides a brief description of the World Values Survey and then an abbreviated codebook that describes the variables included in this subset. A computer diskette containing these data is available from Chatham House for instructors adopting this text for their classes.

World Values Surveys

The World Values Surveys are a series of representative national surveys designed to provide an empirical base for the study of social and cultural change among the publics of societies throughout the world.

These surveys build on a project launched by the European Values Systems Study Group (EVSSG), which carried out a cross-national survey of the publics of ten West European countries in 1981. In 1990, these surveys were expanded and replicated; this time they were designed with input from colleagues in North America, Eastern Europe, Latin America, and Asia. The European surveys were designed and executed under the direction of an EVSSG Steering Committee, consisting of Ruud de Moor, chair; David Barker; Karel Dobbelaere; Loek Halman, secretary; Ronald Inglehart; Jan Kerkhofs; Renate Koecher; Jacques Rabier; Helene Riffault; and Noel Timms. Ronald Inglehart coordinated the non-European surveys and assembled and documented the forty-nation dataset from which this subset is derived.

The 1990–91 World Values Survey examines a broader range of cross-cultural variation than has ever before been available in representative national samples. It was carried out in forty-two nations throughout the world, representing almost 70 percent of the world's population and covering the full range of variation, from societies with per capita incomes as low as $300 per year to societies with per capita incomes well over $20,000 per year, and from long-established democracies with market economies to ex-socialist and authoritarian states. This subset includes the data for four (previously five) nations: the United States, Great Britain, France, western Germany, and eastern Germany. I would like to thank Ronald Inglehart for providing this release of the data. The full data for these nations, and the additional nations, are available from the Interuniversity Consortium for Political and Social Research at the University of Michigan.

Data Acquisition

The data described in this appendix are available from Chatham House Publishers, Inc., to instructors who adopt *Citizen Politics* for classroom use. The data are available on an IBM formatted diskette. The diskette includes data for all four nations and SPSS control cards. To acquire the disk, contact Chatham House Publishers, P.O. Box One, Chatham, NJ 07928.

List of Variables

V01 Nation
V02 Weight

Political Involvement
V03 Discuss political matters
V04 Are you interested in politics
V05 Would sign a petition
V06 Would join a boycott
V07 Would attend a lawful demonstration
V08 Would join an unofficial strike
V09 Would occupy a building
V10 Protest scale

Political Values
V11 Can most people be trusted
V12 Postmaterial values scale—short

V13 Postmaterial values scale—long
V14 Left/Right scale
V15 Party preference
V16 Left/Right party preference

Socioeconomic Attitudes
V17 Attitude toward income inequality
V18 Attitude toward government ownership of business
V19 Attitude toward government guaranteeing well-being
V20 Attitude toward guaranteed employment

Environmental Attitudes
V21 Would give part of my income to prevent pollution
V22 Would pay more taxes to prevent pollution
V23 Government should reduce pollution without costing money
V24 Protecting the environment is less important than often suggested

Discrimination
V25 Job discrimination against women
V26 Job discrimination against the elderly
V27 Job discrimination against immigrants
V28 Job discrimination again the handicapped

Moral Values
V29 Believe in good and evil
V30 Believe in God
V31 Believe in life after death
V32 Believe in devil
V33 Believe in heaven
V34 Believe in hell
V35 Sexual freedom

Gender-related Issues
V36 A working mother can establish relationship with child
V37 Child suffers if mother works
V38 Housework as fulfilling as working for pay
V39 Having a job best way for woman to be independent
V40 Abortion is justifiable

Social Movements
V41 Approve of ecology movement

V42 Approve of antinuclear energy movement
V43 Approve of disarmament movement
V44 Approve of human rights movement
V45 Approve of women's movement
V46 Approve of anti-apartheid movement

Political Support
V47 Proud of nation
V48 Would fight for country
V49 Attitude toward social change
V50 Confidence in legal system
V51 Confidence in press
V52 Confidence in unions
V53 Confidence in police
V54 Confidence in Parliament
V55 Confidence in civil service
V56 Confidence in business
V57 Could do something about unjust law

Social Characteristics
V58 Religious denomination
V59 Frequency of church attendance
V60 Are you religious
V61 Ethnicity
V62 Gender
V63 Age
V64 Education
V65 Respondent's occupation
V66 Town size

Codebook

V01 *Nation*

1	United States	$(N = 1,839)$
2	Great Britain	$(N = 1,484)$
3	West Germany	$(N = 2,101)$
4	France	$(N = 1,002)$
5	East Germany	$(N = 1,336)$

V02 *Weight*
This variable must be used with weight procedures to produce a representative national survey in the United States, Great Britain, and West Germany.

V03 *Discuss politics*
When you get together with your friends, would you say you discuss political matters frequently, occasionally, or never?
1 Frequently
2 Occasionally
3 Never
9 Missing data

V04 *Interest in politics*
How interested would you say you are in politics?
1 Very interested
2 Somewhat interested
3 Not very interested
4 Not at all interested
9 Missing data

V05 *Sign petition*
Now I'd like you to look at this card. I'm going to read out some different forms of political action that people can take, and I'd like you to tell me, for each one, whether you have actually done any of these things, whether you might do it or would never, under any circumstances, do it. Would you sign a petition?
1 Have done
2 Might do
3 Would never do
9 Missing data

V06 *Join boycotts*
Would you join in boycotts?
1 Have done
2 Might do
3 Would never do
9 Missing data

V07 *Attend demonstration*
Would you attend lawful demonstrations?
1 Have done

2   Might do
3   Would never do
9   Missing data

V08   Join strikes

Would you join unofficial strikes?
1   Have done
2   Might do
3   Would never do
9   Missing data

V09   Occupy building

Would you occupy buildings or factories?
1   Have done
2   Might do
3   Would never do
9   Missing data

V10   Protest scale

Number of the actions listed in V05–V09 that respondent has done:
0   None
1   One
2   Two
3   Three or more
9   Missing data

V11   Trust people

Generally speaking, would you say that most people can be trusted or that you can't be too careful in dealing with people?
1   Most people can be trusted
2   Can't be too careful
9   Missing data

V12   Postmaterial values — short

There is a lot of talk these days about what the aims of this country should be for the next ten years. On this card are listed some of the goals which different people would give top priority. Would you please say which one of these you, yourself, consider the most important?

Maintaining order in the nation

Giving people more to say in important government decisions
Fighting rising prices
Protecting freedom of speech

1 Materialist
2 Mixed values
3 Postmaterialist
9 Missing data

V13 *Postmaterial values — long*

There is a lot of talk these days about what the aims of this country should be for the next ten years. On this card are listed some of the goals which different people would give top priority. Would you please say which one of these you, yourself, consider the most important?

Maintaining a high level of economic growth
Making sure this country has strong defense forces
Seeing that people have more to say about how things are done at their jobs and in their communities
Trying to make our cities and countryside more beautiful
Maintaining order in the nation
Giving people more to say in important government decisions
Fighting rising prices
Protecting freedom of speech
A stable economy
Progress toward a less impersonal and more humane society
Progress toward a society in which ideas count more than money
The fight against crime

Responses to the above choices were combined to determine the relative priority of material and postmaterial values:

1 Materialist
2 Less materialist
3 Mixed
4 Postmaterialist
9 Missing data

V14 *Left/Right scale*

In political matters, people talk of "the left" and "the right."

How would you place your views on this scale, generally speaking?
1 Left (1, 2, 3)
2 Center/Left (4, 5)
3 Center/Right (6, 7)
4 Right (8, 9, 10)
9 Missing data

V15 Party preference
If there were a general election tomorrow, which party would you vote for? *Note:* This variable has been coded so that it can be recoded into Left/Right vote: (1–3) Left, (4) Center, (5–8) Right.

United States
1 Democrats
8 Republicans
9 Missing data

Great Britain
1 Labour
4 Liberal Democrats
8 Conservatives
9 Missing data

West Germany
1 SPD
2 Greens
3 SPD
5 FDP
6 CDU/CSU
7 Republikaner
9 Missing data

France
1 Extreme Left, other Left
2 PCF
3 Socialists
4 Greens
5 UDF
6 RPR
7 Other Right (NF, other)
9 Missing data

East Germany
1 PDS
2 Greens/Alliance 90
3 SPD
5 FDP
6 CDU
7 Other right
8 Republikaner
9 Missing data

V16 *Left/Right party vote*
This is a recoded version of V15.
1 Left
2 Right
9 Other party; missing data

V17 *Income inequality*
Now I'd like you to tell me your views on various issues. How would you place your views on this scale? Number 1 means you agree completely with the statement on the left, 10 means you agree completely with the statement on the right, or you can choose any number in between.

1 Incomes should be made more equal
2
3
4 There should be greater incentives for individual effort
9 Missing data

V18 *Gov't own business*
Attitude on government ownership of business
1 Private ownership of business and industry should be increased
2
3
4 Government ownership of business and industry should be increased
9 Missing data

V19 *Individual/government responsibility*
Attitude on individual responsibility versus government responsibility

1 Individuals should take more responsibility for providing for themselves

2

3

4 The state should take more responsibility to ensure that everyone is provided for

9 Missing data

V20 *Guaranteed employment*

Attitude on government guarantees of employment

1 People who are unemployed should have to take any job available or lose their unemployment benefits

2

3

4 People who are unemployed should have the right to refuse a job they do not want

9 Missing data

V21 *Pay for environment*

I would give part of my income if I were certain that the money would be used to prevent environmental pollution

1 Strongly agree

2 Agree

3 Disagree

4 Strongly disagree

9 Missing data

V22 *Taxes for environment*

I would agree to an increase in taxes if the extra money is used to prevent environmental pollution

1 Strongly agree

2 Agree

3 Disagree

4 Strongly disagree

9 Missing data

V23 *Environment not cost*

The Government has to reduce environmental pollution but it should not cost me any money

1 Strongly agree

2 Agree

3 Disagree
4 Strongly disagree
9 Missing data

V24 *Environment not urgent*

Protecting the environment and fighting pollution is less urgent than often suggested
1 Strongly agree
2 Agree
3 Disagree
4 Strongly disagree
9 Missing data

V25 *Jobs—women*

When jobs are scarce, men have more right to a job than women
1 Agree
2 Neither
3 Disagree
9 Missing data

V26 *Jobs—elderly*

When jobs are scarce, people should be forced to retire early
1 Agree
2 Neither
3 Disagree
9 Missing data

V27 *Jobs—immigrants*

When jobs are scarce, employers should give priority to residents over immigrants
1 Agree
2 Neither
3 Disagree
9 Missing data

V28 *Jobs—handicapped*

It is unfair to give work to handicapped people when able-bodied people can't find jobs
1 Agree
2 Neither
3 Disagree

9   Missing data

V29   *Good and evil*
Which of the following statements do you agree with:
A. There are absolutely clear guidelines about what is good and
   evil. These always apply to everyone, whatever the
   circumstances.
B. There can never be absolutely clear guidelines about what is
   good and evil. What is good and evil depends entirely
   upon the circumstances at the time.
1   Agree with statement A
2   Disagree with both
3   Agree with statement B
9   Missing data

V30   *Believe in God*
Does the respondent believe in God?
1   Yes
2   No
9   Missing data

V31   *Believe in afterlife*
Does the respondent believe in life after death?
1   Yes
2   No
9   Missing data

V32   *Believe in devil*
Does the respondent believe in the devil?
1   Yes
2   No
9   Missing data

V33   *Believe in heaven*
Does the respondent believe in heaven?
1   Yes
2   No
9   Missing data

V34   *Believe in hell*
Does the respondent believe in hell?

1 Yes
2 No
9 Missing data

V35 *Sexual freedom*

If someone said that individuals should have the chance to enjoy complete sexual freedom without being restricted, would you tend to agree or disagree?

1 Tend to agree
2 Neither/it depends
3 Tend to disagree
9 Missing data

V36 *Women and children*

A working mother can establish just as warm and secure a relationship with her children as a mother who does not work.

1 Strongly agree
2 Agree
3 Disagree
4 Strongly disagree
9 Missing data

V37 *Child suffers*

A preschool child is likely to suffer if his or her mother works.

1 Strongly agree
2 Agree
3 Disagree
4 Strongly disagree
9 Missing data

V38 *Housework fulfilling*

Being a housewife is just as fulfilling as working for pay.

1 Strongly agree
2 Agree
3 Disagree
4 Strongly disagree
9 Missing data

V39 *Job independence*

Having a job is the best way for a woman to be an independent person.

1 Strongly agree
2 Agree
3 Disagree
4 Strongly disagree
9 Missing data

V40 *Abortion justifiable*
Please tell me whether you think abortion can be always justified, never be justified, or something in between?
1 Never
2
3
4 Always
9 Missing data

V41 *Environmental movement*
There are a number of groups and movements looking for public support. For each of the following movements, which I read out, can you tell me whether you approve or disapprove of this movement?
Ecology or nature protection
1 Strongly approve
2 Somewhat approve
3 Somewhat disapprove
4 Strongly disapprove
9 Missing data

V42 *Antinuclear movement*
Approval of antinuclear energy movement
1 Strongly approve
2 Somewhat approve
3 Somewhat disapprove
4 Strongly disapprove
9 Missing data

V43 *Disarmament movement*
Approval of disarmament movement
1 Strongly approve
2 Somewhat approve
3 Somewhat disapprove

4 Strongly disapprove

9 Missing data

V44 *Human rights movement*

Approval of human rights movement at home or abroad

1 Strongly approve

2 Somewhat approve

3 Somewhat disapprove

4 Strongly disapprove

9 Missing data

V45 *Women's movement*

Approval of women's movement

1 Strongly approve

2 Somewhat approve

3 Somewhat disapprove

4 Strongly disapprove

9 Missing data

V46 *Anti-apartheid movement*

Approval of anti-apartheid movement

1 Strongly approve

2 Somewhat approve

3 Somewhat disapprove

4 Strongly disapprove

9 Missing data

V47 *National pride*

How proud are you to be (respondent's nationality)?

1 Very proud

2 Quite proud

3 Not very proud

4 Not at all proud

9 Missing data

V48 *Fight for country*

Of course, we all hope that there will not be another war, but if it were to come to that, would you be willing to fight for your country?

1 Yes

2 No

9   Missing data

V49   *Social change*

On this card are three basic kinds of attitudes concerning the society we live in. Please choose the one which best describes your own opinion.

1   The entire way our society is organized must be radically changed by revolutionary action
2   Our society must be gradually improved by reforms
3   Our present society must be valiantly defended against all subversive forces
9   Missing data

V50   *Confidence — legal system*

Please look at this card and tell me, for each item listed, how much confidence you have in them: is it a great deal, quite a lot, not very much or none at all?

Do you have confidence in the legal system?

1   A great deal
2   Quite a lot
3   Not very much
4   Not at all
9   Missing data

V51   *Confidence — press*

Do you have confidence in the press?

1   A great deal
2   Quite a lot
3   Not very much
4   Not at all
9   Missing data

V52   *Confidence — unions*

Do you have confidence in trade unions?

1   A great deal
2   Quite a lot
3   Not very much
4   Not at all
9   Missing data

V53   *Confidence — police*

Do you have confidence in the police?

1   A great deal
2   Quite a lot
3   Not very much
4   Not at all
9   Missing data

V54   *Confidence — parliament*
        Do you have confidence in Parliament (Congress)?
1   A great deal
2   Quite a lot
3   Not very much
4   Not at all
9   Missing data

V55   *Confidence — civil service*
        Do you have confidence in the civil service?
1   A great deal
2   Quite a lot
3   Not very much
4   Not at all
9   Missing data

V56   *Confidence — business*
        Do you have confidence in major companies?
1   A great deal
2   Quite a lot
3   Neither / nor
4   Not very much
5   Not at all
9   Missing data

V57   *Could change unjust law*
        If an unjust law were passed by the government, I could do nothing at all about it
1   Agree completely
2   Agree
3   Disagree
4   Disagree completely
9   Missing data

V58   *Religion*
        Do you belong to a religious denomination?

1 Roman Catholic
2 Protestant
3 Jewish
4 Other
5 None
9 Missing data

V59 *Church attendance*

Apart from weddings, funerals, and christenings, about how often do you attend religious services these days?
1 Weekly
2 Monthly
3 A few times a year
4 Never, practically never
9 Missing data

V60 *Feel religious*

Independently of whether you go to church or not, would you say you are:
1 A religious person
2 Not a religious person
3 A convinced atheist
9 Missing data

V61 *Ethnic group*

To which of the following groups does the respondent belong:
1 Caucasian
2 Black
3 South Asian
4 East Asian
5 Arabic
6 Hispanic
7 Other
9 Missing data (in Britain, Germany, and France)

V62 *Gender*

Sex of respondent:
1 Male
2 Female
9 Missing data

V63   *Age*
Can you tell me your date of birth? This means you are ... years old.
1   Under age 30
2   30–44
3   45–59
4   60 or over
9   Missing data

V64   *Education*
At what age did you or will you complete your full-time education, either at school or at an institution of higher education?
1   Lesser educated
2
3
4   Better educated
9   Missing data

V65   *Respondent's occupation*
In which profession/industry do you or did you work? If more than one job, the main job is:
1   Old middle class (owner, professional)
2   New middle class (salaried white collar)
3   Working class
4   Farming
5   Other (other occupation, unemployed)
9   Missing data

V66   *Town size*
Size of town:
1   Under 2,000
2   2,000–5,000
3   5–10,000
4   10–20,000
5   20–50,000
6   50–100,000
7   100–500,000
8   500,000 and more
9   Missing data

Bibliography

ABERBACH, JOEL, AND JACK WALKER. 1970. Political trust and racial ideology. *American Political Science Review* 64:1199–219.

ABRAMSON, PAUL. 1975. *Generational Change in American Politics*. Lexington, Mass.: Heath.

———. 1979. Developing party identification. *American Journal of Political Science* 23:79–96.

———. 1983. *Political Attitudes in America*. San Francisco: Freeman.

ABRAMSON, PAUL, AND JOHN ALDRICH. 1982. The decline of electoral participation in America. *American Political Science Review* 76 :502–21.

ABRAMSON, PAUL, JOHN ALDRICH, AND DAVID ROHDE. 1994. *Change and Continuity in the 1992 Elections*. Washington, D.C.: CQ Press.

ABRAMSON, PAUL, AND RONALD INGLEHART. 1995. *Value Change in Global Perspective*. Ann Arbor: University of Michigan Press.

ABRAMSON, PAUL, AND CHARLES OSTROM. 1991. Macropartisanship: An empirical reassessment. *American Political Science Review* 85:181–92.

———. 1994. Question wording and partisanship. *Public Opinion Quarterly* 58:21–48.

ALDRICH, JOHN, JOHN SULLIVAN, AND E. BORDIDA. 1989. Foreign affairs and issue voting. *American Political Science Review* 83:123–41.

ALMOND, GABRIEL, AND G. BINGHAM POWELL, EDS. 1996. *Comparative Politics Today*. 6th ed. New York: HarperCollins.

ALMOND, GABRIEL, G. BINGHAM POWELL, AND ROBERT MUNDT. 1990. *Comparative Politics*. 2d ed. New York: HarperCollins.

ALMOND, GABRIEL, AND SIDNEY VERBA. 1963. *The Civic Culture*. Princeton: Princeton University Press.

———, EDS. 1980. *The Civic Culture Revisited*. Boston: Little, Brown.

ALT, JAMES. 1984. Dealignment and the dynamics of partisanship in Britain. In *Electoral Change in Advanced Industrial Democracies,* ed. R. Dalton, S. Flanagan, and P. Beck. Princeton: Princeton University Press.

ANDERSON, CHRISTOPHER. 1995. *Blaming the Government: Citizens and the Economy in Five European Democracies*. Armonk, N.Y.: M.E. Sharpe.

ANDERSON, CHRISTOPHER, AND CARSTEN ZELLE. 1995. Helmut Kohl and the CDU victory. *German Politics and Society* 13:12–35.

ARNOLD, DOUGLAS. 1990. *The Logic of Congressional Action*. New Haven: Yale University Press.

ASHFORD, SHEENA, AND NOEL TIMMS. 1992. *What Europe Thinks: A Study of Western European Values.* Brookfield, Vt.: Dartmouth.

BABBIE, EARL. 1990. *Survey Research Methods.* 2d ed. Belmont, Calif.: Wadsworth.

BAGEHOT, WALTER. 1978. *The English Constitution.* London: Oxford University Press.

BAKER, KENDALL, RUSSELL DALTON, AND KAI HILDEBRANDT. 1981. *Germany Transformed: Political Culture and the New Politics.* Cambridge: Harvard University Press.

BARBER, BENJAMIN. 1984. *Strong Democracy.* Berkeley: University of California Press.

BARNES, SAMUEL. 1977. *Representation in Italy.* Chicago: University of Chicago Press.

BARNES, SAMUEL, MAX KAASE, ET AL. 1979. *Political Action.* Beverly Hills, Calif.: Sage.

BARTOLINI, STEFANO, AND PETER MAIR. 1989. *Identity, Competition and Electoral Availability.* New York: Cambridge University Press.

BAUER-KAASE, PETRA. 1994. German unification. In *German Unification,* ed. M.D. Hancock and H. Welsh. Boulder, Colo.: Westview.

BEAN, CLIVE, AND ANTHONY MUGHAN. 1989. Leadership effects in parliamentary elections in Australia and Britain. *American Political Science Review* 83:1165–79.

BECK, PAUL ALLEN. 1984. The dealignment era in America. In *Electoral Change in Advanced Industrial Democracies,* ed. R. Dalton, S. Flanagan, and P. Beck. Princeton: Princeton University Press.

BECK, PAUL ALLEN, AND JOHN CURTICE, EDS. Forthcoming. *Patterns of Political Intermediation.*

BECK, PAUL ALLEN, AND FRANK SORAUF. 1992. *Party Politics in America.* 7th ed. New York: HarperCollins.

BECK, PAUL ALLEN, ET AL. 1992. Patterns and sources of ticket-splitting in subpresidential voting. *American Political Science Review* 86:916–28.

BEEDHAM, BRIAN. 1993. What next for democracy? *The Economist,* 11 September; special supplement, The Future Surveyed.

BELL, DANIEL. 1973. *The Coming of Post-industrial Society.* New York: Basic Books.

BERELSON, BERNARD, PAUL LAZARSFELD, AND WILLIAM McPHEE. 1954. *Voting.* Chicago: University of Chicago Press.

BERGER, SUZANNE. 1979. Politics and anti-politics in Western Europe in the 1970s. *Daedalus* 108:27–50.

BERRY, JEFFREY. 1989. *The Interest Group Society.* Glenview, Ill.: Scott, Foresman.

BETZ, HANS-GEORG. 1994. *Radical Right-wing Populism in Europe.* New York: St. Martin's.

BEYME, KLAUS VON. 1985. *Political Parties in Western Democracies.* New York: St. Martin's.

BISHOP, GEORGE, AND KATHLEEN FRANKOVIC. 1981. Ideological consensus and constraint among party leaders and followers in the 1978 election. *Micropolitics* 2:87–111.

BISHOP, GEORGE, ROBERT OLDENDICK, AND ALFRED TUCHFARBER. 1978. Effects of question wording and format on political attitude consistency. *Public Opinion Quarterly* 42:81–92.

BORRE, OLE. 1984. Critical electoral change in Scandinavia. In *Electoral Change in Advanced Industrial Democracies,* ed. R. Dalton, S. Flanagan, and P. Beck. Princeton: Princeton University Press.

BORRE, OLE, AND DANIEL KATZ. 1973. Party identification and its motivational base in a multiparty system. *Scandinavian Political Studies* 8:69–111.

BORRE, OLE, AND ELINOR SCARBROUGH, EDS. 1995. *Beliefs about the Scope of Government.* Oxford: Oxford University Press.

BOY, DANIEL, AND NONNA MAYER, EDS. 1993. *The French Voter Decides.* Ann Arbor: University of Michigan Press.

BRADY, HENRY, SIDNEY VERBA, AND KAY SCHLOZMAN. 1995. Beyond SES: A resource model of political participation. *American Political Science Review* 89:271–294.

BRODY, RICHARD. 1978. The puzzle of political participation in America. In *The New American Political System,* ed. A. King. Washington, D.C.: American Enterprise Institute.

BRODY, RICHARD, ET AL. 1994. Accounting for divided government. In *Elections at Home and Abroad,* ed. M.K. Jennings and T. Mann. Ann Arbor: University of Michigan Press.

BROWN, BERNARD. 1974. *Protest in Paris.* Morristown, N.J.: General Learning Press.

BUDGE, IAN, IVOR CREWE, AND DAVID FARLIE, EDS. 1976. *Party Identification and Beyond.* New York: Wiley.

BUDGE, IAN, DAVID ROBERTSON, AND D. HEARL. 1987. *Ideology, Strategy and Party Change.* Cambridge: Cambridge University Press.

BURNHAM, WALTER. 1982. The appearance and disappearance of the American voter. In *The Current Crisis in American Politics,* ed. W. Burnham. New York: Oxford University Press.

BUTLER, DAVID. 1995. *British General Elections Since 1945.* Oxford: Blackwell.

BUTLER, DAVID, AND AUSTIN RANNEY, EDS. 1994. *Referendums around the World: The Growing Use of Democracy?* Washington, D.C.: American Enterprise Institute.

BUTLER, DAVID, AND DONALD STOKES. 1969. *Political Change in Britain.* New York: St. Martin's.

———. 1974. *Political Change in Britain.* 2d ed. New York: St. Martin's.

CAMPBELL, ANGUS, PHILIP CONVERSE, AND WILLARD RODGERS. 1979. *The Quality of American Life.* New York: Russell Sage.

CAMPBELL, ANGUS, ET AL. 1960. *The American Voter.* New York: Wiley.

———. 1966. *Elections and the Political Order.* New York: Wiley.

CANTRIL, HADLEY. 1965. *The Patterns of Human Concerns.* New Brunswick, N.J.: Rutgers University Press.

CARMINES, EDWARD, AND JAMES STIMSON. 1980. The two faces of issue voting.

American Political Science Review 74:78–91.

———. 1989. *Issue Evolution: Race and the Transformation of American Politics.* Princeton: Princeton University Press.

CAYROL, ROLAND. 1980. The mass media and the electoral campaign. In *The French National Assembly Elections of 1978,* ed. H. Penniman. Washington, D.C.: American Enterprise Institute.

CERNY, KARL, ED. 1978. *Germany at the Polls.* Washington, D.C.: American Enterprise Institute.

———, ED. 1990. *Germany at the Polls: The Bundestag Elections of the 1980s.* Durham, N.C.: Duke University Press.

CERNY, PHILIP. 1982. *Social Movements and Protest in France.* London: Pinter.

CHARLOT, MONICA. 1980. Women in politics in France. In *The French National Assembly Elections of 1978,* ed. H. Penniman. Washington, D.C.: American Enterprise Institute.

CITRIN, JACK. 1974. Comment. *American Political Science Review* 68:973–88.

CLARKE, HAROLD, AND NITISH DUTT. 1991. Measuring value change in Western industrialized societies. *American Political Science Review* 85:905–20.

CLARKE, HAROLD, ET AL. 1980. *Political Choice in Canada.* New York: McGraw-Hill.

CLUBB, JEROME, WILLIAM FLANIGAN, AND NANCY ZINGALE. 1980. *Partisan Realignment.* Beverly Hills, Calif.: Sage.

COLE, ALEXANDRA. 1996. The Republikaner. In *Germans Divided,* ed. R. Dalton. Washington, D.C.: Berg.

CONOVER, PAMELA, AND STANLEY FELDMAN. 1984. How people organize the political world. *American Journal of Political Science* 28:95–126.

CONRADT, DAVID. 1980. Changing German political culture. In *The Civic Culture Revisited,* ed. G. Almond and S. Verba. Boston: Little, Brown.

CONVERSE, PHILIP. 1964. The nature of belief systems in mass publics. In *Ideology and Discontent,* ed. D. Apter. New York: Free Press.

———. 1966. The normal vote. In *Elections and the Political Order,* ed. A. Campbell et al. New York: Wiley.

———. 1969. Of time and partisan stability. *Comparative Political Studies* 2:139–71.

———. 1970. Attitudes and nonattitudes. In *The Quantitative Analysis of Social Problems,* ed. E. Tufte. Reading, Mass.: Addison-Wesley.

———. 1972. Change in the American electorate. In *The Human Meaning of Social Change,* ed. A. Campbell and P. Converse. New York: Russell Sage Foundation.

———. 1975. Public opinion and voting behavior. In *Handbook of Political Science,* ed. F. Greenstein and N. Polsby. Vol. 4. Reading, Mass.: Addison-Wesley.

———. 1976. *The Dynamics of Party Support.* Beverly Hills, Calif.: Sage.

———. 1980. Comment: Rejoinder to Judd and Milburn. *American Sociological Review* 45:644–46.

———. 1990. Popular representation and the distribution of information. In *Information and Democratic Processes,* ed. J. Ferejohn and J. Kuklinski.

Urbana: University of Illinois Press.

CONVERSE, PHILIP, AND GEORGES DUPEUX. 1962. Politicization of the electorate in France and the United States. *Public Opinion Quarterly* 26:1–23.

CONVERSE, PHILIP, AND GREG MARKUS. 1979. Plus ça change. The new CPS election study panel. *American Political Science Review* 73:32–49.

CONVERSE, PHILIP, AND ROY PIERCE. 1986. *Representation in France.* Cambridge: Harvard University Press.

CONWAY, M. MARGARET. 1991a. *Political Participation in the United States.* 2d ed. Washington, D.C.: CQ Press.

———. 1991b. The study of political participation. In *Political Science: Looking toward the Future,* ed. W. Crotty. Vol. 3. Evanston, Ill.: Northwestern University Press.

CREPAZ, MARKUS. 1990. The impact of party polarization and postmaterialism on voter turnout. *European Journal of Political Research* 18:183–205.

CREWE, IVOR. 1981. Electoral participation. In *Democracy at the Polls,* ed. D. Butler et al. Washington, D.C.: American Enterprise Institute.

———. 1986. On the death and resurrection of class voting. *Political Studies* 34:620–38.

CREWE, IVOR, AND D.T. DENVER, EDS. 1985. *Electoral Change in Western Democracies.* New York: St. Martin's.

CREWE, IVOR, AND ANTHONY KING. 1994. Did Major win? Did Kinnoch lose? In *Labour's Last Chance,* ed. A. Heath et al. Brookfield, Vt.: Dartmouth.

CREWE, IVOR, AND DONALD SEARING. 1988. Mrs. Thatcher's crusade: Conservatism in Britain, 1972–1986. In *The Resurgence of Conservatism in the Anglo-American Countries,* ed. B. Cooper et al. Durham, N.C.: Duke University Press.

CRONIN, THOMAS. 1989. *Direct Democracy: The Politics of Initiative, Referendum and Recall.* Cambridge: Harvard University Press.

CROZIER, MICHEL. 1964. *The Bureaucratic Phenomenon.* Chicago: University of Chicago Press.

CROZIER, MICHEL, SAMUEL HUNTINGTON, AND JOJI WATANUKI. 1975. *The Crisis of Democracy.* New York: New York University Press.

CURTICE, JOHN, AND ROGER JOWELL. 1995. The skeptical electorate. In *British Social Attitudes—the 12th Report,* ed. R. Jowell et al. Brookfield, Vt.: Dartmouth.

CYERT, RICHARD, AND JAMES MARCH, 1963. *A Behavioral Theory of the Firm.* Englewood Cliffs, N.J.: Prentice Hall.

DAHL, ROBERT. 1971. *Polyarchy.* New Haven: Yale University Press.

———. 1984. *A Preface to Economic Democracy.* Berkeley: University of California Press.

———. 1989. *Democracy and Its Critics.* New Haven: Yale University Press.

DAHRENDORF, RALF. 1975. Excerpts from remarks on the ungovernability study. In *The Crisis of Democracy,* ed. M. Crozier et al. New York: New York University Press.

DALTON, RUSSELL. 1977. Was there a revolution? *Comparative Political Studies* 9:459–73.

———. 1984. Cognitive mobilization and partisan dealignment in advanced industrial democracies. *Journal of Politics* 46:264–84.

———. 1985. Political parties and political representation. *Comparative Political Studies* 17:267–99.

———. 1988. *Citizen Politics in Western Democracies*. Chatham, N.J.: Chatham House.

———. 1989. *Politics in West Germany*. Glenview, Ill.: Scott, Foresman.

———. 1991. The dynamics of party system change. In *Eurobarometer: The Dynamics of European Public Opinion*, ed. K. Reif and R. Inglehart. London: Macmillan.

———. 1992. Two German electorates? In *Developments in German Politics*, ed. G. Smith et al. London: Macmillan.

———. 1993a. *Politics in Germany*. New York: HarperCollins.

———, ed. 1993b. *The New Germany Votes: Unification and the Creation of the New German Party System*. Oxford: Berg.

———. 1993c. Review of "Identity, competition and electoral availability," *Comparative Political Studies* 26:246–48.

———. 1993d. Citizens, protest and democracy. *Annals of the American Academy of Political and Social Science* 528.

———. 1994. *The Green Rainbow: Environmental Groups in Western Europe*. New Haven: Yale University Press.

———, ed. 1996. *Germans Divided: The 1994 Bundestagswahl and the Evolution of the German Party System*. Washington, D.C.: Berg.

DALTON, RUSSELL, AND WILHELM BÜRKLIN. 1996. The social bases of the vote. In *Germans Divided*, ed. R. Dalton. Washington, D.C.: Berg.

DALTON, RUSSELL, SCOTT FLANAGAN, AND PAUL BECK, EDS. 1984. *Electoral Change in Advanced Industrial Democracies*. Princeton: Princeton University Press.

DALTON, RUSSELL, AND MANFRED KUECHLER, EDS. 1990. *Challenging the Political Order: New Social and Political Movements in Western Democracies*. New York: Oxford University Press.

DALTON, RUSSELL, AND MARTIN WATTENBERG. 1993. The not so simple act of voting. In *The State of the Discipline*, ed. A. Finifter. Washington, D.C.: American Political Science Association.

DE GRAAF, NAN DIRK. 1988. Postmaterialism and the stratification process. Ph.D. dissertation, University of Utrecht, Holland.

DELLI CARPINI, MICHAEL, AND SCOTT KEETER. 1991. Stability and change in the U.S. public's knowledge of politics. *Public Opinion Quarterly* 55:583–612.

———. Forthcoming. *What Americans Know about Politics and Why It Matters*. New Haven: Yale University Press.

DELLI CARPINI, MICHAEL, AND LEE SIGELMAN. 1986. Do yuppies matter? Competing explanations of their political distinctiveness. *Public Opinion Quarterly* 50:502–518.

DE VAUS, DAVID, AND IAN MCALLISTER. 1989. The changing politics of women. *European Journal of Political Research* 17:241–62.

DOGAN, MATTEI. 1995. Erosion of class voting and the religious vote in Western

Europe. *International Social Science Journal* 47: 525–38.

DOWNS, ANTHONY. 1957. *An Economic Theory of Democracy.* New York: Harper.

DUCH, RAYMOND, AND MICHAEL TAYLOR. 1993. Postmaterialism and the economic condition. *American Journal of Political Science* 37:747–79.

———. 1994. A reply to Abramson and Inglehart's "Education, security and postmaterialism." *American Journal of Political Science* 38:815–24.

DUNLAP, RILEY, GEORGE GALLUP, AND ALEC GALLUP. 1992. *Health of the Planet.* Princeton: Gallup International Institute.

DUNLAP, RILEY, AND ANGELA MERTIG, EDS. 1992. *American Environmentalism: The U.S. Environmental Movement, 1970–1990.* Philadelphia: Taylor and Francis.

DUNLEAVY, PATRICK, AND CHRISTOPHER HUSBANDS. 1985. *British Democracy at the Crossroads.* London: Allen and Unwin.

DYE, THOMAS, AND HARMON ZIEGLER. 1970. *The Irony of Democracy.* Belmont, Calif.: Duxbury.

EASTON, DAVID. 1965. *A Systems Analysis of Political Life.* New York: Wiley.

———. 1975. A reassessment of the concept of political support. *British Journal of Political Science* 5:435–57.

EASTON, DAVID, AND JACK DENNIS. 1969. *Children in the Political System.* New York: McGraw-Hill.

ECKSTEIN, HARRY. 1984. Civic inclusion and its discontents. *Daedalus* 113: 107–46.

EHRMANN, HENRY, AND MARTIN SCHAIN. 1992. *Politics in France.* 5th ed. New York: HarperCollins.

EICHENBERG, RICHARD, AND RUSSELL DALTON. 1993. Europeans and the European community. *International Organization* 47:507–34.

EIJK, CEES VAN DER, AND CEES NIEMOLLER. 1983. *Electoral Change in the Netherlands.* Amsterdam: C.T. Press.

EPSTEIN, LEON. 1980. *Political Parties in Western Democracies.* New Brunswick, N.J.: Transaction Books.

ERIKSON, ROBERT. 1978. Constituency opinion and congressional behavior. *American Journal of Political Science* 22:511–35.

ERIKSON, ROBERT, AND KENT TEDIN. 1995. *American Public Opinion.* 5th ed. Boston: Allyn and Bacon.

ERIKSON, ROBERT, GERALD WRIGHT, AND JOHN MCIVER. 1994. *State House Democracy: Public Opinion and Public Policy in the American States.* New York: Cambridge University Press.

FARAH, BARBARA. 1980. Political representation in West Germany. Ph.D. dissertation, University of Michigan.

FARAH, BARBARA, ET AL. 1979. Political dissatisfaction. In *Political Action,* ed. S. Barnes, M. Kaase, et al. Beverly Hills, Calif.: Sage.

FELDMAN, ELLIOT, AND JEROME MILCH. 1982. *Technocracy versus Democracy.* Boston: Auburn House.

FELDMAN, STANLEY. 1989. Reliability and stability of policy positions. *Political Analysis* 1:25–60.

FENDRICH, JAMES. 1993. *Ideal Citizens: The Legacy of the Civil Rights Movement.* Albany, N.Y.: SUNY Press.

FEREJOHN, JOHN, AND JAMES KUKLINSKI, EDS. 1990. *Information and Democratic Processes.* Urbana: University of Illinois Press.

FINER, S.E. 1980. *The Changing British Party System.* Washington, D.C.: American Enterprise System.

FIORINA, MORRIS. 1981. *Retrospective Voting in American National Elections.* New Haven: Yale University Press.

———. 1990. Information and rationality in elections. In *Information and Democratic Processes,* ed. J. Ferejohn and J. Kuklinski. Urbana: University of Illinois Press.

———. 1992. *Divided Government.* New York: Macmillan.

FLANAGAN, SCOTT. 1982. Changing values in advanced industrial society. *Comparative Political Studies* 14:403–44.

———. 1987. Value change in industrial society. *American Political Science Review* 81:1303–19.

FLANAGAN, SCOTT, ET AL. 1991. *The Japanese Voter.* New Haven: Yale University Press.

FLEURY, CHRISTOPHER, AND MICHAEL LEWIS-BECK. 1993. Anchoring the French voter: Ideology vs. party. *Journal of Politics* 55:1100–1109.

FLICKINGER, R., AND DONLEY T. STUDLAR. 1992. The disappearing voters? Exploring declining turnout in Western European elections. *West European Politics* 15: 1–16.

FLORA, PETER, ED. 1983. *State, Economy and Society in Western Europe, 1918–1975.* Frankfurt: Campus.

FLYNN, GREGORY, AND HANS RATTINGER, EDS. 1985. *The Public and Atlantic Defense.* London: Croom Helm.

FRANKLAND, GENE, AND DONALD SCHOONMAKER. 1992. *Between Protest and Power: The Green Party in Germany.* Boulder, Colo.: Westview Press.

FRANKLIN, MARK. 1985. *The Decline of Class Voting in Britain.* Oxford: Oxford University Press.

FRANKLIN, MARK, TOM MACKIE, AND HENRY VALEN, EDS. 1992. *Electoral Change.* New York: Cambridge University Press.

FRIEDRICH, WALTER, AND HARTMUT GRIESE. 1990. *Jungend und Jugendforschung in der DDR.* Opladen: Westdeutscher Verlag.

FUCHS, DIETER, GIOVANNA GUIDOROSSI, AND PALLE SVENSSON. 1996. Support for the democratic system. In *Citizens and the State,* ed. H. Klingemann and D. Fuchs. Oxford: Oxford University Press.

FUCHS, DIETER, AND HANS-DIETER KLINGEMANN. 1989. The Left-Right schema. In *Continuities in Political Action,* ed. M.K. Jennings and J. van Deth. Berlin: deGruyter.

———. 1996. Citizens and the state. In *Citizens and the State,* ed. H. Klingemann and D. Fuchs. Oxford: Oxford University Press.

FUKUYAMA, FRANCIS. 1992. *The End of History and the Last Man.* New York: Free Press.

GALLUP INSTITUTE. 1976a. *International Public Opinion Polls: Britain.* New

York: Random House.

———. 1976b. *International Public Opinion Polls: France.* New York: Random House.

———. 1995. *Gallup Political and Economic Index.* London: Gallup.

GELB, JOYCE. 1989. *Feminism and Politics: A Comparative Perspective.* Berkeley: University of California Press.

GLASS, DAVID. 1985. Evaluating presidential candidates: Who focuses on their personal attributes? *Public Opinion Quarterly* 49:517–34.

GLUCHOWSKI, PETER. 1983. Wahlerfahrung und Parteiidentifikation. In *Wahlen und politisches System: Analysen aus Anlass der Bundestagswahl 1980,* ed. M. Kaase and H. Klingemann. Opladen: Westdeutscher Verlag.

———. 1987. Lebensstile und Wandel der Wählerschaft in der Bundesrepublik Deutschland. *Aus Politik und Zeitgeschichte,* 21 March, 18–32.

GOLDTHORPE, JOHN. 1980. *Social Mobility and Class Structure in Modern Britain.* Oxford: Clarendon Press.

GRABER, DORIS. 1988. *Processing the News: How People Tame the Information Tide.* 2d ed. New York: Longman.

———. 1993. *Mass Media and American Politics.* 4th ed. Washington, D.C.: CQ Press.

GREEN, MARK, ET AL. 1984. *Who Runs Congress?* 4th ed. New York: Dell.

GURR, T. ROBERT. 1970. *Why Men Rebel.* Princeton: Princeton University Press.

HAMMOND, JOHN. 1986. Yuppies. *Public Opinion Quarterly* 50:487–501.

HARDING, STEVE. 1986. *Contrasting Values in Western Europe.* London: Macmillan.

HARMEL, ROBERT, AND KENNETH JANDA. 1982. *Parties and Their Environments.* New York: Longman.

HASTINGS, ELIZABETH, AND PHILIP HASTINGS, EDS. 1989. *Index to International Public Opinion, 1987–88.* Westport, Conn.: Greenwood.

HEATH, ANTHONY, ROGER JOWELL, AND JOHN CURTICE. 1985. *How Britain Votes.* New York: Pergamon.

———. 1991. *Understanding Political Change: The British Voter 1964–1987.* New York: Pergamon Press.

———. 1994. *Labour's Last Chance: The 1992 Election and Beyond.* Brookfield, Vt.: Dartmouth.

HEATH, ANTHONY, AND DORREN MCMAHON. 1992. Changes in values. In *British Social Attitudes: The 9th Report,* ed. R. Jowell et al. Brookfield, Vt.: Dartmouth.

HEATH, ANTHONY, AND ROY PIERCE. 1992. It was party identification all along. *Electoral Studies* 11:93–105.

HEIDENHEIMER, ARNOLD, AND PETER FLORA, EDS. 1981. *The Development of the Welfare State.* New Brunswick, N.J.: Transaction Books.

HEIDENHEIMER, ARNOLD, HUGH HECLO, AND CAROLYN ADAMS. 1990. *Comparative Public Policy.* 3d ed. New York: St. Martin's.

HELD, DAVID. 1987. *Models of Democracy.* Stanford: Stanford University Press.

HERZOG, DIETRICH, AND BERNHARD WESSELS, EDS. 1990. *Abgeordnete und Bürger.* Opladen: Westdeutscher Verlag.

HESS, ROBERT, AND JUDITH TORNEY. 1967. *The Development of Political Attitudes in Children.* Chicago: Aldine.

HIGLEY, JOHN, ET AL. 1979. *Elites in Australia.* London: Routledge and Kegan Paul.

HIMMELWEIT, HILDE, ET AL. 1981. *How Voters Decide.* London: Academic Press.

HOFFMANN, STANLEY. 1974. *Decline or Renewal?* New York: Viking.

HOFFMANN-LANGE, URSULA. 1992. *Eliten, Macht und Konflikt in der Bundesrepublik.* Opladen: Leske + Budrich.

HOLLIFIELD, JAMES. 1993. *Immigrants, Markets and States.* Cambridge: Harvard University Press, 1993.

HOLMBERG, SÖREN. 1974. *Riksdagen Representerar Svenska Folket.* Lund: Studentlittertur.

———. 1989. Political representation in Sweden. *Scandinavian Political Studies* 12:1–35.

———. 1994. Party identification compared across the Atlantic. In *Elections at Home and Abroad,* ed. M.K. Jennings and T. Mann. Ann Arbor: University of Michigan Press.

HOSKIN, MARILYN. 1991. *New Immigrants and Democratic Society.* New York: Praeger.

HOUT, MICHAEL, ET AL. 1996. The democratic class struggle in the United States, 1948–1992. *American Sociological Review.*

HUCKFELDT, ROBERT, AND CAROL KOHFELD. 1989. *Race and the Decline of Class in American Politics.* Urbana: University of Illinois Press.

HUNTINGTON, SAMUEL. 1974. Postindustrial politics: How benign will it be? *Comparative Politics* 6:147–77.

———. 1975. The democratic distemper. *Public Interest* 41:9–38.

———. 1981. *American Politics: The Promise of Disharmony.* Cambridge: Harvard University Press.

———. 1984. Will more countries become democratic? *Political Science Quarterly* 99:193–218.

———. 1991. *The Third Wave.* Norman: University of Oklahoma Press.

HURWITZ, JON, AND MARK PEFFLEY. 1987. How are foreign policy attitudes structured? *American Political Science Review* 81:1099–1120.

IGNAZI, PIERO. 1992. The silent counter-revolution. *European Journal of Political Research* 22:3–34.

INGLEHART, MARGARET. 1981. Political interest in West European women. *Comparative Political Studies* 13:299–326.

INGLEHART, MARITA. 1991. Gender differences in sex-role attitudes: A topic without a future? In *Eurobarometer: The Dynamic of European Public Opinion,* ed. K. Reif and R. Inglehart. London: Macmillan.

INGLEHART, RONALD. 1977. *The Silent Revolution.* Princeton: Princeton University Press.

———. 1979. Political action. In *Political Action,* ed. S. Barnes, M. Kaase, et al. Beverly Hills, Calif.: Sage.

———. 1981. Post-materialism in an environment of insecurity. *American Politi-*

cal Science Review 75:880–900.

———. 1984. Changing cleavage alignments in Western democracies. In *Electoral Change in Advanced Industrial Democracies,* ed. R. Dalton, S. Flanagan, and P. Beck. Princeton: Princeton University Press.

———. 1990. *Culture Shift in Advanced Industrial Society.* Princeton: Princeton University Press.

———. 1991. Trust between nations: Primordial ties, societal learning, and economic development. In *Eurobarometer: The Dynamic of European Public Opinion,* ed. K. Reif and R. Inglehart. London: Macmillan.

———. 1995. Public support for environmental protection. *PS — Political Science and Politics* 28:57–72.

———. Forthcoming. *Modernization and Postmodernization: Cultural, Economic, and Political Change in 43 Nations.* Princeton: Princeton University Press.

INGLEHART, RONALD, AND PAUL ABRAMSON. 1994. Economic security and value change, 1970–1993. *American Political Science Review* 88:336–54.

INGRAM, HELEN, AND STEVEN SMITH, EDS. 1993. *Public Policy for Democracy.* Washington, D.C.: Brookings Institution.

INKELES, ALEX, AND DAVID SMITH. 1974. *Becoming Modern: Individual Change in Six Developing Countries.* Cambridge: Harvard University Press.

JACKMAN, ROBERT. 1972. Political elites, mass publics, and support for democratic principles. *Journal of Politics* 34:753–73.

———. 1987. Political institutions and voter turnout in the industrialized democracies. *American Political Science Review* 81:405–24.

JACOBY, WILLIAM. 1991. Ideological identification and issue attitudes. *American Journal of Political Science* 35:178–205.

JENNINGS, M. KENT. 1987. Residues of a movement: The aging of the American protest generation. *American Political Science Review* 81:367–82.

———. 1992. Ideological thinking among mass publics and political elites. *Public Opinion Quarterly* 56:419–41.

JENNINGS, M. KENT, AND THOMAS MANN, EDS. 1994. *Elections at Home and Abroad.* Ann Arbor: University of Michigan Press.

JENNINGS, M. KENT, AND GREG MARKUS. 1984. Partisan orientations over the long haul. *American Political Science Review* 78:1000–1018.

JENNINGS, M. KENT, AND RICHARD NIEMI. 1973. *The Character of Political Adolescence.* Princeton: Princeton University Press.

———. 1981. *Generations and Politics.* Princeton: Princeton University Press.

JENNINGS, M. KENT, AND JAN VAN DETH, EDS. 1989. *Continuities in Political Action.* Berlin: deGruyter.

JOWELL, ROGER, AND RICHARD TOPF. 1988. Trust in the establishment. In *British Social Attitudes: The 5th Report,* ed. R. Jowell, S. Witherspoon, and L. Brook. Brookfield, Vt.: Gower.

JUDD, CHARLES, JON KROSNICK, AND MICHAEL MILBURN. 1981. Political involvement and attitude structure in the general public. *American Sociological Review* 46:660–69.

JUDD, CHARLES, AND MICHAEL MILBURN. 1980. The structure of attitude systems in the general public. *American Sociological Review* 45:627–43.

KAASE, MAX. 1982. Partizipative revolution: Ende der Parteien? In *Bürger und Parteien*, ed. J. Raschke. Opladen: Westdeutscher Verlag.

———. 1989. Mass participation. In *Continuities in Political Action,* ed. M.K. Jennings and J. van Deth. Berlin: deGruyter.

———. 1994. Is there personalization in politics? *International Political Science Review* 15:211–30.

———. 1996. Looking ahead. In *Germans Divided.* ed. R. Dalton. Washington, D.C.: Berg.

KAASE, MAX, AND HANS-DIETER KLINGEMANN. 1994. The cumbersome way to partisan orientations in a "new" democracy. In *Elections at Home and Abroad,* ed. M.K. Jennings and T. Mann. Ann Arbor: University of Michigan Press.

KATZ, RICHARD, ED. 1987. *The Future of Party Government.* Berlin: deGruyter.

KATZENSTEIN, MARY, AND CAROL MUELLER, EDS. 1987. *The Women's Movement of the United States and Western Europe.* Philadelphia: Temple University Press.

KAVANAUGH, DENNIS. 1980. Political culture in Great Britain. In *The Civic Culture Revisited,* ed. G. Almond and S. Verba. Boston: Little, Brown.

KEITH, BRUCE, ET AL. 1992. *The Myth of the Independent Voter.* Berkeley: University of California Press.

KERR, HENRY. 1990. Social class and party choice. In *People and Their Polities,* ed. R. Sankiaho et al. Helsinki: Finnish Political Science Association.

KEY, V.O. 1966. *The Responsible Electorate.* Cambridge, Mass.: Belknap Press.

KIEWIET, D.R. 1983. *Macroeconomics and Micropolitics.* Chicago: University of Chicago Press.

KINDER, DONALD. 1983. Diversity and complexity in American public opinion. In *Political Science: The State of the Discipline,* ed. A. Finifter. Washington, D.C.: American Political Science Association.

———. 1986. Presidential character revisited. In *Political Cognitions,* ed. R. Lau and D. Sears. Hillsdale, N.J.: Lawrence Erlbaum.

KINDER, DONALD, AND D.R. KIEWIET. 1981. Sociotropic politics. *British Journal of Political Science* 11:129–61.

KINDER, DONALD, AND DAVID SEARS. 1985. Public opinion and political action. In *The Handbook of Social Psychology,* ed. E. Aronson and G. Lindzey. Vol. 2. Reading, Mass.: Addison-Wesley.

KINDER, DONALD, ET AL. 1980. Presidential prototypes. *Political Behavior* 2:315–37.

KIRKPATRICK, JEANE. 1976. *The New Presidential Elite: Men and Women in National Politics.* New York: Russell Sage Foundation and Twentieth Century Fund.

KITSCHELT, HERBERT. 1989. *The Logics of Party Formation.* Ithaca: Cornell University Press.

KLANDERMANS, BERT, ED. 1991. *Peace Movements in Western Europe and the United States.* Greenwich, Conn.: JAI Press.

KLEIN, ETHEL. 1987. The diffusion of consciousness in the United States and

Western Europe. In *The Women's Movements of the United States and Western Europe,* ed. M. Katzenstein and C. Mueller. Philadelphia: Temple University Press.

KLINGEMANN, HANS-DIETER. 1979. Measuring ideological conceptualizations. In *Political Action,* ed. S. Barnes, M. Kaase, et al. Beverly Hills, Calif.: Sage.

———. 1983. Einstellungen zur SPD und CDU/CSU 1969–1980. In *Wahlen und Politisches System,* ed. M. Kaase and H. Klingemann. Opladen: Westdeutscher Verlag.

KLINGEMANN, HANS-DIETER AND DIETER FUCHS, EDS. 1996. *Citizens and the State.* Oxford: Oxford University Press.

KLINGEMANN, HANS-DIETER, RICHARD HOFFERBERT, AND IAN BUDGE. 1994. *Parties, Policy and Democracy.* Boulder, Colo.: Westview.

KNIGHT, KATHLEEN. 1992. Ideology and the American electorate. In *Perspectives on Texas and American Politics,* ed. K. Tedin, D. Lutz, and E. Fuchs. Dubuque, Iowa: Kendall/Hunt.

KNUTSEN, ODDBJORN. 1987. The impact of structural and ideological cleavages on West European democracies. *British Journal of Political Science* 18: 323–52.

KORNHAUSER, WILLIAM. 1959. *The Politics of Mass Society.* New York: Free Press.

KROSNICK, JON. 1991. The stability of political preferences. *American Journal of Political Science* 35:547–76.

KUKLINSKI, JAMES. 1978. Representativeness and elections. *American Political Science Review* 72:165–77.

KUKLINSKI, JAMES, ROBERT LUSKIN, AND JOHN BOLLAND. 1991. Where is the schema? *American Political Science Review* 85:1341–57.

LANE, JAN-ERIK, AND SVANTE ERRSON. 1991. *Politics and Society in Western Europe.* 2d ed. Newbury Park, Calif.: Sage.

LANE, ROBERT. 1962. *Political Ideology.* New York: Free Press.

———. 1973. Patterns of political belief. In *Handbook of Political Psychology,* ed. J. Knutson. San Francisco: Jossey-Bass.

LAVER, MICHAEL, AND W. BEN HUNT. 1992. *Policy and Party Competition.* New York: Routledge.

LAWSON, KAY, AND PETER MERKL, EDS. 1988. *When Parties Fail.* Princeton: Princeton University Press.

LAZARSFELD, PAUL, BERNARD BERELSON, AND HAZEL GAUDET. 1948. *The People's Choice.* New York: Columbia University Press.

LEDUC, LAWRENCE. 1981. The dynamic properties of party identification. *European Journal of Political Research* 9:257–68.

LEEGE, DAVID, LYMAN KELLSTEDT, ET AL. 1993. *Rediscovering the Religious Factor in American Politics.* Armonk, N.Y.: M.E. Sharpe.

LEWIS-BECK, MICHAEL. 1984. France: The stalled electorate. In *Electoral Change in Advanced Industrial Democracies,* ed. R. Dalton, S. Flanagan, and P. Beck. Princeton: Princeton University Press.

———. 1988. *Economics and Elections.* Ann Arbor: University of Michigan Press.

LEWIS-BECK, MICHAEL, AND ANDREW SKALABAN. 1992. France. In *Electoral Change,* ed. M. Franklin et al. New York: Cambridge University Press.

LIJPHART, AREND. 1979. Religious vs. linguistic vs. class voting. *American Political Science Review* 73:442–58.

———. 1981. Political parties. In *Democracy at the Polls,* ed. D. Butler et al. Washington, D.C.: American Enterprise Institute.

———. 1984. *Democracies.* New Haven: Yale University Press.

LIPPMANN, WALTER. 1922. *Public Opinion.* New York: Harcourt, Brace.

LIPSET, SEYMOUR MARTIN. 1981a. *Political Man: The Social Bases of Politics.* Baltimore: Johns Hopkins University Press.

———. 1981b. The revolt against modernity. In *Mobilization, Center-Periphery Structures and Nation-Building,* ed. P. Torsvik. Bergen: Universitetsforlaget.

LIPSET, S.M., AND STEIN ROKKAN, EDS. 1967. *Party Systems and Voter Alignments.* New York: Free Press.

LIPSET, S.M., AND WILLIAM SCHNEIDER. 1983. *The Confidence Gap.* New York: Free Press.

LIPSKY, MICHAEL. 1968. Protest as a political resource. *American Political Science Review* 62:1144–58.

LOVENDUSKI, JONI. 1986. *Women and European Politics: Contemporary Feminism and Public Policy.* Amherst: University of Massachusetts Press.

LUPIA, ARTHUR. 1994. Shortcuts versus encyclopedias. *American Political Science Review* 88:63–76.

LUSKIN, ROBERT. 1987. Measuring political sophistication. *American Journal of Political Science* 18:361–82.

MCALLISTER, IAN. 1991. Party voters, candidates and political attitudes. *Canadian Journal of Political Science* 24:237–68.

———. 1992. *Political Behaviour: Citizens, Parties and Elites in Australia.* Melbourne: Longman Cheshire.

———. 1996. Leadership. In *Comparing Democracies,* ed. L. LeDuc, R. Niemi, and P. Norris. Newbury Park, Calif.: Sage.

MCCLOSKY, HERBERT. 1964. Consensus and ideology in American politics. *American Political Science Review* 58:361–82.

MCCLOSKY, HERBERT, ET AL. 1960. Issue conflict and consensus among party leaders and followers. *American Political Science Review* 54:406–27.

MCCLOSKY, HERBERT, AND ALIDA BRILL. 1983. *Dimensions of Tolerance: What Americans Believe about Civil Liberties.* New York: Russell Sage Foundation.

MCCORMICK, JOHN. 1991. *British Politics and the Environment.* London: Earthscan.

MCINTOSH, MARY, AND MARTHA MACIVER. 1994. The structure of foreign policy attitudes in East and West Europe. Paper presented at the annual meeting of the International Studies Association.

MACKIE, THOMAS, AND RICHARD ROSE. 1982. *International Almanac of Electoral History.* 2d ed. London: Macmillan.

MACKUEN, MICHAEL. 1981. Social communication and the mass policy agenda. In *More Than News,* ed. M. MacKuen and S. Coombs. Beverly Hills, Calif.: Sage.

MacKuen, Michael, Robert Erikson, and James Stimson. 1989. Macropartisanship. *American Political Science Review* 83:1125–42.

———. 1992. Peasants or bankers? *American Political Science Review* 86: 597–611.

MacRae, Duncan. 1967. *Parliament, Parties, and Society in France, 1946–1958.* New York: St. Martin's.

Mann, Thomas. 1978. *Unsafe at Any Margin.* Washington, D.C.: American Enterprise Institute.

Margolis, Michael. 1979. *Viable Democracy.* New York: St. Martin's.

Markus, Gregory B. 1988. The impact of personal and national economic conditions on the presidential vote. *American Journal of Political Science* 32: 137–54.

Marsh, Alan. 1974. Explorations in unorthodox political behavior. *European Journal of Political Research* 2:107–31.

———. 1977. *Protest and Political Consciousness.* Beverly Hills, Calif.: Sage.

Maslow, Abraham. 1954. *Motivations and Personality.* New York: Harper & Row.

Michelat, Guy. 1993. In search of Left and Right. In *The French Voter Decides,* ed. D. Boy and N. Mayer. Ann Arbor: University of Michigan Press.

Middendorp, C.P. 1991. *Ideology in Dutch Politics.* Assen/Maastricht: Van Gorcum.

Milbrath, Lester. 1984. *Environmentalists: Vanguard of a New Society.* Albany: SUNY Press.

Milbrath, Lester, and M.L. Goel. 1977. *Political Participation.* New York: Rand McNally.

Miller, Arthur. 1974a. Political issues and trust in government. *American Political Science Review* 68:951–72.

———. 1974b. Rejoinder. *American Political Science Review* 68:989–1001.

Miller, Arthur, and Stephen Borrelli. 1991. Confidence in government during the 1980s. *American Politics Quarterly* 19:147–73.

———. 1992. Policy and performance orientations in the United States. *Electoral Studies* 11:106–21.

Miller, Arthur, Patricia Gurin, and Gerald Gurin. 1979. Electoral implications of group identification and consciousness. Paper presented at the annual meeting of the American Political Science Association, New York.

Miller, Arthur, and Ola Listhaug. 1990. Political parties and confidence in government. *British Journal of Political Science* 29:357–86.

Miller, Arthur, and Martin Wattenberg. 1985. Throwing the rascals out. *American Political Science Review* 79:359–72.

Miller, Arthur, Martin Wattenberg, and Oksana Malanchuk. 1986. Schematic assessments of presidential candidates. *American Political Science Review* 80:521–40.

Miller, Warren. 1976. The cross-national use of party identification as a stimulus to political inquiry. In *Party Identification and Beyond,* ed. I. Budge, I. Crewe, and D. Farlie. New York: Wiley.

———. 1988. *Without Consent: Mass-Elite Linkages in Presidential Politics.* Lexington: University Press of Kentucky.

————. 1991. Party identification, realignment, and party voting: Back to the basics. *American Political Science Review* 85:557–68.

MILLER, WARREN, AND M. KENT JENNINGS. 1986. *Parties in Transition: A Longitudinal Study of Party Elites and Party Supporters.* New York: Russell Sage Foundation.

MILLER, WARREN, AND TERESA LEVITIN. 1976. *Leadership and Change.* Cambridge, Mass.: Winthrop.

MILLER, WARREN, AND DONALD STOKES. 1963. Constituency influence in Congress. *American Political Science Review* 57:45–56.

MILLER, WILLIAM. 1977. *Electoral Dynamics in Britain Since 1918.* London: Macmillan.

————. 1990. *Media and Voters: The Audience, Content and Influence of Press and Television at the 1987 General Election.* New York: Oxford University Press.

MILLER, WILLIAM, ET AL. 1990. *How Voters Change: The 1987 British Election Campaign in Perspective.* New York: Oxford University Press.

MOON, DAVID. 1990. What you use depends on what you have. *American Politics Quarterly* 18:3–24.

MONROE, ALAN. 1979. Consistency between public preferences and national policy decisions. *American Politics Quarterly* 7:3–21.

MORRIS, RICHARD. 1995. What informed public? *Washington Post National Weekly Edition,* 10–16 April, 36.

MULLER, EDWARD. 1972. A test of a partial theory of potential for political violence. *American Political Science Review* 66:928–59.

————. 1979. *Aggressive Political Participation.* Princeton: Princeton University Press.

MULLER, EDWARD, AND THOMAS JUKAM. 1977. On the meaning of political support. *American Political Science Review* 71:1561–95.

MÜLLER-ROMMEL, FERDINAND, ED. 1989. *New Politics in Western Europe.* Boulder, Colo.: Westview.

MÜLLER-ROMMEL, FERDINAND, AND GEOFFREY PRIDHAM. 1991. *Small Parties in Western Europe.* Newbury Park, Calif.: Sage.

NIE, NORMAN, WITH KRISTI ANDERSEN. 1974. Mass belief systems revisited. *Journal of Politics* 36:340–91.

NIE, NORMAN, AND JAMES N. RABJOHN. 1979. Revisiting mass belief systems revisited. *American Journal of Political Science* 23:139–75.

NIE, NORMAN, SIDNEY VERBA, AND JOHN PETROCIK. 1979. *The Changing American Voter.* Cambridge: Harvard University Press.

NIE, NORMAN, ET AL. 1988. Participation in America: Continuity and change. Paper presented at the annual meeting of the Midwest Political Science Association.

NIEMI, RICHARD, AND M. KENT JENNINGS. 1991. Issues and inheritance in the formation of party identification. *American Journal of Political Science* 35:970–88.

NIEMI, RICHARD, JOHN MUELLER, AND TOM SMITH. 1989. *Trends in Public Opinion: A Compendium of Survey Data.* Westport, Conn.: Greenwood.

NIEMI, RICHARD, AND HERBERT WEISBERG, ED. 1993. *Controversies in Voting*. 3d ed. Washington, D.C.: CQ Press.

NIEUWBEERTA, PAUL. 1995. *The Democratic Class Struggle in Twenty Countries, 1945–1990*. Amsterdam: Thesis Publishers.

NOELLE-NEUMANN, ELISABETH. 1967. *The Germans, 1947–1966*. Allensbach: Institut für Demoskopie.

———. 1981. *The Germans, 1967–1980*. Westport, Conn.: Greenwood.

NOELLE-NEUMANN, ELISABETH, AND EDGAR PIEL, EDS. 1984. *Allensbacher Jahrbuch der Demoskopie, 1978–1983*. Munich: Saur.

NORPOTH, HELMUT. 1978. Party identification in West Germany. *Comparative Political Studies* 11:36–61.

———. 1983. The making of a more partisan electorate in West Germany. *British Journal of Political Science* 14:53–71.

———. 1992. *Confidence Regained: Economics, Mrs. Thatcher, and the British Voter*. Ann Arbor: University of Michigan Press.

NORPOTH, HELMUT, AND DIETER ROTH. 1996. Timid or prudent?: The German electorate in 1994. In *Germans Divided*, ed. R. Dalton. Washington, D.C.: Berg.

NUNN, CLYDE, ET AL. 1978. *Tolerance for Nonconformity*. San Francisco: Jossey-Bass.

PAGE, BENJAMIN. 1978. *Choices and Echoes in Presidential Elections*. Chicago: University of Chicago Press.

PAGE, BENJAMIN, AND ROBERT SHAPIRO. 1983. Effects of public opinion on public policy. *American Political Science Review* 77:175–90.

———. 1992. *The Rational Public: Fifty Years of Trends in Americans' Policy Preferences*. Chicago: University of Chicago Press.

PAPPI, FRANZ URBAN. 1990. Klassenstruktur und Wählerverhalten im sozialen Wandel. In *Wahlen und Wähler: Analysen aus Anlass der Bundestagswahl 1987*, ed. M. Kaase and H. Klingemann. Opladen: Westdeutscher Verlag.

PARRY, GERAINT, GEORGE MOYSER, AND NEIL DAY. 1992. *Political Participation and Democracy in Britain*. Cambridge: Cambridge University Press.

PATEMAN, CAROLE. 1970. *Participation and Democratic Theory*. Cambridge: Cambridge University Press.

———. 1980. The civic culture: A philosophical critique. In *The Civic Culture Revisited*, ed. G. Almond and S. Verba. Boston: Little, Brown.

PEFFLEY, MARK, AND JON HURWITZ. 1985. A hierarchical model of attitude constraint. *American Journal of Political Science* 29:871–90.

PENNIMAN, HOWARD, ED. 1975a. *Britain at the Polls*. Washington, D.C.: American Enterprise Institute.

———. 1975b. *France at the Polls*. Washington, D.C.: American Enterprise Institute.

———. 1980. *The French National Assembly Elections of 1978*. Washington, D.C.: American Enterprise Institute.

———. 1981. *Britain at the Polls, 1979*. Washington, D.C.: American Enterprise Institute.

PERCHERON, ANNICK, AND M. KENT JENNINGS. 1981. Political continuities in

French families. *Comparative Politics* 13:421–36.

PIERCE, JOHN, KATHLEEN BEATTY, AND PAUL HAGNER. 1982. *The Dynamics of American Public Opinion.* Glenview, Ill.: Scott, Foresman.

PIERCE, JOHN, ET AL. 1992. *Citizens, Political Communication and Interest Groups.* New York: Praeger.

PIERSON, PAUL. 1994. *Dismantling the Welfare State?* New York: Cambridge University Press.

PIVEN, FRANCES FOX, AND RICHARD CLOWARD. 1989. *Why Americans Don't Vote.* New York: Pantheon Books.

POGUNTKE, THOMAS. 1993. *Alternative Politics.* Edinburgh: University of Edinburgh Press.

POMPER, GERALD, ED. 1989. *The Election of 1988.* Chatham, N.J.: Chatham House.

——, ED. 1993. *The Election of 1992.* Chatham, N.J.: Chatham House.

POPKIN, SAMUEL. 1991. *The Reasoning Voter.* Chicago: University of Chicago Press.

POOL, I. DE SOLA. 1983. *Technologies of Freedom.* Cambridge, Mass.: Belknap Press.

POWELL, G. BINGHAM. 1980. Voting turnout in thirty democracies. In *Electoral Participation,* ed. R. Rose. Beverly Hills, Calif.: Sage.

——. 1982. *Contemporary Democracies.* Cambridge: Harvard University Press.

——. 1986. American voting turnout in comparative perspective. *American Political Science Review* 80:17–44.

PROTHRO, JAMES, AND CHARLES GRIGG. 1960. Fundamental principles of democracy. *Journal of Politics* 22:276–94.

PUTNAM, ROBERT. 1995. Bowling alone. *Journal of Democracy* 6:65–78.

QUIGLEY, CHARLES. 1991. *Civitas: A Framework for Civic Education.* Calabasas, Calif.: Center for Civic Education.

RAHN, WENDY M., ET AL. 1990. A social-cognitive model of candidate appraisal. In *Information and Democratic Processes,* ed. J. Ferejohn and J. Kuklinski. Urbana: University of Illinois Press.

RANNEY, AUSTIN, ED. 1985. *Britain at the Polls, 1983.* Durham, N.C.: Duke University Press.

REIF, KARLHEINZ, AND RONALD INGLEHART, EDS. 1991. *Eurobarometer: The Dynamic of European Public Opinion.* London: Macmillan.

REPASS, DAVID. 1971. Issue saliency and party choice. *American Political Science Review* 65:389–400.

RICHARDSON, BRADLEY, AND SCOTT FLANAGAN. 1984. *Politics in Japan.* Boston: Little, Brown.

RIESMAN, DAVID, ET AL. 1950. *The Lonely Crowd.* New Haven: Yale University Press.

ROBERTSON, DAVID. 1976. *A Theory of Party Competition.* New York: Wiley.

ROCHON, THOMAS. 1988. *Mobilizing for Peace.* Princeton: Princeton University Press.

ROHRSCHNEIDER, ROBERT. 1993a. Environmental belief systems in Western Europe. *Comparative Political Studies* 26:3–29.

———. 1993b. New party versus old left realignments. *Journal of Politics* 55:682–701.

ROHRSCHNEIDER, ROBERT, AND DIETER FUCHS. 1995. A new electorate? *German Politics and Society* 13:100–22.

ROKEACH, MILTON. 1973. *The Nature of Human Values*. New York: Free Press.

ROKKAN, STEIN. 1970. *Citizens Elections Parties*. Oslo: Universitetsforlaget.

ROLLER, EDELTRAUD. 1996. Political agendas and beliefs about the scope of government. In *Beliefs about the Scope of Government,* ed. O. Borre and E. Scarbrough. Oxford: Oxford University Press.

ROSE, RICHARD, ED. 1974. *Electoral Behavior*. New York: Free Press.

———. 1980. *Politics in England*. 3d ed. Boston: Little, Brown.

———. 1982. *The Territorial Dimension in Politics*. Chatham, N.J.: Chatham House.

———. 1984. *Do Parties Make a Difference?* Chatham, N.J.: Chatham House.

———. 1989. *Politics in England*. 5th ed. New York: HarperCollins.

ROSE, RICHARD, AND IAN MCALLISTER. 1986. *Voters Begin to Choose*. Beverly Hills, Calif.: Sage.

———. 1990. *The Loyalties of Voters*. Newbury Park, Calif.: Sage.

ROSE, RICHARD, AND DEREK URWIN. 1969. Social cohesion, political parties and strains in regimes. *Comparative Political Studies* 2:7–67.

———. 1970. Persistence and change in Western party systems since 1945. *Political Studies* 18:287–319.

ROSENBERG, SHAWN, AND PATRICK MCCAFFERTY. 1987. The image and the vote: Manipulating voters' preferences. *Public Opinion Quarterly* 51:31–47.

ROSENSTONE, STEVEN. 1983. *Forecasting Presidential Elections*. New Haven: Yale University Press.

ROSENSTONE, STEVEN, AND JOHN HANSEN. 1993. *Mobilization, Participation and Democracy in America*. New York: Macmillan.

SARTORI, GIOVANNI. 1968. Representational systems. *International Encyclopedia of the Social Sciences* 13:470–75.

———. 1976. *Parties and Party Systems*. New York: Cambridge University Press.

SCHLOZMAN, KAY, NANCY BURNS, AND SIDNEY VERBA. 1994. Gender and the pathways to participation. *Journal of Politics* 56:963–90.

SCHUMACHER. E.F. 1973. *Small Is Beautiful*. New York: Harper & Row.

SCHUMAN, HOWARD, AND STANLEY PRESSER. 1981. *Questions and Answers in Attitudinal Surveys*. New York: Academic Press.

SCHUMAN, HOWARD, CHARLOTTE STEEH, AND LAWRENCE BOBO. 1985. *Racial Attitudes in America*. Cambridge: Harvard University Press.

SCHUMPETER, JOSEPH. 1943. *Capitalism, Socialism and Democracy*. London: Allen & Unwin.

SCOTT, JACQUELINE, MICHAEL BRAUN, AND DUANE ALWIN. 1993. The family way. In *International Social Attitudes: The 10th BSA Report,* ed. R. Jowell et al. Brookfield, Vt.: Dartmouth.

SEMETKO, HOLLI, AND KLAUS SCHOENBACH. 1994. *Germany's Unity Election*. Cresskill, N.J.: Hampton Press.

SEMETKO, HOLLI, ET AL. 1991. *The Formation of Campaign Agendas.* Hillsdale, N.J.: Lawrence Erlbaum.

SENNETT, R. 1978. *The Fall of Public Man: On the Social Psychology of Capitalism.* New York: Vintage Books.

SHANKS, MERRILL, AND WARREN MILLER. 1990. Policy direction and performance evaluations. *British Journal of Political Science* 20:143–235.

———. 1991. Partisanship, policy and performance. *British Journal of Political Science* 21:129–97.

SHAPIRO, ROBERT, AND LAWRENCE JACOBS. 1989. The relationship between public opinion and public policy. In *Political Behavior Annual,* ed. Samuel Long. Boulder, Colo.: Westview.

SHIVELY, W. PHILLIPS. 1979. The development of party identification among adults. *American Political Science Review* 73:1039–54.

SMITH, ERIC R.A.N. 1989. *The Unchanging American Voter.* Berkeley: University of California Press.

SMITH, STEVEN, AND DOUGLAS WERTMAN. 1992. *U.S.–West European Relations during the Reagan Years: The Perspective of West European Publics.* New York: St. Martin's.

SMITH, TOM, AND PAUL SHEATSLEY. 1984. American attitudes toward race relations. *Public Opinion* 7:14ff.

SNIDERMAN, PAUL, RICHARD BRODY, AND JAMES KUKLINSKI. 1984. Policy reasoning and political values. *American Journal of Political Science* 28:74–94.

SNIDERMAN, PAUL, RICHARD BRODY, AND PHILIP TETLOCK. 1991. *Reasoning and Choice.* New York: Cambridge University Press.

SNIDERMAN, PAUL, AND THOMAS PIAZZA. 1993. *The Scar of Race.* Cambridge: Harvard University Press.

SNIDERMAN, PAUL, ET AL. 1991. The fallacy of democratic elitism. *British Journal of Political Science* 21:349–70.

STANLEY, HAROLD, AND RICHARD NIEMI. 1991. Partisanship and group support, 1952–1988. *American Politics Quarterly* 19:189–210.

———. 1994. *Vital Statistics of American Politics.* 4th ed. Washington, D.C.: CQ Press.

STIMSON, JAMES. 1991. *Public Opinion in America: Moods, Cycles and Swings.* Boulder, Colo.: Westview.

STIMSON, JAMES, MICHAEL MCKUEN, AND ROBERT ERIKSON. 1995. Dynamic representation. *American Political Science Review* 89:543–65.

STOKES, DONALD. 1963. Spatial models of party competition. *American Political Science Review* 57:368–77.

STOKES, DONALD, AND WARREN MILLER. 1962. Party government and the saliency of Congress. *Public Opinion Quarterly* 26:531–46.

STOUFFER, SAMUEL. 1955. *Communism, Conformity and Civil Liberties.* New York: Doubleday.

STRATE, JOHN, ET AL. 1989. Life span civic development and voting participation. *American Political Science Review* 83:445–63.

STREEK, W. 1987. Vielfalt und Interdependenz. *Kölner Zeitschrift für Soziologie und Sozialpsychologie* 39:471–95.

SULLIVAN, DENNIS, AND ROGER MASTERS. Happy warriors: Leaders' facial displays, viewers' emotions and political support. *American Journal of Political Science* 32:345–68.

SULLIVAN, JOHN, JAMES PIERESON, AND GEORGE MARCUS. 1978. Ideological constraint in the mass public. *American Journal of Political Science* 22:233–49.

SULLIVAN, JOHN, ET AL. 1982. *Political Tolerance and American Democracy.* Chicago: University of Chicago Press.

TAAGEPERA, REIN, AND MATTHEW SHUGART. 1989. *Seats and Votes: The Effects and Determinants of Electoral Systems.* New Haven: Yale University Press.

TATE, KATHERINE. 1993. *From Politics to Protest.* Cambridge: Harvard University Press.

TAYLOR, CHARLES, AND MICHAEL HUDSON. 1972. *World Handbook of Social and Political Indicators.* New Haven: Yale University Press.

TAYLOR-GOOBY, PETER. 1993. What citizens want from the state. In *International Social Attitudes: The 10th BSA Report,* ed. R. Jowell et al. Brookfield, Vt.: Dartmouth.

TEIXEIRA, RUY. 1992. *The Disappearing American Voter.* Washington, D.C.: Brookings Institution.

THOMAS, JOHN. 1980. Ideological trends in Western political parties. In *Western European Party Systems,* ed. P. Merkl. New York: Free Press.

THOMMASEN, JACQUES. 1976. *Kiezers en gekozenen in een representative demokratie.* Alphen aan den Rijn: Samson.

———. 1994. Empirical research into political representation. In *Elections at Home and Abroad,* ed. M.K. Jennings and T. Mann. Ann Arbor: University of Michigan Press.

TILLY, CHARLES. 1969. Collective violence in European perspective. In *Violence in America,* ed. H. Graham and T. Gurr. New York: Bantam.

———. 1975. Revolutions and collective violence. In *Handbook of Political Science,* ed. F. Greenstein and N. Polsby. Vol. 3. Reading, Mass.: Addison-Wesley.

TILLY, CHARLES, ET AL. 1975. *The Rebellious Century.* Cambridge: Harvard University Press.

TIMES/MIRROR CENTER FOR THE PEOPLE AND THE PRESS. 1991. *The Pulse of Europe: A Survey of Political and Social Values and Attitudes.* Washington, D.C.: Times/Mirror Center.

TOCQUEVILLE, ALEXIS DE. 1966. *Democracy in America.* New York: Knopf.

TOPF, RICHARD. 1989. Political change and political culture in Britain: 1959–87. In *Contemporary Political Culture,* ed. J. Gibbins. London: Sage.

———. 1996a. Electoral participation. In *Citizens and the State,* ed. H. Klingemann and D. Fuchs. Oxford: Oxford University Press.

———. 1996b. Beyond electoral participation. In *Citizens and the State,* ed. H. Klingemann and D. Fuchs. Oxford: Oxford University Press.

TOPF, RICHARD, PETER MOHLER, AND ANTHONY HEATH. 1989. Pride in one's country: Britain and West Germany. In *British Social Attitudes: Special International Report,* ed. R. Jowell, S. Witherspoon, and L. Brook. Brookfield, Vt.: Gower.

TUFTE, EDWARD. 1978. *Political Control of the Economy*. Princeton: Princeton University Press.

ÜHLINGER, HANS-MARTIN. 1989. *Politische Partizipation in der Bundesrepublik*. Opladen: Westdeutscher Verlag.

UHLANER, CAROLE. 1989. Rational turnout. *American Journal of Political Science* 33:390–422.

USLANER, ERIC, AND RONALD WEBER. 1983. Policy congruence and American state elites. *Journal of Politics* 45:186–93.

VAN DETH, JAN. 1983. Ranking and ratings: The case of materialist and postmaterialist value orientations. *Political Methodology* 9:407–31.

VAN DETH, JAN, AND RAYMOND HORSTMANN, EDS. 1989. *Dutch Parliamentary Election Studies: Data Source Book 1971–1989*. Amsterdam: Steinmetz Archive.

VAN DETH, JAN, AND J. JANSSEN. 1994. Party attachments and political fragmentation in Europe. *European Journal of Political Research* 25:87–109.

VAN DETH, JAN, AND ELINOR SCARBROUGH, EDS. 1996. *The Impact of Values*. Oxford: Oxford University Press.

VERBA, SIDNEY, AND NORMAN NIE. 1972. *Participation in America*. New York: Harper & Row.

VERBA, SIDNEY, NORMAN NIE, AND J.O. KIM. 1971. *The Modes of Democratic Participation*. Beverly Hills, Calif.: Sage.

———. 1978. *Participation and Political Equality*. New York: Cambridge University Press.

VERBA, SIDNEY, AND GARY ORREN. 1985. *Equality in America*. Cambridge: Harvard University Press.

VERBA, SIDNEY, KAY SCHLOZMAN, AND HENRY BRADY. 1995. *Voice and Equality: Civic Voluntarism in American Politics*. Cambridge: Harvard University Press.

WAHLKE, JOHN, ET AL. 1962. *The Legislative System*. New York: Wiley.

WALD, KENNETH. 1983. *Crosses on the Ballot*. Princeton: Princeton University Press.

———. 1993. *Religion and Politics in America*. 2d ed. New York: St. Martin's.

WALKER, JACK. 1991. *Mobilizing Interest Groups in America*. Ann Arbor: University of Michigan Press.

WALLAS, GRAHAM. 1908. *Human Nature in Politics*. London: Constable.

WATANUKI, JOJI. 1991. Social structure and voting behavior. In *The Japanese Voter*, ed. S. Flanagan et al.. New Haven: Yale University Press.

WATTENBERG, MARTIN. 1991. *The Rise of Candidate-Centered Politics*. Cambridge: Harvard University Press.

———. 1996. *The Decline of American Political Parties, 1952–1994*. Cambridge: Harvard University Press.

WEIL, FREDERIC. 1991. Structural determinants of political tolerance. *Research in Political Sociology* 5:299–323.

WEISBERG, HERBERT, ED. 1995. *Democracy's Feast: Elections in America*. Chatham, N.J.: Chatham House.

WEISBERG, HERBERT, AND DAVID KIMBALL. 1995. Attitudinal correlates of the

1992 presidential vote. In *Democracy's Feast,* ed. H. Weisberg. Chatham, N.J.: Chatham House.

WEISBERG, HERBERT, AND JERROLD RUSK. 1970. Dimensions of candidate evaluation. *American Political Science Review* 64:1167–85.

WEISSBERG, ROBERT. 1978. Collective versus dyadic representation in Congress. *American Political Science Review* 72:535–47.

WESSELS, BERNHARD. 1993. Politische Repräsentation als Prozess gesellschaftlich-parlamentarischer Kommunikation. In *Parlament und Gesellschaft,* ed. D. Herzog et al. Opladen: Westdeutscher Verlag.

———. 1994. Gruppenbindung und rationale Faktoren als Determinaten der Wahlentscheidung in Ost- und West Deutschland. In *Wahlen und Wähler,* ed. H. Klingemann and M. Kaase. Opladen: Westdeutscher Verlag.

WESTHOLM, ANDERS, AND RICHARD NIEMI. 1992. Political institutions and political socialization. *Comparative Political Studies* 25:25–41.

WESTLE, BETTINA. 1992. Politische Partizipation. In *Die EG-Staaten im Vergleich: Strukturen, Prozesse, Politikinhalte,* ed. O. Gabriel. Opladen: Westdeutscher Verlag.

WILCOX, CLYDE. 1991. Support for gender equality in West Europe. *European Journal for Political Research* 20:127–47.

WITTKOPF, EUGENE. 1990. *Faces of Internationalism: Public Opinion and Foreign Policy.* Durham, N.C.: Duke University Press.

WOLFINGER, RAYMOND, AND STEVEN ROSENSTONE. 1980. *Who Votes?* New Haven: Yale University Press.

WRIGHT, JAMES. 1976. *The Dissent of the Governed.* New York: Academic Press.

WYCKOFF, MICHAEL. 1987. Measures of attitudinal consistency as indicators of ideological sophistication. *Journal of Politics* 49:148–68.

YOUNG, KEN. 1992. Class, race and opportunity. In *British Social Attitudes: The 9th Report,* ed. R. Jowell et al. Brookfield, Vt.: Dartmouth.

ZALLER, JOHN. 1992. *The Nature and Origins of Mass Opinion.* New York: Cambridge University Press.

ZELLE, CARSTEN. 1995. Social dealignment vs. political frustration. *European Journal for Political Research* 27:319–45.

ZIEGLER, HARMON. 1993. *Political Parties in Industrial Democracy.* Itasca, Ill.: Peacock.

ZIMMERMAN, MICHAEL. 1990. Newspaper editors and the creation-evolution controversy. *Skeptical Inquirer* 14:182–95.

———. 1991. A survey of pseudoscientific sentiments of elected officials. *Creation/Evolution* 29:26–45.

ZUCKERMAN, ALAN. 1982. New approaches to political cleavage. *Comparative Politics* 15:131–44.

Index